AGES IN CONFLICT

COLUMBIA STUDIES
OF SOCIAL GERONTOLOGY AND AGING

COLUMBIA STUDIES
OF SOCIAL GERONTOLOGY AND AGING
Abraham Monk, General Editor

Ages in Conflict

A Cross-Cultural Perspective on Inequality Between Old and Young

Nancy Foner

Columbia University Press

New York   1984

Library of Congress Cataloging in Publication Data

Foner, Nancy, 1945–
    Ages in conflict.

    (Columbia studies of social gerontology and aging)
    Includes bibliographical references and index.
    1. Aged—Cross-cultural studies.   2. Conflict of
generations—Cross-cultural studies.   I. Title.
II. Series.
GN485.F66   1984   305.2′6   83-26157
ISBN 0-231-05696-6 (alk. paper)
ISBN 0-231-05697-4 (pbk. : alk. paper)

Columbia University Press
New York   Guildford, Surrey
Copyright © 1984 Columbia University Press
All rights reserved

Printed in the United States of America

Contents

Acknowledgments

In the course of writing this book, I received help from a number of people and institutions. My thanks go, first, to Karen Blu, Loretta Fowler, David Kertzer, Roger Sanjek, and Peter Swerdloff, who read and commented on drafts of the manuscript, in part or in whole. I also owe a debt to the Research Foundation of the State University of New York for a grant and fellowship used for the preparation of the manuscript.

My largest debt is to my mother, Anne Foner. It was through reading her publications and through personal conversations that I first became interested in the subject of age inequality. Her paper with David Kertzer, applying insights from the age stratification model to age-set societies, made it clear to me that a perspective on age inequality had much to offer to the study of societies other than our own.

Not only did my mother spark my enthusiasm for the study of age inequality in nonindustrial societies, but she also helped me in many ways as I wrote this book. She read the manuscript several times, even when busy with her own writing and teaching obligations, and provided a steady stream of valuable suggestions and criticisms.

My mother helped me to complete the manuscript; the birth of my daughter held it up for several months. To the two generations, Anne and Alexis, I dedicate this book.

Introduction

This is a book about conflict and tension. It deals with strains that are generated by age inequalities in nonindustrial societies throughout the world. The key actors are old people. And the principal issue is how they come into conflict with younger adults because of their position in their society's age hierarchy.

The study thus takes as its starting point the idea that age is a basis of structured inequality or social stratification. The major premise is that age inequalities have crucial implications for old people's lives and for their social relations. The book pulls together strands from the ethnographic literature to explore the quality of relations between old and young in nonindustrial societies when there are marked inequalities between the two ages. What is the relationship between age inequalities and intergenerational conflict? In what ways are the tensions between old and young expressed? Why is it that these tensions are often latent or suppressed? And how do age inequalities and relationships between old and young change over time?

These questions enable us to get at important aspects of old age and the social relations of old people. But they are questions that have not been systematically addressed by anthropologists who study old age. Viewing the old as part of a system of age inequality is not yet a feature of gerontological anthropology. The growing number of anthropologists who have, in recent years, investigated old age in different cultures have thus far had other concerns.[1] As in Leo Simmons' (1945) pioneering study, *The Role of the Aged in Primitive Society*, the issue that has received the most attention is the status and treatment of the old: how and why the old are afforded relatively high status and good treatment in some societies and not others (see, for example, Amoss and Harrell 1981; Cowgill and Holmes 1972; J. Goody 1976a; Maxwell and Silverman 1970; Press and McKool 1972). A number of anthropologists have also challenged the universal applicability of certain sociological and psychological theories of aging in light of ethnographic data, most notably the disengagement hypothesis (Cumming and Henry 1961), which postulates that old age inevitably involves a process of mutual withdrawal between old people and their society (for example, Clark 1973; Myerhoff and Simić 1978; Vatuk 1980). Many anthropologists have explored societal or self-conceptions of aging in various cultures (for example, Amoss and Harrell 1981; Clark and Anderson 1967; Fry 1980; Kleemeier 1961; Myerhoff 1978; Myerhoff and Simić 1978). And those who look at Western societies have often studied old-age communities through traditional participant-observation techniques to find out what it is like to live in them (see Byrne 1974; Jacobs 1974; Johnson 1971; Keith 1977, 1979).

All these topics are obviously important and much work still needs to be done on them. Indeed, this study sheds light on such familiar concerns as the conditions that lead to advantages or disadvantages in old age in different cultures and the way the elderly, as well as younger people, view old age. But something crucial is missing in the anthropological literature on old age: a systematic analysis of age inequalities in nonindustrial societies. A perspective that emphasizes age as a basis of structured inequality opens up new lines of inquiry and highlights social processes that have been given relatively little consideration in cross-cultural studies of old age. It not only points out the need to view the old in relation to younger people but also makes us aware of the possibility of strain and conflict between them.

Age Inequality and Anthropology

If this book is going to look at the consequences of inequalities between old and young, what are the models available in the anthropological literature for such an enterprise?

Despite the salience of age inequalities in the nonindustrial world, there has been no systematic attempt in anthropology to build a model of age inequality—or, for that matter, of age and aging (for a beginning effort to stimulate the development of a theory of age and aging in anthropology, see Keith and Kertzer 1984). Anthropological theorizing on social inequality has tended to focus on the kinds of institutionalized inequalities found in complex societies, such as class, caste, and racial divisions. Some anthropologists even speak of societies as egalitarian where the division of labor is mainly on the basis of age, sex, and personal characteristics. In the past few years, anthropologists have broadened their focus on inequality as they have begun to explore and develop theoretical approaches to explain the extent and nature of sexual inequalities (see, for example, Friedl 1975; Ortner and Whitehead 1981; Reiter 1975; Rosaldo 1980; Rosaldo and Lamphere 1974; Sanday 1981; Schlegel 1977). Age, however, has been left behind.

"In anthropology," Gerald Berreman writes in the introduction to a recent collection of essays on social inequality, "age is far more neglected than sex as a basis for stratification. . . . Social differentiation and grouping by age have been of considerable interest to anthropologists working in non-Western societies, but inequality has not been an important feature of that interest" (1981:21). As a rule, age is simply treated as a basis of differentiation—a criterion for assigning people to different roles. That these roles are not just different, but are unequally rewarded and valued, is often passed over in general statements about age.

Now it is true that a number of French anthropologists in the Marxist tradition have included inequalities between elders and young men in their theoretical models. Although their work provides useful insights, it cannot serve as a general guide to the analysis of age inequalities—or the specific case of inequalities between old and young.

Age per se is peripheral to the main concerns of French Marxist anthropologists. What they want to determine is whether classes in the Marxian sense exist in precapitalist societies (for example, Meillassoux 1981; Rey 1979; Terray 1972, 1975). They therefore debate whether relations between privileged elders (men who control land, cattle, goods intended for bridewealth, and young men's labor) and subordinate juniors in lineage-based societies constitute class relations.[2] Whatever their position on this issue, Marxist anthropologists have, in the course of the debate, focused attention on the way younger men are "exploited" by elders. And because these scholars are sensitive to the potential for class struggle, they raise questions about the likelihood of rebellion or concerted radical action by younger men.

But the French Marxist anthropologists are so worried about whether or not elder–junior distinctions are class divisions that they overlook many critical features of inequalities between old and young. Indeed, they only pinpoint one kind of age inequality: the situation in which elders are advantaged and youths disadvantaged. They do not include in their models cases in which the old are relatively disadvantaged and younger adults have the upper hand—a not unfamiliar situation in nonindustrial societies. Moreover, they only consider the possibility that relations between old and young are class relations in certain types of societies: lineage-based nonindustrial societies. And they are not concerned with structured inequalities between old and young women.[3]

That anthropologists have not developed a general and comprehensive approach to analyzing inequality between old and young does not mean, of course, that they do not provide rich documentation of the forms that such inequality takes in a variety of settings. Many ethnographic reports provide detailed material that is the backbone of the present work. Then, too, a number of anthropologists have looked beyond one particular society to generalize about the way certain kinds of structural arrangements generate strains between older and younger people. These analyses are a source in this study as well (see especially R. LeVine 1965 on intergenerational tensions in African extended families). For a general model of age inequality, however, we must leave the confines of anthropology and turn to the sociological literature.

The Age Stratification Perspective: A Guide for Analysis

The approach of this study is based on the age stratification model developed by Matilda White Riley and her associates (1972) to provide a comparative framework for analyzing and describing age systems. The age stratification perspective is the most comprehensive model of age systems in the sociology of age. It shows how age is built into social systems, pointing to the impact of structural as well as dynamic aspects of age systems at both the individual and societal levels. What is important here is that the age stratification perspective emphasizes inequality as a central aspect of age systems.[4]

As a contribution to the sociology of age, it is not surprising that the age stratification model was elaborated and illustrated with Western industrial societies in mind. This Western emphasis is probably the main reason that anthropologists of aging have largely ignored it.[5] However, the age stratification perspective can in fact broaden our understanding of age and aging in nonindustrial societies. It offers a systematic and inclusive approach to age inequality and so suggests a new way to analyze and interpret cross-cultural material on old age—a new way to look at relations between old and young in different societies.

What is age stratification? First of all, age stratification implies the notion of an age hierarchy. The term "stratification" is simply a way to refer to structured social inequality.[6] Age stratification means that individuals in a society, on the basis of their location in a particular age stratum, have unequal access to valued social roles and social rewards. It does not imply that individuals need be aware that age is a basis of social inequality. But from the outside looking in, we can see that because of their age some people have the opportunity, as C. Wright Mills put it, to "have more of what there is to have": more power, wealth, and prestige than others (cited in A. Foner 1975:146).

Age stratification theorists recognize that age stratification is a form of social inequality in its *own right*. In fact, they analyze the parallels and contrasts between age, sex, and class stratification, demonstrating both the uniqueness of age stratification and its kinship to other forms of stratification (see A. Foner 1975, 1979). The age stratification model proposes that *all* societies are stratified by age and thus allows an examination of age inequalities in both industrial and nonindustrial societies. It also permits comparisons between the two kinds of societies.

Just as all societies are stratified by age, so too all individuals in a society are part of the age stratification system. In terms of old age, this means considering old women as well as old men and the disadvantaged as well as privileged elders.

When age systems are seen as systems of social inequality, the old are viewed as part of the whole age system rather than in isolation. The very existence of an age hierarchy assumes that individuals in one age stratum are better or worse off in certain ways than individuals in other age strata. Members of the various age strata in a society (socially recognized divisions based on age), as age stratification theorists write, not only differ in age or life stage.[7] As I already have said, they also differ in their access to roles that are unequally rewarded by wealth, prestige, or power. It is important, then, to know how valued roles and social rewards are allocated among *all* the age strata in a society and not only among the old.

Moreover, once the perspective of age inequality is introduced, the possibility of conflict and tensions between age strata arises. Of course, we know from our own society that social inequalities—based on class, race, or sex, for instance—do not inevitably produce open conflict between the advantaged and disadvantaged. But the potential for discord is ever present (see A. Foner 1979). Thus, those at the top of the age hierarchy may be resented by those below, while downwardly mobile individuals, who have suffered social losses with age, may resent more successful younger people and be bitter about their own declines.

In sum, an understanding that inequalities among age strata are part of the fabric of any society directs us to issues and topics that shed light on the structure and ramifications of age inequality in general and, specifically in terms of the concerns of this work, inequalities between old and young in nonindustrial societies.

Organization of This Book

This book, then, explores questions not typically addressed by anthropologists who study old age. Do inequalities between old and young lead to tensions and conflicts? Which relationships are particularly vulnerable to strain? Do the disadvantaged young or disadvantaged old develop "age-stratum consciousness" and struggle together with age peers to further their age-related interests? What factors reduce discord or enhance solidarity between old and young, thereby mitigating or preventing open age conflicts?

The chapters that follow bring together material embedded in ethnographic reports to explore these questions systematically and to elucidate the nature of age stratification in nonindustrial societies.

The analysis starts out in chapters 2, 3, and 4 with a look at the bases—and consequences—of inequality between old and young. For age inequalities have a profound impact on the lives of old as well as young people. The main theme of the three chapters is how age inequalities create strains and tensions between old and young. Chapters 2 and 3 explore the quality of relations between old and young in societies where the old are at the top of the age hierarchy. Chapter 4 discusses cases in which the elderly experience serious social losses.

When I speak of strains and tensions between old and young, I refer to suppressed or latent resentment, antagonism, frustration, and hostility. Sometimes these strains and tensions lead to overt conflict or "interpersonal behavior consciously directed toward injuring a person (or group) or interfering with his attainment of goals" (R. LeVine 1961:5; compare Coser 1956). Chapters 5 and 6 consider the many ways that conflict between old and young is openly expressed in different cultures, including witchcraft accusations and suspicions. These chapters also look at the other side of the coin. Tensions and opposition between old and young do not necessarily result in open flare-ups and struggles. Nor do the disadvantaged old or young rise up in revolt to alter age systems that make their lives so difficult. Chapters 5 and 6 thus address a vital issue in any study of social inequality: the sources of accommodation between the haves and have-nots. The chapters examine the factors that reduce age-related tensions and encourage cooperation and accommodation between old and young. And they investigate the factors that forestall or mute bitter age conflicts when such tensions are marked.

In chapter 7 I turn to the subject of change. Inequalities and tensions between old and young, after all, change over time. In analyzing the structure of age inequalities and conflicts in chapters 2 through 6, the ethnographic material presented, unless otherwise noted, refers to the period when the anthropologist was in the field. This period, of course, is but one point in time. Age inequalities and tensions observed then may well have been different in earlier days and may also have subsequently undergone important alterations.

The age stratification model makes us aware that the particular age inequalities and tensions experienced by one cohort of old people are often quite different from those experienced by previous or later cohorts of the old. For members of a cohort (individuals born in the same time period) are affected by specific historical events and social changes that occur as they grow up and mature.

Drawing on studies that specifically discuss change, very often with considerable historical data, chapter 7 reviews some of the major changes of the past century that have affected the opportunities available to and the social relations between old and young in nonindustrial societies. This review suggests the different experiences that successive cohorts have undergone. The chapter shows how changes in the last hundred years or so—such as the imposition of colonial rule, the emergence of wage labor, and the introduction of Christianity—have influenced the roles old and young fill and the social rewards they receive. It analyzes the way ideas about age-related roles and age relations have shifted and discusses whether tensions and conflicts between old and young have become more or less serious.

The final chapter draws together the main threads of the analysis. In addition, it raises new questions about how changes even earlier than those discussed in chapter 7 affected the relative status of old and young before contact or colonial rule. It also speculates about some changes that might alter age inequalities in years to come. Last but not least, chapter 8 examines the relations between age and other forms of inequality.

Although there are scattered references throughout this book to the social position of old people in the United States today, my concern in this work is with other cultures. Why, it might be asked, should we spend so much time investigating the effects of age inequality on the lives and social relations of old people in nonindustrial societies instead of looking in our own backyard—especially when the problems of the elderly are so pressing in contemporary America?

The study of the way age inequalities influence the old— and their relations with the young—in different cultures is not only fascinating in itself, it is also important. Looking at other cultures reminds us that ways of thinking and doing things in this society represent but one of many possible patterns. Cross-cultural comparisons make clear that the position the old occupy in this society—and the kinds of relations they have with the young here—are neither inevitable nor "natural." The analysis of age inequality in nonindustrial societies also shows that it is an oversimplification to idealize old age in these societies. To those who think of the old in the nonindustrial world only as wise and powerful elders who are respected and honored, this book offers a sobering corrective. The chapters that follow point out that privileged and influential elders often have severely strained relations with the young—and that younger people may express their resentment and hostility toward the old quite openly. Moreover, the old in nonindustrial societies frequently lose prestige and power in the family and community, and they may end up in a most unfortunate position.

A study of inequality between old and young that looks beyond American or European society is also crucial for developing general theoretical propositions about age inequality. To understand fully the nature of age stratification it is essential to consider its forms and consequences in human societies throughout the world—not just in Western industrial countries.

Some Points of Procedure

It is possible to go about a comparative or cross-cultural study in a variety of ways. In this book, I have picked a method that suits the questions and problems at hand.

To begin to explore the many possible consequences of age inequality for relations between old and young, I have relied heavily on studies that provide detailed material on age inequalities and age relations. All in all, I have drawn on material from over sixty nonindustrial societies. By nonindustrial societies I mean those where the economy is based on hunting and gathering, pastoralism, or farming, including the nonindustrial sectors of industrial societies (J. Goody 1976a:117). I consider a broad range of nonindustrial societies from various parts of the world and at different stages of technological development. I even look far back in time, making occasional forays into America's and Western Europe's preindustrial past.

The method I have used to gather ethnographic material does not rely on a random sample of cultures. Had I followed this alternative method, the present work would have been seriously weakened. A random sample of cultures would have inevitably included too many societies for which descriptions of inequalities and relations between old and young are sketchy at best—and excluded ethnographic studies that offer detailed information on these topics. It is even possible that certain kinds of age inequalities or strains between old and young or certain ways of expressing or reducing age conflict would have been completely missed.

In any case, I am not concerned here with making statistical generalizations. The aim is not, for example, to figure out on the basis of quantitative data the number or type of societies where the old fill certain kinds of valued roles or where certain conflict-reducing factors come into play. Rather, the goal is to begin to understand the myriad and complex ways that age inequalities can influence relations between old and young. At this stage, this goal is best met by mining the rich available ethnographic material to uncover the sources of strain as well as cooperation between old and young, to learn about the conflicts as well as accommodations between them. This is not to dismiss the value of quantitative studies. Indeed, by pulling together ethnographic data to start making sense of age inequality in nonindustrial societies, the present work will, I believe, suggest propositions that can in the future be tested through quantitative methods.

In investigating the quality of intergenerational relations in the chapters that follow,[8] the focus will be on the structural sources of conflict and amity rather than on individual factors involved in particular cases. Not that individual variation is unimportant. Each person's special circumstances and idiosyncrasies are the stuff out of which lives are built and relationships made. Some old people are more resourceful than others, for example. Some are irascible, others easygoing. Indeed, anthropologists of aging are increasingly sensitive to the way individuals' unique life experiences play a role in shaping their actions and ideas (for example, Myerhoff and Simić 1978).

Despite the peculiarities of each individual and each social relationship, certain structural limitations and potential tension points can be discerned in every society. In other words, given the structure of social relations in a society, there is a range of possibilities that restricts old people's (or certain categories of old people) quest for success, whatever their personalities. And there are *potential* strains between certain old and young people, whatever their individual characters.[9] Thus, I examine how structured age inequalities put the old at an advantage or disadvantage in obtaining highly valued roles and rewards and how these inequalities provide fertile ground for strain and conflict with the young.

If I have repeatedly spoken of the young–old dichotomy, this is not because a two-strata model predominates in non-industrial societies. While Shakespeare waxed lyrical about the seven ages of man—from the mewling and puking infant to second childishness—in some societies only three or four life stages are differentiated. For example, beyond infancy a man may pass through boyhood, mature adulthood, and elderhood. The age stratification perspective takes as its starting point culturally defined life stages. The number of life stages (or age strata) distinguished and the age-related boundaries of these stages differ across cultures and, within the same culture, over time.

There is, then, cultural variation in who is, and who is not, old. The way physically mature persons who are not old are classified also differs from culture to culture. We in our society may think of such people as adolescents, youths, young adults, or mature adults, depending on their chronological age, but in other cultures the divisions are quite different. Just what these divisions are is not always reported, however. Although some ethnographic accounts tell us how people distinguish various life stages over the entire life course, more often they do not. What we do know is that certain physically mature individuals are not considered old. When I use the term "young" or "younger people" in this book, it is these people I have in mind.

Difficult as it often is to determine, it is nevertheless necessary to have an idea of what old age "is" in nonindustrial societies before going on to examine relations with younger people—since the old are the key players in this study. How old age is defined is thus the subject of chapter 1.

AGES IN CONFLICT

1
What Is
Old Age?

Growing old is inevitable. Indeed, certain biological processes of aging seem to be a feature of human life around the world. But although everyone grows older, the particular ways individuals age and the meanings they attach to the life course are not universal. And the way the life course is divided—including the markers that delineate old age—is highly variable.

Our own cultural conceptions of age and aging are just that: our own. Because we in present-day America assume that certain characteristics make a person "old" does not mean that individuals in other cultures hold the same view. Far from it. The criteria people use to decide who is, or is not, old vary widely from place to place. Definitions of old age can also shift from one historical period to another.

It thus seems appropriate to begin a study of old age and age relations by making clear that old age is a cultural concept and by discussing some of the ways people in other cultures demarcate old age as a distinct life stage.[1]

Definitions of Old Age:
Some Problems

As outside observers, we can, of course, legitimately define old age operationally in one way or another. Such a distinction, though not made by the people being studied, may well be relevant for our understanding of their social relations. But the way people themselves view the life course and later years is crucial. It is not just that perceived life-stage divisions are usually significant markers of social roles. The way old age is defined may mold "personal plans, hopes and fears," shaping the way individuals in different cultures age and modifying the values attached to life and death (Riley 1978:49).

Yet studying cultural definitions of old age is not a simple matter, if only because ethnographers have generally not paid much attention to informants' definitions of old age. Often we are left wondering what particular ethnographers mean when they say someone is "old." Many times we cannot tell whether they refer to their own or their informants' view when they use the term "old." I myself, in previous writings on Jamaicans (Foner 1973, 1978), have been guilty of this practice. In some cases, arbitrary chronological boundaries are used and we do not know what relation these bear to the people's perceptual models.

Even when anthropologists do refer to folk conceptions of old age, it is impossible to determine to what extent the anthropologists' own cultural biases influence the way they present native models of old age. As David Schneider comments about anthropological studies of kinship: "When we read about kinship in some society foreign to our own we have only the facts which the author chooses to present to us, and we usually have no independent source of knowledge against which we can check his facts" (1968:vi).

Despite these limitations, it is worth examining those accounts in which anthropologists do present folk definitions of old age. It is useful to pull together cross-cultural material on perceptions of old age to show how biological and social factors shape cultural definitions of what old age "is" and who is old.

I start out this chapter by briefly discussing how old age is defined in our own society—both today and in the past—before turning to other cultures. Changes in physical structure and physiological functioning, social roles, and chronological age, as I will show, have marked off the boundaries of old age, albeit in different ways, through the years and across cultures.

Old Age in America

The Present

When is old? is no easy question to answer in present-day America. Ask it of a fairly large number of Americans and a variety of answers will undoubtedly be given. This is not only because several criteria define old age in our own society. The boundaries marking off old age are not clear-cut. Views of what constitutes old age may vary for different subgroups within our complex society and also shift with the situational context.

To be sure, a combination of various characteristics—chronological age, physical changes in the later years, and the role shifts of retirement from work and becoming a grandparent—seem to be involved in Americans' definitions of old age. But determining when a person actually becomes—or is—"old" is often problematic because there is no one consistent definition of old age. Social researchers use sixty-five as the chronological benchmark of old age, but if administrative eligibility for retirement, pensions, or social security is the criterion of old age, this may be variously set from ages in the seventies down to ages in the forties (Riley and A. Foner 1974). Others may see grandparenthood as a marker of old age, but grandparents in their forties are, as Kalish notes, hardly unusual (1975:3). As for Americans in their sixties and older, substantial proportions simply do not consider themselves old.

Indeed, Bernice Neugarten (1974) has suggested that Americans are beginning to think of the old in terms of two age categories: the young-old and the old-old.[2] The young-old, approximately fifty-five to seventy-five years old, as well as the old-old, seventy-five years and older, are relatively free from the responsibilities of work and parenthood. But compared with the old-old, the young-old are relatively healthy and vigorous as well as relatively comfortable in economic terms.

The Past

One thing is clear in the United States today, however. Old age is seen as a distinct life stage with particular problems. Has this always been true in this country?

In the wake of Aries' (1962) study of childhood in French history, historians have become increasingly sensitive to the fact that the conception of what constitute meaningful life stages shifts, to use Hareven's (1978) phrase, with historical time. In terms of the age stratification perspective, the number of age strata and their age-related boundaries not only vary cross-culturally but, within Western society, historically.

Aries argued that in Western European society childhood was not viewed as a discernible period of life, with special needs and characteristics, until about the seventeenth century. In medieval times, the awareness that children were distinct from adults was absent; children belonged to adult society as soon as they could live without the constant care of their mothers or nannies (Aries 1962:128). The word "child" did not have the same meaning it has today; "people said 'child' much as we say 'lad' in everyday speech" (Aries 1962:128). Indeed, meaningful social distinctions in way of life, dress, and work or play seem to have been clearly drawn only among three age strata: infancy; adulthood; and old age.

According to many historians, our current concept of adolescence, too, is relatively new. In the United States, Joseph Kett (1977) has suggested that adolescence did not begin to assume its present meaning until the late nineteenth century, when schooling was prolonged and entry into the work force delayed. In the middle decades of the nineteenth century the word "adolescent" was generally unfamiliar. When formally defined, it had a different meaning than it does today: Roget's *Thesaurus* in 1854 equated adolescence with "being out of one's teens," with manhood, virility, and maturity (Kett 1977:143). "If adolescence is defined as the period after puberty during which a young person is institutionally segregated from casual contacts with a broad range of adults," Kett observes, "then it can scarcely be said to have existed at all [in early nineteenth-century America]" (Kett 1977:36). In this period, boys might have left home to work as early as age eight or nine. By about fifteen, they were usually fully incorporated into the labor force.

When American historians write about old age in the past, they do not agree as to how long it has been a meaningful life stage. On the one hand, Tamara Hareven argues that in America old age has not always been recognized as a distinct and sharply differentiated life stage with specific social and psychological problems.[3] In preindustrial America, she says, adulthood flowed into old age without institutionalized disruptions (1978:205). The two major adult social roles—parenthood and work—generally stretched out over an entire lifetime without an "empty nest"[4] or compulsory retirement. This continuity over adult life has changed, however, in the last hundred years or so. The gradual ousting of older people from the labor force and the decline in their parental functions in the later years of life have led to increasing age segregation and a new awareness of old age (Hareven 1978:207).

Other historians, however, emphasize continuities between past and present—and that Americans have considered old age as a special life stage from the earliest days of this country. Although old age has not always been associated with complete retirement from work or with the absence of child-rearing functions, this does not mean it was not viewed as a distinct period of human development.

David Hackett Fischer, for one, emphatically states that there has been no "discovery" of old age in the modern world comparable to historians' "discovery" of childhood and adolescence (1978:12). Old age has long been perceived as a stage within a life continuum with chronological boundaries. Similarly, in his study of old age in America since 1790, Andrew Achenbaum asserts that Americans have always viewed old age as a distinct phase of the life course and that the chronological boundaries of old age have remained relatively stable (1978:1–2).

Research on seventeenth- and eighteenth-century New England supports the contention that old age is, as Achenbaum puts it, an age-old phenomenon in America (1978:2). John Demos (1978) shows that old age has been perceived as a distinct life stage since colonial times. "The culture at large," he writes of early New England, "recognized old age as a distinct time of life." So, too, elderly people were conscious of their own aging: "They thought about it and talked about it, and in various ways they acted from a particular sense of age-appropriate needs and requirements" (1978:261).

According to various written statements and legislative decrees, old age in early New England was defined chronologically as life after sixty. One town, for example, voted to exempt older persons from certain civic duties and established "sixty years of age" as the official cut-off point (Demos 1978:249). But not all official documents were so specific, and many New Englanders, Demos suggests, probably did not know or care precisely how old they were (1978:261). In any case, age norms were loosely applied and were very flexible. More important than chronological criteria, he says, were the physical markers of old age.[5] Old age was measured by the survival—or decline—of physical capacity: "There is no doubting the depth of the association between age and physical depletion in the minds of New Englanders" (Demos 1978:262). As for retirement, men past sixty in early New England did as a rule reduce their activities in work or public service, although such withdrawal was voluntary, gradual, and partial.[6]

Uncovering how ordinary Americans defined the boundaries of old age in the past is fraught with difficulties, and historians, by necessity, must rely on fragmentary evidence. There are also practical problems in deciding who to include in the category "old." Even historians who indicate there was no precise chronological benchmark of old age in the past

usually end up using rather arbitrary chronological boundaries for statistical purposes.[7]

Just how arbitrary such boundaries can be is highlighted
by Janet Roebuck's (1979) analysis of old-age definitions in
England. Researchers who select sixty and sixty-five, she says,
sometimes justify this decision by assuming that the state had
logical reasons for adopting sixty and sixty-five to mark the
onset of old age. The state's choice of these chronological
benchmarks, however, was determined by such factors as the
cost of pension programs and the demand to get older people
out of the labor market, with no real consideration given to
the definition of old age as such.

The study of cultural beliefs in days gone by in preliterate societies—where the people themselves have left no written records behind—is even more problematic than it is in
Western European and American society. But anthropologists
are also interested in the present. Indeed, this is usually their
primary concern. And in investigating cultural perceptions in
the present they have an advantage over historians. Anthropologists can get to know and talk with living people to begin
to understand how individuals in different cultures delineate
old age.

Not that all anthropologists who refer to old age tell us
how this life stage is defined. And we know hardly anything
about the variability of old-age definitions in nonindustrial
societies—whether, in other words, some criteria are used or
emphasized in certain situations and not in others. Yet there
is a growing body of material detailing the distinctive characteristics that guide individuals in different cultures in judg-
ing who is, or is not, "old." It is to these criteria that I now
turn.

Old Age Across Cultures

Old age, according to anthropological accounts, is recognized
as a distinct life stage in a wide variety of cultures. Some an-

thropologists claim that such a distinction is well nigh universal. In the introduction to an edited volume on aging in different cultures, Cowgill asserts that some people are considered "old" in all societies: they are so identified in the nomenclature of the people, and they are associated with specific roles (1972:4). Pamela Amoss and Stevan Harrell make a similar statement in the opening pages of a more recent collection of ethnographic accounts of old age. "Every known society," they write, "has a named social category of people who are old—chronologically, physiologically, or generationally. In every case these people have different rights, duties, privileges, and burdens from those enjoyed or suffered by their juniors" (1981:3).

What is not constant, of course, are the criteria by which people decide who is old—or the sharpness of the boundaries marking off old age. "The divisions between [age] strata," Riley and her associates note, "may be variously specified, either precisely or approximately, and in terms either of the chronological age of the members (as in census age categories) or of their stage of biological, psychological or social development" (1972:6). The following analysis does not include psychological criteria of old age (see Erikson 1963). Instead, I focus on the chronological, physical, and social-role criteria that mark off those considered old.[8]

Chronology

It is often difficult to separate empirically chronological and physical criteria delineating old age. As people grow older, certain processes of physiological deterioration are inevitable so that those in the final decades of the normal life span are likely to experience certain kinds of physical and mental disabilities (Amoss and Harrell 1981:2). As we will see, the physical changes that come with the passing years often signal the onset of old age. Indeed, the old are nearly always those who have passed the prime years of physical health and vigor. Chronological age—the rough or precise calculation of the amount of time that has elapsed since an individual's birth—can be involved in defining people as old. In fact, in their analysis of a worldwide sample of societies from the Human Relations Area Files, Glascock and Feinman (1980) found that chronology was the second most common criterion employed in the definition of old age, although they question the reliability of the ethnographic literature on this point.[9]

In literate societies, absolute chronological age may mark the onset of old age. A frequent benchmark of old age in present-day America is the sixty-fifth birthday. In traditional Japan, a formal ceremony, held on an individual's sixty-first birthday, signaled the transition to old age. Putting on a bright kimono symbolized the new feeedom from responsibilities of middle adulthood (Plath 1972:147).

Of course, most preliterate societies do not keep close track of age. In preliterate societies, as Jack Goody notes, "there is no conceptualization of absolute age calculated by time elapsed from a fixed position such as date of birth, since the reckoning of a birthday and its annual commemoration of time past, age attained, is dependent upon the existence of a calendrical system based upon an era, i.e., a point at which time begins, at least for the purpose of time-reckoning" (1976a:125). Fortes (1984) tells us, for example, that the Tallensi were culturally blind to facts of chronological age and had no notion of specific ages for entry into, or exit from, particular roles. Many anthropologists relate their difficulties in discovering exact chronological ages of older persons in the societies they studied. Colson and Scudder lament that few Gwembe villagers knew when they were born (1981:131). To estimate older peoples' ages, Colson and Scudder found out birth order and then extrapolated from the birthdates of those few people whose births could be fixed. Such a procedure of course is subject to error, and the anthropologists say that the ages they assigned could be off by as much as five or ten years.

Individuals in nonindustrial societies may not know their exact chronological ages, but this does not mean that the passage of time goes unordered or unmeasured. Chronological age, as I use the term, need not entail a knowledge of absolute age; approximate chronological age may be calculated in a variety of ways. People may reckon age "comparatively (he was born before me), in relation to some irregular natural event (before the flood), or in some loose way by reference to the passage of the seasons (he has seen eighty summers)" (J. Goody 1976a:125). Age may also be figured in relation to the occurrence of certain public ceremonies or other important events. The Gusii, for instance, had a system of naming each year after a major event in that period so they knew what year they were born in and circumcised. Those who shared particular named years of birth and/or circumcision recognized each other as age-mates (R. LeVine 1980:92).

In some societies, membership in an age set provides a way to estimate age. Of course, age sets can include individuals of widely varying ages—ten to fifteen years apart, for example. But informal distinctions within age sets can provide a way to calculate age. The Mursi of Ethiopia know a person's relative age without having to express it in years:

In fact, most people can tell instantly and accurately the relative ages, to within less than one-year intervals, of the other members of their local community, whether male or female. This is achieved through the ceremonial of the age organization. What happens, briefly, is that boys and girls go through, in local groups of age-mates, a number of grades before entering that of adulthood. A boy begins his passage through the grades at the age of about seven, in the company of his closest local age-mates. As he gets older he will enter age groups of wider and wider age span, but, within these wider groups, distinctions based on intervals of as little as one year between successive intakes to a particular grade of boys are remembered and are thus available to allow fine distinctions to be made, when necessary, between one man and another on the basis of age. (Turton and Ruggles 1978:592)

Relative age—seniority and juniority by birth order—is in fact crucial for social relations in many societies. But to know someone is older than yourself or others is not the same as labeling him or her as old. This leads us back to the issue of chronology and old-age definitions. What I want to emphasize is that having lived a certain amount of time—however it is conceptualized and whatever this span may be—is probably of some account in defining old age in many nonindustrial societies. Indeed, physical changes and role shifts that are supposed to mark off old age do not always make a person "old" if he or she is chronologically young. I should note, too, that although people in many societies do not calculate old age in terms of years, those they consider old are often chronologically young (or middle-aged) by our standards, in their forties, for instance. Interviews with the Asmat of New Guinea, to take one example, indicated that they considered persons over about forty-five as "old" (Van Arsdale 1981:118).

Physical Changes and Role Shifts

Chronological age, however it is reckoned, may, then, have something to do with definitions of old age in non-Western societies. Physical changes and shifts in social roles are generally even more important in delineating old age in these societies.

Physical Structure and Functioning. Individuals at different life stages, we know, show important differences in both physical structure and physiological functioning. Wrinkled skin and gray hair are two changes in physical appearance connected to the organic processes of aging. Many other internal physiological changes associated with aging—the decline in the number and quality of vital cells, for example—are manifested externally as well.

Research on old age in modern industrial societies has demonstrated that strength and endurance among the old are lower than among younger adults. Old people also tend to have poorer health than the young. While the aged have fewer acute illnesses, they are more subject to such chronic conditions as failing vision and hearing, rheumatism and arthritis, and heart disease and high blood pressure. When compared with younger people, older people are more likely to show deficits in sensory and perceptual skills, in complex sensorimotor coordination, in certain forms of memory, and in various aspects of intellectual functioning (Riley and A. Foner 1974:548; see Riley and A. Foner 1968).

It is true, of course, that as we learn more about biological changes in the later years in different populations we may find that declines in physiological functioning that are accepted as normal in modern Western countries are not inevitable concomitants of aging in many non-Western societies (Beall 1984). Yet whatever the cultural variations in the physical condition of people in the later years, many ethnographers note that one or another of the various physical signs of aging mark the beginning of old age in particular cultures. Indeed, in many societies physical differences distinguish two categories of old people. The old are often differentiated from the very old—those "with body feeble and the mind hazy" who are infirm and decrepit (Simmons 1945:177).[10]

The Links Between Physical and Role Changes. Since physical changes are, in reality, often closely associated with shifts in social roles, it is hard to separate empirically one from the other. I suggest that physical changes usually take on meaning as important signposts of old age precisely because they are connected with significant role changes. Thus, if a person did not change social roles when his or her hair whitened or strength began to wane, for instance, then white hair and decreasing stamina might not be significant markers of old age.

At the same time, biological factors such as decreasing muscular strength obviously set limits on the roles individuals can play in their later years. Social scientists who emphasize the importance of functional definitions of old age in nonindustrial societies make this point quite clearly. Margaret Clark, for instance, says that while chronological age is an important index of old age in our own culture, in less complex societies, old age is often defined in functional terms: "This is to say, when biological deterioration sets in, as this affects productivity, mobility, strength—in short, when the individual's capacity to contribute to the work and protection of the group to which he belongs is substantially changed" (1968:438). Physical declines, in other words, force individuals to restrict their activities and render them incapable of performing certain roles. Keep in mind, however, that these changes in role patterns tend to be gradual, involving a tapering off of activities rather than an abrupt shift from one day to the next (see Riley 1976:208).

Among the Quechua Indians described by Allan Holmberg, two signs of old age—in addition to such indicators as the presence of grandchildren—were declining physical strength, which meant one could not carry heavy burdens up and down the mountains, and failing eyesight, which prevented traveling at night (1961:88–89). When these signs of age appeared, men and women began to reduce their workload and ceased doing heavy agricultural labor.

To the Inuit (Eskimo) of northern Canada, those who were no longer fully productive workers were considered old. Men became old when they were unable to hunt all year round—usually, by Guemple's (1980) calculations, when they were about fifty. Thus, one year a man was adult; the next, when he did not have the strength for rigorous winter hunting, he was labeled old. For women, becoming old was more gradual. Their declining physical capabilities were not so obvious since their productive work was less demanding and more varied. Generally they were classified as old when they were about sixty.

Similarly, people were thought old among the Coast Salish of Washington State and British Columbia in precontact times when they could no longer perform the full range of adult tasks appropriate to their sex and station (Amoss 1981:230). That is, men could no longer hike miles to kill game and pack it home again; and women found it hard to bend and stoop to pick berries and dig roots. Then they would shift the major part of these jobs to younger relatives.

Even when Coast Salish women could still easily produce and process food, they were considered old for certain purposes when they could no longer bear children. In other societies, too, menopause marks the onset of old age for women, for example, the Asmat (Van Arsdale 1981:118). Menopause is obviously a physiological change, but it is linked to shifts in social roles. Although women often continue child-rearing functions well past menopause by caring for grand-children and other young ones, at this point they cease to be mothers of their own infants.

The above examples/emphasize that physical changes come first, followed by shifts in social roles. Anthropologists who have studied other societies, however, stress the primacy of role changes in defining old age. Indeed, Glascock and Feinman (1980) found that changes in social role were the main bases for defining old age in the societies they sampled—although their classification scheme suggests that role shifts marking off old age were often linked to physical changes.[11]

On a general theoretical level, in terms of the age stratification perspective, Riley and her associates note that partitions of the population by age acquire sociological meaning as age strata "only as they index socially significant aspects of people and roles" (1972:399). Individuals in various age strata are differentiated by sequences of roles they have already experienced, currently occupy, and may expect to move into. "Partitions between strata are further differentiated by the social roles that are normatively prescribed, proscribed, or permitted to members of these strata" (Riley, Johnson, and A. Foner 1972:399). While these partitions are categories constructed by social scientists to understand social patterns, similar distinctions may well be made by the people being studied. In other words, as individuals assume specific and meaningful new social roles, they may be defined as old. And once defined as old, there may be further formal rules as well as informal norms and beliefs about the kinds of roles and activities appropriate for them (Riley, Johnson, and A. Foner 1972:403).

A few cases highlight the importance of role changes in defining old age. According to Austin Shelton, individuals were considered aged among the rural Igbo of Nigeria when they began mainly to receive rather than provide goods and services and when they received their first share of distributed goods and services (1972:32–33). This time of life was linked with observable physical changes, such as graying hair,[12] and also with changed family roles associated with children's maturity. It normally occurred after a person's children had married and begun to raise their own children. The aged, in fact, were often referred to according to their role in society. Old men could be called "those who rule" and "those who are headmen"; old women were referred to as "aged mother" by their daughter's children and as "great aged mother" by the children of their daughter's sons.

In many societies, grandparenthood is a sign of old age, and old people may be called by terms which mean "grandfather" or "grandmother" (see, for example, Adams 1972:106). Among the Coast Salish, as I mentioned, physical functioning was important in defining old age. But a person was also thought to have become "old" on the birth of his or her first grandchild (Amoss 1981:230).

In Sylvia Vatuk's (1975) study of Indian women in a former agricultural village, now part of metropolitan Delhi, perceptions of what old age "is" were actually an important subject of investigation. Partly because the women she studied did not know their exact chronological age, she decided not to select arbitrarily a chronological age to set off the old from younger people. Instead, Vatuk included in her study of old women those who considered themselves, and were considered by others, to be old. She found that self-perception and the perception of others as old differed from one individual to another and tended to depend on such external physical signs of aging as tooth loss and graying hair. The general consensus, however, was that marriage of one's children, especially sons, marked the beginning of old age for women (Vatuk 1975:143). This was more important than the passing of a specific number of years. Vatuk labels the marriage of sons a life-cycle criterion of old age, but she also indicates that marriage of sons (or adopted sons) meant that a woman assumed a new role in the family: she became a mother-in-law. And soon a grandmother. For when sons married they brought their wives—and later grandchildren—into her household. Now an old woman, with married sons, she usually ceased having sexual relations with her husband, for it was considered shameful for parents to engage in sex while a son and his wife were also doing so in the same house.

Elders

The examples presented so far show how people in a number of different societies define old age. Another issue related to old-age definitions needs clarification. What does the term "elder" mean? In reading about nonindustrial societies, the term "elder" frequently crops up. Does the term refer to old men? To older men? To generational seniors?

Just as there is no one definition of old age applicable to all societies, so, too, no one definition of elder can cover all possible cases. Definitions of eldership differ from place to place, and I can only give some idea of the range of variation. Important here is that being an elder is not necessarily synonymous with old age. It is not a given that all elders in a particular society will be old or that all old men will be considered elders. Being an elder, for instance, may simply denote comparative age. Among the Suku of Zaire, the term "elder" literally meant anyone older than oneself—an older sibling, for instance, or anyone in a senior generation (Kopytoff 1971a:131). Elsewhere, an elder is a man with a combination of characteristics—generational seniority as well as advanced age, influence, and/or wealth.

The Lugbara case is interesting in that it shows how age considerations affected the way eldership was viewed. Among the Lugbara, the elder was the official head of the locally based cluster of patrilineally related kin. He owed his position to generational seniority. He was supposed to be the eldest son of the senior (or first) wife of his predecessor. To fill all his duties, however, the elder should also have been senior in years.[13] If the "true" elder was young (or weak or poor), he could have been replaced in some situations by a close kinsman who was older (or strong-willed or wealthy), who became holder of overall secular authority, "a kind of regent in everyday matters" (Middleton 1965:27). The regent might also have been referred to as an elder (Middleton 1960:12).

In one family cluster in the early 1900s, the "true" elder, Ondua, succeeded to the position when he was only in his early twenties. Although he held the mystical power of eldership, his authority was not accepted throughout the lineage and secular authority was exercised by older men until Ondua was in his forties. Then Ondua succeeded to full authority as elder (Middleton 1960:121). Whether the Lugbara then considered Ondua to be old is not clear; Middleton does not tell us how the Lugbara defined old age. That elderhood was associated with being old is suggested, however, by the fact that subordinate family heads, though distinguished from "real" elders, might be called elders if they were old (Middleton 1960:10).

Still another meaning of the term "elder"—quite different from that described by Middleton for the Lugbara—is found in societies with age-set systems. In these societies, elders are men in senior age grades. As we shall see, however, elders in age-set societies are not always considered old.

Age-Set Societies

Formal Group Transitions to Old Age

Age-set societies hold a particular fascination for anthropologists of aging. In these societies age is explicitly used as a major element in social organization. Age, it can be clearly seen, plays a crucial role in the allocation of social roles and rewards. Age-set societies are of especial interest in investigating the way changes in social roles demarcate old age. In societies without age sets, entering old age is an individual matter, a question of each person becoming old as his or her physical state, chronological age, or social roles change. In age-set societies, however, the formal transition to old age—or at least the official assumption of important social roles associated with old age—is often an organized and collective affair.

What are age-set societies? As the term implies, they are

characterized by age sets. *Age sets* are named groups of individuals, usually males, of similar age,[14] which are formed at a specific point in the life course. Once a set is formed, sometime in youth, it lasts the bulk of the life course. Age-set members, moreover, formally proceed together from one age grade to another. These group transitions through a series of age-graded roles are generally marked by formalized procedures and accompanied by considerable public ceremony. An age set, then, is a publicly recognized group of age-mates. *Age grades*, by contrast, are socially defined life stages—youth, warrior, and elder, for instance—each associated with a set of distinctive social roles and with different social rewards. The number of age grades can, of course, vary from society to society. But in all age-set societies, as individuals formally move through successive age grades with members of their age set, they assume or give up such significant roles as ritual or political office as well as a wide array of social privileges ranging from the right to marry to the power to curse others (A. Foner and Kertzer 1978:1084–1085).

Age-set systems, as I have described them, are relatively rare, with most found in Africa, particularly East Africa. Adequate documentation is available for some two dozen African age-set systems (A. Foner and Kertzer 1978:1083). This documentation is far more extensive for men's than women's age-set systems. Indeed, in most African age-set societies, age-set systems directly involve only men. Age-set systems are not only more common but are also more socially significant for men than for women. Besides, almost all of the ethnographic literature explores how men's age sets work, and we know little about women's age sets (Kertzer and Madison 1981).

Where age-set systems are found, they can influence the way individuals become old. In a number of age-set societies certain age grades are associated with old age. And an individual formally makes the transition to these grades—and thus officially assumes the roles of an old person—at communally ritualized times, together with his age-mates. In some age-set societies, for example, the final age grade is occupied by men who are considered old. And there is sometimes a grade, or a subgrade, to delineate very old men. Among the Masai, the "ancient elders" was one of the grades (Gulliver 1968:157). The Samburu distinguished "really old men" from others in the elders grade by special terms, though Spencer says that these "really old men" did not constitute a separate grade (quoted in Stewart 1977:148).

Informal Transitions to Old Age

Formal group transitions to old age are a dramatic feature of some age-set systems. But not all. There is a danger of exaggerating the importance of formal age grades in defining old age in age-set societies. Although age grades demarcate many meaningful life stages, they do not always formally mark off old age. And an exclusive focus on the formal rules of age-set systems draws our attention away from the way people actually make the transition to old age. Age-mates do not necessarily enter old age en masse: they may become old at different times than their fellow age-set members, each at his own pace. Thus, knowing a man's age set and the position of this set in the age-grade hierarchy may not indicate whether he is considered old or what age-grade roles he actually fills.

Available evidence suggests that criteria independent of age-set membership and age-grade location may signal the onset of old age in age-set societies. What these criteria are in specific age-set societies is unclear, but it seems likely that, as in other nonindustrial societies, one or more of the following criteria are involved in determining whether an individual is thought to be old: physical changes; approximate chronological age; and role changes (such as grandparenthood) that are not specifically allocated by age-grade level. Simply because men in age-set societies belong to age sets that move through specific grades does not, then, preclude other characteristics delineating old age.

Not all age-set societies, for one thing, have a formal, or even informal, age grade that is clearly associated with and demarcates old age. In a number of age-set societies, those considered old or very old belong to an age grade with younger men so that the age grade as a whole is not identified with old men. In fact, the final age grade of the life course, elder status, might typically be reached well before what is regarded as old age, often much earlier for some men in the age-set system than others (A. Foner and Kertzer 1978:1092). Even when an age grade is identified with old age, some men considered old may not yet have formally moved into it. Regardless of their official age grade, however, these old men may act in ways suited to members of the age grade of old men. The formal and informal entry to old age may thus be two quite different things.

It is worth exploring more fully the disjunction between formal rules governing age-set transitions and the actual timing of transitions—a subject, by the way, of increasing interest as anthropologists begin to synthesize what we know about and develop theoretical models to understand age-set systems (Baxter and Almagor 1978; A. Foner and Kertzer 1978; Kertzer 1978; Stewart 1977). The discrepancy between the formal and informal transition to various age grades can arise because of the long interval between age sets. As a result of these long intervals, each age grade is formally occupied by men of disparate ages, some of whom may be deemed "old enough," in terms of their physical, chronological, or social age, to move on to the next grade.

Thus, in some age-set societies each named age set can include men initiated over an extended period—about fourteen years among the Samburu and Arusha, to mention two societies we will discuss again. In general, men on the edges of two adjacent sets are likely to be closer to each other in age than they are to members of their own set at its other extreme (see Baxter and Almagor 1978:6). Because of the wide age range of set members, men are not always officially in a grade that fits their physical condition, chronological age, or various family and economic roles. The oldest members of one age set, for instance, may have to wait until quite late to become official elders, whereas the youngest members of the same set will be catapulted into elderhood at a relatively young age.

In terms of old age, men defined as old on the basis of

physical criteria, certain social roles, or chronological age—but who are not yet officially in grades associated with old men—will want to assume prestigious grade roles still formally denied them. In other cases, old men's desire to depart from their official grade roles is related to their sheer physical inability to continue in these roles. Possibly, too, relatively young men who are in grades associated with old men will be reluctant to assume their official grade roles, especially if these roles are poorly regarded.

Often, however, a degree of flexibility is allowed in the operation of the age-grade system (A. Foner and Kertzer 1978; Stewart 1977). Men in an age set may be permitted to make role transitions at different times rather than as a group with their age-set mates. In addition, there is sometimes a gradual period of transition so that men begin to assume some of the roles of the next age grade before they have officially moved into it. There is reason to think that physical state, social roles, and/or chronological age are crucial in determining which age-grade privileges and responsibilities men in fact assumed.

The Arusha of Tanzania show how men often informally assumed age-grade roles that were in tune with their physical state and social position, despite their official age grade (Gulliver 1963). Among the Arusha, as I said, each age set had an age range of about fourteen years. Although officially men often occupied grades that were not appropriate to their stage of physical development or their economic and family careers, in reality they could depart from their official age-grade roles. Thus, knowing a man's formal age grade might not be a good guide to what grade roles he actually occupied or, I suspect, to whether he was considered old.

Ideally, an Arusha age set advanced as a group through a series of five defined age grades: junior murran; senior murran; junior elders; senior elders; and retired elders. Progress from one grade to the next was defined by specific ceremonies. In practice, however, all members of a single set did not necessarily assume the same age-grade roles. Nor were actual shifts in age-grade roles made by whole sets at specific times through rites of passage. Ceremonial events, supposed to mark formally age-grade changes, in fact mainly gave public recognition to established changes for most men in an age set, bringing formal categories in line with actual roles (Gulliver 1963:39). At certain times, many—sometimes most—members of an age set did not fill the age-grade roles that by ideal standards they should have filled.

What happened was that men began to take on roles of a senior age grade in order to bring their age-grade roles in line with their physical state and other social roles. At the end of the period during which circumcision was forbidden and before a new set was formed, for example, older uninitiated youths acted as if they were junior murran because they were physically ready to do so. "Such youths are more than mere boys," Gulliver writes, "many are about twenty years old. They would formerly, say Arusha today, have already been out with raiding parties, and would have been reasonably competent with spear and shield. They are, despite sanctions, already involved in sexual liaisons, and some may be betrothed. They disdain herding work and occupy themselves hedonistically like murran, even sometimes wearing murran-type decoration" (1963:42).

As for older men, many junior elders in 1956–1958 were doing the advising and consulting that was supposed to be the senior elders' job. Some junior elders' claims for senior eldership were probably buttressed by their advanced age. Like many senior elders, they had consolidated their families, herds, and farms. Their older sons were now adult and their older daughters were marrying, thereby creating useful affinal ties. Perhaps, too, they considered themselves old. At least this is one reason they used to justify moving up the age-grade hierarchy ahead of schedule. "We are getting old now," a junior elder spokesman publicly said, explaining why some junior elders were giving up certain responsibilities associated with their official age grade. "We have no time for all this work and no energy for it. Let the (senior) murran do it! It is their time now!" (Gulliver 1963:41). By the same token, many official senior elders were acting like retired elders. They had stopped attending public assemblies and were reluctant to engage in politico-jural affairs that did not directly involve them personally (Gulliver 1963:41).

Just how the Arusha defined old age is an open question. The retired elders grade seemed to be associated with old age; men in this grade were described by younger men as "too old for anything" (Gulliver 1963:38). Whether the senior elders grade was associated with old age is unclear. (Senior elders were typically in their fifties and early sixties; retired elders in their early sixties and over.) But it hardly seems likely that official age grade signaled the onset of old age. Rather, I suspect that men defined as old—in terms of physical state, social roles, and perhaps approximate chronological age—began to assume the grade roles thought appropriate for old men.

In the Arusha case, age-set members could be as much as fourteen years apart because of the long interval between the inauguration of sets. In other age-set societies, different factors can account for age sets consisting of men of a wide age range. In these societies as well, it seems unlikely that all men of an age set, formally occupying an age grade, are considered old.

When initiation into an age set requires substantial expense, economic considerations affect the timing of initiation and therefore which set a youth enters (A. Foner and Kertzer 1978:1091; Stewart 1977:223–224). An individual's social or physical maturity often influences when he joins an age set. Stewart notes that two boys of the same age might be at different levels of maturity: "In such cases it must happen from time to time that they are enrolled in different sets" (1977:203). Once recruitment of the age set's membership was completed, however, members officially made subsequent role transfers at the same time. Thus, Anne Foner and David Kertzer point out that a person who was initiated at a comparatively young age could also in many systems retire early: "For example, where individual A was one of the oldest recruits to the age set and individual B was one of the youngest, they would both 'retire' at the same time, but individual A might be forty-eight and individual B just thirty-eight at retirement" (1978:1091).

Generation-Set Systems

Age sets, then, sometimes group men of disparate ages, including some who are, and some who are not, considered old. Generation sets, found in a number of East African societies, often consist of men who are even further apart in social, physical, or chronological age. Indeed, there is every reason to think that old age is not defined by the generation-set system but rather by changes in physical condition, social roles, and/or chronological age.

Not surprisingly, generation sets are an unreliable guide to whether an individual is considered old. In generation-set systems, a man is assigned generation-set membership by virtue of genealogical factors, not age. The generation set a man joins is determined by the generation set his father is in; the son's generation-set membership is specified by a fixed number of sets following that of his father. Among the Karimojong, for example, where only two generation sets (one senior and one junior) were recognized as being in existence at any one time, a young man could not be initiated while his father belonged to the junior generation set (Dyson-Hudson, cited in A. Foner and Kertzer 1978:1091).

The formal rules of generation-set systems inevitably cause discrepancies between age and generation-set membership. Genealogical generations group men of disparate stages of development and social positions so that, for example, brothers thirty years apart in age will belong to the same generation set. Set members of widely different ages share in the same rewards—or social losses—that come with generation-set membership. Many young men among the Boran of Ethiopia, for instance, "retired"[15] alongside elderly men who belonged to the same generation set (Legesse, cited in A. Foner and Kertzer 1978:1091). In societies where generation sets move through a series of age grades, some men may never even reach the most senior grade. Since a man must wait until the appropriate generation set (as defined by a specified number of sets distant from his father's) is open for recruitment, he may be relatively old by the time he can enter a set and occupy a grade at the beginning of the age-grade cycle. And he may not live long enough to proceed through all the grades of the system (Kertzer 1978:373).

To be sure, various practices reduce the discrepancies between generation-set membership, on the one hand, and physical, social, and/or chronological age, on the other. In some societies, restrictions limit the number of years during which men can sire legitimate children so that they cannot, for example, marry until relatively late. Rules that eliminate the phenomenon of young fathers reduce the likelihood that sons will be too old for their designated generation set. Some East African generation-set systems permit shifting. An individual who is a younger member of his generation might be below what is considered the proper age for members of that group, especially when the group is in an age grade suitable for older men. He is therefore allowed to enroll in a junior generation set (Stewart 1977:100–101).

Moreover, in some societies with generation-set systems, the disjunction between age and generation-set membership is alleviated somewhat because age-grade and/or age-set systems also operate independently of the generation-set system (see A. Foner and Kertzer 1978:1091–1092). Among the Kikuyu, the ruling generation set, which at any one time included some very young men and excluded some older men, had certain distinct privileges. However, as participants in the age-grade system, older men who were in the generation set junior to the ruling set could take part in the various elders' councils. By paying fees they could also acquire most of the privileges of the ruling generation. As for men who belonged to the retired generation set, as long as they were healthy and vigorous they continued, along with members of the ruling set, as active members of the judicial council (Stewart 1977:188–189).

Finally, the conflict between age and generation-set membership is reduced because generation sets can have quite limited functions. Baxter and Almagor argue that generation as well as age sets in East African societies do not control productive resources (1978:10, 13–14). Rights in herds rest with families, not sets, and older men's control of stock, wives, and management decisions ensures their privileges and authority in the family, whatever their set. Set membership is important only insofar as "age-suitability for the task, age-grading and set rules fit in with the labour requirements of the family herd and the need to fill essential familial roles" (Baxter and Almagor 1978:13).

Nonetheless, even though various factors can lessen the disjunction between age and generation-set membership, this disjunction is often quite glaring. What is important here is that characteristics other than generation-set memberhip—and position of this set in a hierarchy of graded roles—delineate old age.

Conclusion

Not all societies have such complicated and inherently contradictory ways to group people as those with generation-set systems. Yet societies vary widely in the way individuals are defined as old. Despite this variety, certain common patterns emerge. As I have repeatedly emphasized, definitions of old age involve one or more of the following factors: physical characteristics and physiological processes associated with aging; approximate or absolute chronological age; and the social roles an individual is expected, permitted, or required to play in the later years.

It is partly because definitions of old age are either lacking or poorly specified in most accounts—and because these definitions vary from one society to another—that cross-cultural comparisons of old age are so difficult. Leo Simmons (1945), in his well-known cross-cultural study of old age in primitive societies, recognized this problem too. He decided to consider "a person as 'old' whenever he was so regarded and treated by his contemporaries" (1945:16). That this is what the ethnographers and other observers meant when they used the word "old" in the reports Simmons uses is, however, far from clear. Indeed, many of the writers he relies on did not know the native language or live in the society for very long. Yet at present there is little we can do to improve on Simmons's decision.

Thus in the following chapters, I will, when possible, report what the ethnographer means by the term "old" in his or her account. If I offer no definition this is because none was supplied by the anthropologist. Many times I will simply use the term "older" to refer to relative age. With the understanding, then, that definitions of old age are culturally variable, let us turn to the kinds of inequalities that are found between old and young in nonindustrial societies and the tensions that such inequalities produce.

2
Consequences
of Age Inequality: I

Old Men at the Top

For young people in many nonindustrial societies the best, as Browning had it, is yet to be. To reach old age is the crowning achievement of a lifetime. That old people are likely to enjoy considerable influence, prestige, and wealth is not just happenstance. Certain advantages systematically come with old age in a great number of societies.

When the old reap many benefits, however, their situation is not trouble free. Problems often arise with the young. The counterpart to old people's powers and privileges is young people's less fortunate position. The young are frequently bursting over with envy and resentment or at least are ambivalent toward the old in control. There is, in short, a negative side to power and privilege, and the elderly at the top of the age hierarchy often find that relations with younger people are in a state of uneasy peace and sometimes open conflict.

This chapter and the one that follows develop these themes. The two chapters point, first of all, to the sources of old people's privileges, power, and wealth in nonindustrial societies. In this analysis, it is important to bear in mind that, while the old in many places have the opportunity to occupy highly valued roles and to accumulate social rewards, the later years are not necessarily an enviable time for *all* old people. Some of the elderly were on top at an earlier point in their old age but have had to give up valued roles, or at least actively functioning in these roles. Most commonly this occurred because they experienced severe physical or mental declines, as we shall see in chapter 4. This chapter and the next, however, refer to individuals who can still attend physically and mentally to their essential daily needs and who do not need custodial care, though they may no longer be fully productive economically and may partly depend on others for their livelihood (Amoss and Harrell 1981:3).

Even where the still active old are relatively privileged vis-à-vis younger adults, all are not equally successful. Some old people have an unfair head start, being eldest sons or having prosperous parents, to name two possible advantages. Others who are, for example, members of certain kinship groups may be the only ones who can qualify for powerful political roles. Such factors as luck, skill, and personality also influence an old person's achievements. All of the still active old in many societies do acquire some rewards. But growing old simply gives individuals the opportunity to compete for others. Stated somewhat differently, age limits the competition for rewards and valued roles, and younger people often have to wait their turn to compete.

This waiting period can be a frustrating time for the young. While they are eager to come into their own, all too often older people stand in the way. The second and major theme of these two chapters is thus the consequences of age inequality for intergenerational relations. Strains are likely to arise when the young find themselves subject to and constrained by old people's authority and when they, unlike the elderly, have only limited and perhaps even no chances to gain the key rewards their society has to offer.

So far these general comments apply to old men as well as to old women. Yet the scope of the prestige, power, and wealth of elderly men and women in nonindustrial societies is not the same. And the particular young people who typically have the most tense relations with old men are rarely those who have serious conflicts with old women. This chapter is thus devoted to old men at the peak of the age hierarchy; chapter 3 focuses on old women.

Bases of Inequality

Before probing the effects of age inequalities on relations between old and young men, the stage must be set: What are the rewards and valued roles that old men reap?[1]

Old men often have greater opportunity than younger men to control material resources and other property, to accumulate wives, and to exercise authority in the household as well as in the wider community. In many societies, old men also predominate in ritual offices. And they often have extensive ritual and practical knowledge. This expertise, in addition to their other privileges and powers, usually brings old men a great deal of esteem.

Bear in mind that where old men, as a group, are privileged and powerful as compared to younger men, old men (or certain categories of old men) may not have access to all of these rewards. In the case of plural wives, this asset is obviously out of the question where polygyny is not practiced—though, as we shall see, it is a linchpin of old men's privileged position in many places.

Control Over Material Resources

Control of material resources (either through outright ownership or trusteeship and managerial rights) is an important benefit that comes with age in many nonindustrial societies.

In hunting and gathering societies, it is true, economic resources are largely open and there are generalized rights to exploit a territory so that the young are relatively independent of older men for acquiring rights in productive resources

(J. Goody 1976a:118). And there are few valuable possessions in such societies that anyone, young or old, accumulates or waits to inherit.

In farming and pastoral societies, however, old men frequently have the power to allocate and transfer land and livestock. In farming societies, rights to farmland are acquired from senior kinsmen who often formally hold on to these rights well into old age and perhaps until death. In pastoral societies, too, young men acquire livestock from senior kin, who may retain ultimate control over the family herd into their later years. The young are thus often beholden to old men for their very livelihood, especially when the resources under old men's control are in scarce supply. Even in horticultural societies where land is fairly easily available, old men's control of scarce movable property such as crops, money, or cattle is frequently a key to their economic power.

Young men may depend on senior relatives for resources for reproductive as well as productive purposes. In many societies, marriage is arranged through substantial bridewealth payments—livestock, other goods, and nowadays often cash—to the bride's relatives. It is senior kin who control the wherewithal needed for a man's bridewealth payments, and this gives them the power to delay young men's marriages. Where senior relatives control the resources that make up bridewealth—or dowries for daughters—they can influence not only the timing of marriage but whom their dependents will wed.

While older men are obliged to provide junior male kin with bridewealth, they are also on the receiving end. Senior kin obtain bridewealth when their own female dependents—daughters or sister's daughters, for example—marry, and this in many cases is an important resource at their command.

Old men's control of material resources and the right to distribute the produce of their household's collective labor gives them the means to obtain other valued goods and to expand their influence over people. Old men often take additional wives, as we shall see. Terray makes much of the ability of compound heads among the Abron and Kulango of West Africa to exchange produce for, among other things, such prestige goods as jewelry and loincloths (1975:107). Although they have no economic utility, prestige goods, as the term implies, bring social honor. A man may bask in the glory of owning and displaying them and by so doing make clear his superior social rank.

Generosity, not accumulation of goods, is what is valued in many places, however. Here, too, old men's control of economic resources (as well as their ability to call on the help of many people) often makes it possible for them to give lavishly at public gatherings. And bestowing gifts on individuals and providing others with help enable an old man to expand his political supporters.

Human Resources

"Among most if not all nonindustrial people," writes Sally Falk Moore, "access to human beings is the greatest wealth and power there is" (1978:67). Indeed, it is often hard to separate old men's control over material resources from their "people power." In nonindustrial societies, the ability to command the labor and support of others often underpins old men's wealth, prestige, and influence. Where land is readily available, labor cannot be hired, most property is not durable, and rudimentary technology limits the amount of land any one person can cultivate or food that he or she can gather, those who can call on many people have a definite edge. They are the ones with the means to entertain or acquire prestige goods, to build up political support, and even to retire from the more arduous productive tasks.

Building up large families and followings is thus a key to success in nonindustrial societies. Old men, for one thing, have time on their side. Aging provides the opportunity to establish durable relations with kin, descendants, and social debtors and allies who can be relied on in times of need and for political support. Old men also frequently control the material—as well as reproductive—resources needed to attract followers and accumulate dependents. Polygyny is important here. In polygynous societies, it is usually older men who are adding wives, while younger men must wait (sometimes until their thirties) to marry for the first time. This is often because older men control the wherewithal to marry, or sometimes because other restrictions prevent younger men from marrying until relatively late.

If, as Moore writes, social relations in nonindustrial societies are the most long-lived and reliable riches, then wives may be the most valued treasures (1978:67). Wives, for one thing, are valuable work hands. And women, of course, are reproducers as well as producers. The more wives a man has, the more children he is likely to sire. Sons (or sons-in-law) as well as daughters (or daughters-in-law) are an important source of labor in farming, hunting, fishing, herding, and domestic work. Sons (or sons-in-law) may also defend the home front and its resources from outside attack.

Having many wives and many descendants means a larger work team and more food for the household and thus a surplus with which to entertain visitors, to obtain prestige goods, and to attract clients. Hospitality is often important to a man's prestige, and formal or informal influence frequently depends at least partly on the ability to give economic assistance to others. Older men may even be able to withdraw from heavier and more time-consuming productive tasks and use their leisure time for political or other pursuits.

The ability to bestow or marry daughters also brings wealth, prestige, and power in many places. In Australian hunting and gathering societies, older men accumulated power through control of wives for themselves as well as potential wives for others—called gerontogamy by Gardner (1968:209). In many African societies and elsewhere, daughters bring in bridewealth. In some societies, sons-in-law provide fathers-in-law with labor for months and even years in the form of brideservice. Where sons-in-law join their wives' people at marriage, they may give fathers-in-law more lasting help.

Many wives and many descendants are, in themselves, a source of prestige. Polygny also provides older men with important affinal ties. The more wives a man has, the more people there are with whom he can exchange services and gifts and on whom he can depend for political and economic support. And it is not only a man's wives' relatives who expand his networks. He is able to gain allies and create, or cement, durable social relations through the marriage of his children or other dependents.

Positions of Authority

It is already clear that older men, as controllers of material resources and as husbands, senior kin, and affines, have authority over people.

In many societies, much of an older man's authority stems from his position as head of an extended family, which he occupies on the basis of age and seniority. Compared to our own society, domestic groups in nonindustrial societies are more likely to include several generations of kin. Family members are also involved in joint productive activities. In many places, successful men, by the time they are old, have a sizable number of relatives under their wing, including, children, daughters-in-law or sons-in-law, grandchildren, and perhaps several wives as well. Older men who head extended family units commonly have the authority not only to allocate resources and labor but to settle disputes and punish offenders in the group (see R. LeVine 1965:190). In addition, they usually represent the family in relations with other groups. And they tend to have a good deal of say in determining just what juniors in the family can and cannot do. Even when an old man's heirs move out to set up their own households, he frequently retains considerable authority over these juniors.

Old men in many societies also have greater access than younger men to roles that bring authority beyond the domestic group. Sometimes, age itself is a criterion for leadership. Or aging is important because it gives men the time to build up the support, skills, and wealth needed for political success. Genealogical seniority is also often a key qualification and here, too, age is an advantage, for by the time a man is old most of his own senior male relatives are dead.

We thus read of old men in many societies predominating in the community in formal and informal leadership roles; in councils as well as less formal assemblies; in voluntary associations and secret societies. In these and other roles, old men often sit in judgment in disputes. Men sometimes even hold onto political office up to the very end. "Where 'blood' (or filiation) is part of the requirement of office and legitimizes the choice of incumbent," Jack Goody writes, "a man may well be separated from his position only by death" (1976a:127).

The extent of old men's authority outside the domestic group varies widely, of course, both within and between societies. Looking across cultures, it is clear that old men's authority is very restricted in many simpler societies so that even those in formal leadership positions cannot make decisions without community consensus. At the other extreme, old men in certain official positions in centralized states have substantial authority over vast numbers of people.

It should also be borne in mind that in societies where old age is associated with political leadership, not all old men rise to positions of power beyond the domestic group. Seniority as well as age often has a lot to do with who becomes leaders of wider kinship groups. Remember the Lugbara case, where the elder in the family cluster was the eldest son of his predecessor. In age-set societies, age-set membership and age-grade location affect who assumes certain community-wide powers, so that only men in certain elders' grades, for instance, qualify for particular responsibilities. Such factors as personal ability and wealth also determine which old men will be the influentials within an age set, kinship group, or community. And in some societies political office is restricted to men of certain descent groups so that some old men are clearly out of the running.

Ritual Roles and Mystical Powers

Ritual powers are often closely connected to authority in the household and community. In nonindustrial societies, growing old tends to bring with it certain ritual powers so that the old have ritual benefits and occupy ritual positions that are denied, or are less available, to younger folks. Indeed, it is through their control of ritual and religious knowledge, Amoss and Harrell write, that the old gain a special measure of respect almost everywhere (1981:14–15).

In societies with ancestor cults, for example, the elders "are not only the nearest to the ancestors in genealogical terms (and in this respect are living ancestors with 'one foot in the grave'), they are also progenitors of the maximum number of descendants, the apical ancestors of the living" (J. Goody 1976a:128). Senior living kin are thus the appropriate persons to conduct sacrifices and communicate with deceased ancestors, and these seniors are very often old. Even in societies without ancestor cults, the old are often believed to be close to deities or to have other mystical powers. The belief in old men's (or certain old men's) mystical powers not only enhances their prestige. Old people's threat to use these powers to harm the living is an important sanction at their command. Old men in many societies, for example, are believed to have the power to curse certain juniors. Old men's control of ritual knowledge and their direction of crucial rituals also backs up their authority in the community or in the family.

As with formal political positions, usually only certain old men qualify for or choose to fill ritual offices. Younger men, too, may occupy important ritual positions. Yet in many societies aged practitioners are especially powerful and influential. Old men are often found as curers and diviners, for example, or as priests and ceremonial leaders at important rituals.

Knowledge and Experience

The old are often felt to be suited to certain ritual roles because they have, over the years, accumulated ritual expertise and religious lore. Ritual knowledge is just one aspect of old people's expertise, however. In societies without writing, the old are repositories of wisdom about everyday practical affairs as well.

Because they have lived a long time, the elderly are important sources of information about the past and therefore about the way things should be done. It is they, for example, who may know how to perform certain ceremonies and who can remember genealogies and family histories so crucial in mediating disputes.

Because the old are generally regarded as possessors of knowledge, wisdom, and experience, they are often sought after, according to Simmons, to interpret puzzling and mysterious phenomena, diagnose and treat diseases, and provide comfort and guidance to the distraught and bereaved:

Faced with common perplexities, distressing anxieties, and personal crises of every kind, people have turned for help and counsel to the "old wise ones." . . . Where writing and records have been unknown . . . a lucid mind, a good memory, and a seasoned judgment, even when housed in a feeble frame, have been indispensable and treasured assets to the group. (1945:131)

Useful as the old are as storehouses of information, there is sometimes a less beneficent side to their knowledge. The knowledge gained through years of experience frequently justifies their ritual and political dominance as well as the respect they receive from younger people. Indeed, the elderly are not always willing to share what they know. They sometimes guard their privileged knowledge of ritual matters and of family and community history in order to buttress their control over the young (see Murphy 1980 on the Kpelle of Liberia).

Prestige

Property, polygyny, formal authority, as well as ritual powers and wisdom are all sources of old men's prestige. Perhaps, too, there is something to the notion that the old in nonindustrial societies are esteemed because they are relatively rare. As compared to modern industrial societies, there tend to be fewer old people as a proportion of the population in nonindustrial societies that are relatively untouched by modern developments in health and sanitation (Amoss and Harrell 1981:6).[2] To live to a ripe old age in these societies may be considered an achievement worthy of respect.

Age and seniority, in themselves, may be bases of prestige. In many societies men expect deferential behavior from those junior in generation. The older a man is, the more people who are junior to him—and the more who owe him respect. Juniors, for example, are often required to greet and speak to seniors in a respectful manner. And old men, on the basis of age and seniority, frequently receive other prerogatives, such as the best or largest portion of food or seats of honor at public ceremonies.

Of course, deferential behavior can be an empty formality and even disregarded when an old man has none of the other qualities that bring prestige. Even when old men are powerful and wealthy, the fact that younger folks are expected to show them deference often masks underlying tensions. It is to these tensions that I now turn. By looking at specific cases, the following pages will flesh out the picture of inequalities between old and younger men.

Strains Between Old and Young Men

All is not smooth sailing for old men at the top. They may cherish their privileges, but, as in any system of inequality, relations with the less advantaged are frequently marked by strain. While old men are piling up rewards, young men, at least for the time being, are often on the losing end. Old men want to preserve their advantages. And the young, subject to their elders' authority and deprived of valued resources and roles, often resent old men's prerogatives and the restraints under which they themselves labor.

How disadvantaged young men in different societies experience age inequality varies, of course. No two societies, or two individuals for that matter, are exactly alike. Young men may even accept their disadvantaged position as right and proper, as I will discuss in chapter 5. My main concern here, however, is with how inequalities between old and young men create strains between them. Despite cultural and individual differences, certain kinds of inequalities and resulting strains emerge with startling similarity in different social and cultural settings.

Close Kin and Affines

In many nonindustrial societies, strains between old and young men are most pronounced between those who are closely related by particular kinship or affinal ties. Serious tensions commonly develop where young men are constrained by the authority of certain old relatives or affines and, in many cases, are waiting to succeed them.

Fathers and Sons in Patrilineal Societies. Relations between fathers and sons are a good place to begin. Of course, these relations are not always strained. Patterns of descent, residence, and inheritance have much to do with the nature of the father–son bond. Whether sons succeed, inherit from, and are subject to the commands of fathers clearly influences relations between them.

Relations between fathers and sons are particularly strained in patrilineal societies. Since most societies of the world have adopted a predominantly patrilineal mode of descent and inheritance, tensions and clashes between fathers and sons have been frequently reported. In patrilineal societies, descent is traced principally through the male line on the father's side, and a man inherits property and position in his father's patriline. Virilocal residence tends to be the rule: a woman lives with her husband's people after marriage. In patrilineal societies this means that she usually joins the homestead or village of her husband's father (patrilocal residence).

What are the sources of tension and rivalry between fathers and sons in patrilineal societies? One source of the younger man's resentment before he marries is his economic dependence on his father. As heads of family groups, fathers are usually in charge of allocating economic resources to sons, so that young men are dependent on fathers not only for a livelihood but for the material resources needed to take a first wife. Although a young man is eager to come out from under, it is often difficult for him to become more independent. Accounts of many societies describe how a young man's very ability to marry hinges on his father's willingness and readiness to allocate resources to him. Fathers are not always so willing or ready, instead wanting to use their resources for their own aggrandizement (such as marrying more wives themselves) and to delay providing their son's bridewealth. Another possible difficulty in polygynous societies is an older man's fear that his bachelor sons will commit adultery with his younger wives (R. LeVine 1965:193).

When young men are unmarried, their fathers, of course, may not yet be old. But it is not unusual for men to be old when one of their bachelor sons is becoming adult and is hankering after more independence. And since men in many societies do not marry until relatively late—in their late twenties or early thirties—fathers are often old when their sons (or certain sons) "tie the knot."[3]

Marriage does not necessarily end young men's discontent and troubles with their fathers. Indeed, strains and rivalry between them frequently become more acute as young men mature and marry and as fathers age. As sons marry and grow older, they often want more autonomy and become more impatient to replace their fathers. Aging fathers, for their part, sense the threat from below and want to protect their position as long as possible. Eventually, they know, their sons will succeed them in positions of authority, as controllers of certain economic resources, and perhaps even as sexual partners to their younger wives.[4] They also know that their adult sons are capable of taking over immediately. A man may fear that when he becomes physically or mentally incompetent his sons will presume upon their inheritance, thereby undermining his own authority and position (R. LeVine 1965:195).

When an older man and his married son live in the same dwelling group (the same house or group of houses that make up a homestead or compound), the son is subject to his father's constant authority. In the Indian village of Gaon, for example, sons who stayed with their father often continued to wait on him, obeying his every whim, even when they had grown children. One such man remarked, with slightly bitter humor, that he was a servant in his own home (Orenstein 1965:56).

In many societies a son cannot move away until his father approves, and the question of timing can be a bone of contention between them. Sometimes, sons are not supposed to move away at all. In Turkish villages, for instance, married sons were expected to stay in their father's household until he died. A tug of war, Stirling says, inevitably occurred, with sons and their wives pressing to escape and fathers pressing to keep sons loyally attached (1965:119). Typically, fathers won out, and sons, despite their desire for independence, remained in a subordinate position at home. The older man owned the land and house and, as long as he was mentally capable, controlled household affairs.[5] Even the self-important headman in one village, a man of about thirty-five, who gave the impression of running his household, was, in fact, an underling at home. His old, still vigorous father was the real head of the household, and he had great influence on his son's public conduct as well. In rural Turkey, one son, usually the eldest, became the new household head when the father died, and eventually the younger sons left to set up their own independent households. In societies where only one son is expected to stay with the father, it is he who must wait for his father's death or extreme incapacity before he can fully take charge.

Even where young married men are residentially independent of fathers, their continued dependence on these older men in many societies can rankle. For one thing, they may still be obliged to provide labor for their father's household. When a man married among the Anlo Ewe of southern Ghana, he was expected to establish his own compound. He was given part of his father's land (or uncleared bush adjoining it) to use. But this did not liberate a young man from his father's authority. A son built his compound at a place chosen by his father—usually not far from the father's compound so that he could help his father when needed. And help he did. The father's farming needs came first, and he had a claim on his son's labor at weeding, sowing, and hoeing times (Nukunya 1969:32–40).

Issues of property control and inheritance often loom large. The Taita of Kenya said that the rivalry between a man and his son increased when the young man became a father and householder (Harris 1978:63, 110). As the Taita saw it, a man thought his son hoped for his death so that he could come into his inheritance. As for the son, the Taita said that he resented every reminder of his subordination, particularly the requirement that he not build up publicly his own wealth in livestock and thus be accused of trying to surpass his father. Sons complained that aging fathers grew more and more difficult, denying the sons rights to land and the produce of herds in order to cling to control as long as possible.

That young men are often waiting to come into their full inheritance is clearly a cause of strain between fathers and sons in many societies. A tale told among the pastoral Bedouin of Cyrenaica (Libya), where a man did not acquire proprietary rights in animals and land until his father died, suggests the tensions that stemmed from sons' impatience to inherit. A man, according to the tale, returned to camp after a long absence and was informed of the deaths of various kinsmen. In each case, he expressed his condolences. Finally, when told that his father had died, he replied, "Praise be to God, my property is free" (Peters 1978:325, 348).

Even in instances where senior men allocate land or other property in their lifetime to their sons, they often retain considerable property—the land they themselves farm, for example—which the young are eager to inherit. Among the Igbo of Nigeria, clashes between fathers and sons were most likely to occur when the father was in his late fifties and sixties and his sons were in their late thirties or forties, with almost-grown children themselves. By this time, the older man had usually distributed some of the family land to his grown sons. But if he was a strong and forceful person, he probably had kept back some of the better land, which he still farmed. In such cases, sons were likely to resent their father's continued control of the farmland and their inability to use this land for their own economic benefit (Shelton 1972:42).

If young men in many societies resent their economic dependence on, and demands for labor and financial assistance from, fathers, there are also other grounds for discontent. The older man's jural and ritual authority can restrict his sons' independence even after the young men marry and become fairly autonomous residentially. Young men are often unable to take certain actions—transferring land allocated to them, for example—without consulting with and gaining the approval of their fathers. In many societies, a young man cannot assume certain ritual powers or roles until his father dies.

Of course, a young man's subordination to his father— and an older man's dread of being replaced by his sons—rarely leads to unalloyed hostility between them. A complex mixture of feelings tends to characterize the bond between fathers and sons, a "tangle of attachments, reciprocities, tensions, and suppressed antagonisms," as Fortes reports in his classic study of the Tallensi of Ghana (1949:234). A closer look at father–son relations among the Tallensi shows the "ambivalent antagonisms" between them and offers another illustration of how older men's economic, jural, and ritual authority creates tensions with their sons.

Sons, among the Tallensi, were obliged to love, honor, and respect their fathers. This was not necessarily a burdensome duty. Sons were usually deeply attached and loyal to their fathers. At the same time, young men were severely constrained as long as their fathers were alive.

Tale fathers had numerous powers over their sons, which continued well into the fathers' old age. Fathers were said, in fact, to "own" their sons. A son, for instance, needed his father's approval to marry, and the older man could cause his son's marriage to break down by holding back the bridewealth. Even if a young man provided the means of payment, he could not get a wife unless his father accepted responsibility for the bridewealth. Once married and on the way to economic independence, a young man still came under his father's domination in many ways. He could not set out on his own without his father's blessing and consent, and it could take five or six years of pressuring before the older man gave way. Even when he had set up on his own, a son could be, and often was, called on to work his father's land.[6] And a man's property still formally belonged to his father. Any sheep, goats, or cattle he acquired, through his own efforts or for his daughter's bridewealth, were housed in his father's, not his own, homestead (Fortes 1949:206).

Wherever a son lived, he was subject to his father's ritual authority. The Tallensi believed that the ancestors' mystical protection was essential. Access to the ancestors was limited, however. A man could not make sacrifices to his dead patrilineal ancestors in his own right as long as his father was alive. Even when his father died, he approached the ancestors through the intermediation of his father's spirit. Just as a living father had the legitimate power to curse his sons, so when he died he could also cause harm to disobedient or offending junior kin. The anger of dead ancestors was, in fact, more feared than that of the living. A man could defy his living father and be forgiven. Not so with a dead father, who was owed "reverence and submission in surpassing degree" (Fortes 1949:173).

Tensions arose between a father and any of his adult sons, but the sharpest strains were between a man and his eldest son. The eldest son was the nearest to the succession and had the most to gain by his father's death. Since he was furthest along the road of social and economic maturity, the eldest son, of all a man's children, most effectively symbolized the filial generation (Fortes 1949:230). A man's eldest son was at once his crowning glory and a threat to his own authority. As his eldest son matured, married, and fathered his own children, the more the father felt that his eldest son threatened his dominance and seemed to be waiting in the wings to take over.

Tale fathers were quite open about strains with eldest sons. "Your oldest son is your rival" said the men. An elder told Fortes, "Look at my oldest son. He would not care if I should die tomorrow. Then he would inherit all my possessions"

(1949:225). The mystical concept of *Yin*, or personal Destiny, also expressed the latent antagonism between fathers and eldest sons:

> There is, they say, an inborn antagonism between the *Yin* of a father and the *Yin* of his eldest son. While the son is still young his *Yin* is weak, but as he grows older his *Yin* grows more powerful and wants to make him master of his own affairs. The son's *Yin* wants to destroy the father's *Yin*; but the father's *Yin* desires the father to live and be well and remain master of the house. It wishes to continue to receive sacrifices from the father. Therefore it will try to destroy the son's *Yin*, and if it is the stronger *Yin* it will cause misfortune and perhaps death to the son. (Fortes 1949:227)

While a man's father was alive, the son was not supposed to act in any way that suggested a desire to usurp the older man's place. Lest eldest sons have delusions of grandeur, symbolic avoidances between fathers and eldest sons made plain to the younger man that he was not his father's equal. From early childhood, certain taboos regulated relations between the two. A first-born son, for instance, could not eat from the same dish as his father, wear his father's clothes, use his father's bow, or look into his father's granary. When the first-born son married, he and his father were not supposed to meet face to face in the gateway of their common homestead. These symbolic avoidances thus required the younger man to behave in a way that showed he did not covet his father's position (Fortes 1949:223–227; 1970:173–174).

Yet eldest sons did, of course, look forward to the day when they would be their own masters. According to Fortes (1970), rituals and beliefs connected with dead ancestors eased the younger men's guilt at supplanting their fathers. Having to perform rituals that "metamorphose fathers into ancestors" provided an occasion when sons were forced to accept their triumph as a duty: "It is reassuring for a son to know that it is by his pious submission to ritual that his father is established among the ancestors forever. He sees it is as the continuation of submission to the authority that was vested in his father before his death" (1970:193).[7]

Relations between eldest sons and fathers carry the potential for strain in other patrilineal societies where the eldest son is the most likely to be his father's successor. This does not mean that relations between fathers and other sons are trouble free. Young men's economic, ritual, or jural subordination to fathers can create strains—no matter what the son's birth order. And sometimes middle or younger sons have special difficulties. Among the Chagga, for example, middle sons—the least favored with regard to land allocation—were likely to have strained relations with fathers (Moore 1975). In societies where youngest sons remain to care for aged fathers, they, too, often have a hard time. Living so close to, and being obliged to look after, the old men can present problems (see chapter 4).

Mother's Brothers and Sister's Sons in Matrilineal Societies. Strains between fathers and sons, of course, are not confined to patrilineal societies. Conditions are ripe for latent, as well as overt, antagonism between them whenever sons are constrained by their father's authority and where sons are slated to inherit property from and to succeed their fathers—in societies, for example, where descent is traced equally through females and males (bilateral descent systems). Where descent is traced through women, however, relations between fathers and sons are more relaxed.[8]

In matrilineal societies, a man's heir and successor is his sister's, rather than his own, son. From a young man's perspective, his mother's brother is commonly the villain of the piece. When a man will inherit from and succeed his mother's brother—and when his mother's brother has authority over him—relations between the two are often strained.[9]

The sources of tension are much the same as those I discussed for fathers and sons in patrilineal societies. Sisters' sons often resent their economic dependence on and obligations to maternal uncles—the duty to provide labor, for example—and their subjection to maternal uncles' authority. As potential heirs, they are rivals of their mother's brothers.

"A sister's son is his mother's brother's enemy, waiting

for him to die so that he may inherit," was a saying among the Ashanti of Ghana (Fortes 1950:272). The word "enemy" overemphasizes the negative, however. "Ambivalence" is the word Fortes uses to sum up the quality of relations between mother's brothers and sister's sons (1950:272). The two frequently lived and worked together in "the most amicable way." Yet older men were concerned about their replacement by the generation below. And young men might bristle under their mother's brother's authority. A man's oldest living mother's brother was his legal guardian with considerable authority over him—the right to demand financial assistance, for example. Adult nephews often criticized their maternal uncle for squandering what should be preserved as their inheritance or for making unfair demands.

Among the Ashanti, young men were often living with their maternal uncles after adolescence, some having been there since childhood. In the case of the Nayars of Central Kerala, in the days before British conquest, all young men lived with their maternal uncles from childhood and throughout their adult years. To be sure, men were away a good deal of the time from about the age of sixteen to fifty, attending military exercises and fighting. When they were at home in their villages, however, they lived in matrilineal extended households headed by the eldest male member, known as the *karanavan*. Younger men were subject to the *karanavan's* awesome authority (among his many powers, he managed the household's property and served as legal guardian for juniors), and they owed him, as well as other old maternal uncles, loyalty and obedience. Deep hostility, Gough writes, characterized the relationship between a man and his mother's brothers (1961:349). She says that occasional stories were still told in the 1950s of nephews who even poisoned or stabbed their maternal uncles (see chapter 5 on avoidance prohibitions between them).

Residential patterns in matrilineal societies are quite variable, however, and the Nayar arrangements are in fact very rare. In many matrilineal societies, a boy grows up with both of his parents in his father's group, although he is expected to join his maternal uncle when he reaches puberty or marries. In others, he lives apart from his maternal uncles not only during childhood but for much, sometimes all, of his adult life. This is a key difference between matrilineal and patrilineal societies. In patrilineal societies, a boy grows up with and perhaps even spends the rest of his life in, or near to, his father's household. In matrilineal societies, men are less likely to live with their maternal uncles, and when they do, they usually live with maternal uncles for a shorter time. Out of sight does not mean out of mind. Living apart limits the opportunities for interaction and open conflict between mother's brothers and sister's sons, but difficulties over succession and authority do not disappear.

A good example of a matrilineal society where young men do not live under the immediate authority of their maternal uncles is the Suku of Zaire (Kopytoff 1964, 1965, 1971b). Wherever a Suku man's father lived, so went his son. Relations between fathers and sons tended in fact to be warm and harmonious. Not so between nephews and maternal uncles. Young men's lineage membership was crucial, and the authority of maternal uncles was keenly felt. Suku men belonged to lineages, composed of about forty matrilineal kin (of about three or four living generations) who claimed descent from a common ancestor. Younger adult men were subject to the jural and economic authority of lineage elders, who were mostly their real and classificatory mother's brothers,[10] and eventually succeeded these men at the helm.

Young men often chafed under the authority of their maternal uncles. As the ruling subgroup of the lineage, elders made demands on sororal nephews for contributions so that they could discharge such duties as paying bridewealth and fines for lineage members. Having had longer to amass wealth, lineage elders contributed more in times of need, but they also claimed more when new wealth was allocated among lineage members. Indeed, at a man's death his inheritance reverted to the lineage as a whole and the elders handled its distribution.

Younger men's residential separation from their maternal uncles had its compensations, of course. In their youth and early middle age, men usually preferred to live away from the authority and constant demands of their lineage elders. But the separation was far from complete. Men of the lineage, though dispersed in different villages, apparently lived no more than about ten miles from the lineage center—the village where the lineage head (the oldest living male) lived and where important lineage ritual activities were conducted. As a man approached maturity and his economic and political interests became more closely bound to lineage membership, he began to make periodic visits to his maternal uncles. Later on, at his father's death and when he was coming close to being a lineage elder, he might even return to the lineage center.

While younger men often found lineage elders' dominance hard to bear, older men regarded junior male kin as a threat from below. "A sister's son is like a dog you own," went one proverb. "You think he is sitting obediently at your feet while in fact he is about to gnaw at your leg-bone" (Kopytoff 1971b:74). A sick man preferred to be cared for by his son rather than his sister's son. His own son had nothing to gain materially by his death. His sister's son, however, might be impatient to move up the ladder of authority and take control of lineage property (Kopytoff 1964:104).

Fathers-in-law and Sons-in-law. It is not unusual for tensions between fathers and sons or mother's brothers and sister's sons to increase as the younger men mature and marry. In the case of fathers-in-law and sons-in-law, a young man's marriage is just the beginning of troubles with his father-in-law.

In patrilineal societies, the usual pattern is for a woman to join her husband so that a man is not expected to live under the authority of his father-in-law. When fathers-in-law and sons-in-law in such societies live nearby, however, and when the young man owes the older man bridewealth payments, labor, or other services, the relationship tends to be subject to strain. The son-in-law is junior in age and generation to his father-in-law and indebted to the older man for providing him with a wife. Bridewealth payments often stretch out over a long period of time. They may also be quite high.

Among the patrilineal Gisu of Uganda, where bride-wealth in the 1950s equaled more than a year's cash income, a young man paid bridewealth in installments over several years (La Fontaine 1962). As long as the payments were not completed, he was obliged to provide small services and assistance to his father-in-law whenever called upon. One man, for example, had to bicycle seventeen miles to buy nails for the house his father-in-law was building. Not surprisingly, young men preferred a relatively distant father-in-law who would be too far away to make too many demands. "If my wife's home is near," said one man, "then her father and brothers are always visiting me, or they are always asking her to go home and help them. In each case this means presenting them with a fowl. I can't afford it" (La Fontaine 1962:100). The economics of bridewealth, however, meant that most men married close to home. Older men took into account the potential services of a son-in-law when they set the bridewealth amount. Knowing they would benefit less from the services of a distant son-in-law, older men exacted higher bridewealth in such cases.

It was not only that Gisu fathers-in-law demanded various services while bridewealth payments were outstanding. There was always the risk that the older man would press for the remaining bridewealth due. Fathers-in-law were legally within their rights to demand payment of the balance of the bridewealth at any time, and if the son-in-law did not comply, they could even dissolve the marriage or seize the son-in-law's property. Although young men owed their fathers-in-law respect and deference, it is not hard to see why there were undercurrents of resentment.

Now it was frequently the case among the Gisu that a young man with outstanding bridewealth debts was beholden to a father-in-law who was not yet old. By the time his father-in-law was old, a son-in-law was likely to owe no, or few, bridewealth payments and the period of heavy demands from the older man was over. It was the younger man's turn to ask his father-in-law for favors. As the father-in-law withdrew from an active role in political life, relations between the two became "more equable" and the younger man looked to his father-in-law to use his prestige and influence to help him (La Fontaine 1962:106).

Difficulties arising from bridewealth indebtedness lasted much longer in some societies—among the traditional Kpelle of Liberia, usually for the duration of the marriage (Bledsoe 1980:105–106). Few young Kpelle men could afford to pay a full bridewealth when they were betrothed. Instead, payments went on and on, with every gift counting as an installment. "The man," Caroline Bledsoe writes, "remains in a state of long-term obligation to his in-laws, who feel they can ask him for financial help at any time" (1980:105–106). It should be noted, too, that in some places bridewealth debts could be compounded by other debts to fathers-in-law, loans for land, for example (see Harris 1962). And in some societies, it appears that even after the bridewealth was fully paid, demands from fathers-in-law for labor and other services continued. Indeed, among the Nyoro of Uganda, proverbs likened a father-in-law to the Nyoro equivalent of a bottomless pit (Beattie, cited in Mair 1971:139).

But bridewealth payments are not always the source of troubles between a man and his father-in-law. Indeed, in matrilineal societies bridewealth, if paid, is usually small. Instead of bridewealth payments, a man might be expected to provide labor for a woman's relatives for several months or years to earn rights to her as a wife. This practice, known as brideservice, is found not only in some matrilineal societies. In some patrilineal societies where virilocal residence is the dominant or desired pattern, poor young men who cannot afford bridewealth or a large payment on bridewealth often have no alternative but to work for their fathers-in-law in order to get a wife. Some poor or aged parents among the Kpelle actually refused bridewealth in order to secure a son-in-law's labor:

Parents who want labor from a son-in-law may give their daughter to an impecunious young man for only a token payment, but they require him to perform a lengthy brideservice and share whatever he earns in the outside world with them. Though he eventually escapes these burdens as he grows older and his in-laws die, his labor and support last as long as the in-laws can stretch them out. (Bledsoe 1980:106–107)

This description clearly suggests strains between sons-in-law and fathers-in-law. Like bridewealth, brideservice, as Bledsoe puts it, was a boon to older people (1980:97). Also like bridewealth, it was a sore affliction to young men.

Brideservice sometimes lasts for a relatively short period. In societies where a young man is expected to join his wife's people after marriage (uxorilocal residence), he can find himself under the direct authority of his father-in-law for many long years. Among the Kagwahiv of the Brazilian Amazon, young men often lived in local groups headed by their father-in-law, who occasionally held onto this leadership position well into old age. Kracke (1978) describes in detail the ambivalence, including rebellious feelings and resentments, that one son-in-law harbored toward his father-in-law, a man of about seventy who, despite his advanced age, was still the headman of one, albeit declining, local group. Although uxorilocal residence is a common arrangement in a few patrilineal societies, like the Kagwahiv, it is far more frequent in matrilineal societies. Among the Western Apache, for example, a man usually lived in the same family cluster (but in a separate dwelling) as his father-in-law. Until he became "too old"—and one of his sons-in-law probably took his place—the father-in-law was the leader of the family cluster and the son-in-law was under strong economic obligation to him. Tensions between the two, however, were generally masked by the strict respect relationship that regulated their interactions. They could not joke together, and they were always supposed to maintain a reserved manner and use moderated voices when talking to each other (Goodwin 1942:131, 250, 255–256).

So far I have stressed several possible sources of trouble between fathers-in-law and sons-in-law: the younger man's indebtedness to his father-in-law; the father-in-law's demands for labor and services; and subjection to the father-in-law's authority on a daily basis in residential groups. In the northern Thai village of Chiangmai, the issue of succession was an added difficulty: jural authority in the family passed from father-in-law to son-in-law (J. Potter 1976; S. Potter 1977).

Although men (as well as women) in Chiangmai inherited land from their parents, it was customary for men to sell out their rights in their parents' property to their sisters and brothers-in-law. For at marriage a man usually went to live with his bride's parents and his main interests shifted to her family. Ideally, a man and his wife only lived in her parents' house for a short time—a few months to several years—before moving into their own house. But this house was in the same courtyard or as near the parental home as possible. The husband of the youngest or only daughter never moved out. He, along with his wife and children, remained in his in-law's house. Ultimately, his wife inherited the house and its grounds as well as her share of the rest of the family property. And the resident son-in-law succeeded his father-in-law as head of the household.[11]

The crucial structural conflicts in Chiangmai village tended to be between these two men (S. Potter 1977:18). It was a classic case of the dominant and dominated. A young man worked in his wife's parents' fields under his father-in-law's direction and supervision. He even had to depend on his father-in-law for help in obtaining land to rent. His position might be especially difficult if he had married into another village. Cut off from his own family, he was at the mercy of his wife's parents, relatives, and fellow villagers.

A man was supposed to work willingly for his father-in-law and submit to the older man's authority. The situation was potentially explosive. "The father-in-law," says Jack Potter, "is able to exploit his son-in-law's labor and to exercise his control over him, a situation which is resented by the younger man" (1976:125). An avoidance taboo kept the lid on these tensions, however. The two practically never spoke to each other and avoided each other's presence as far as possible. The younger man, in addition, tried to save to buy his own house and land as soon as possible.

While the younger man wanted to come out from under, the father-in-law wanted to stay in charge. Since he controlled the land, he had the definite edge. Sons-in-law who moved out of their in-laws' house and bought their own land did achieve considerable autonomy. And the husband of the youngest (or only) daughter assumed more authority as his father-in-law aged. Yet the older couple were loathe to cede formal ownership of the land and often held on even after they had retired and had handed over the farm management to their resident daughter and son-in-law. Writes Jack Potter: "A constant struggle occurs in almost all village families between young people who wish to take over formal authority in the family and the wife's parents who wish to retain control over the family and formal ownership of their land as long as possible" (1976:126). Full independence for all the sons-in-law might only be achieved when the old couple died and formal titles to shares of land were given.

This could mean a long wait. Father Good, a man well past fifty who was married to the sole surviving daughter in one family, was finally released from subordination to his father-in-law when this man, Grandfather Ten Thousand, died. Father Good, at this time, had been married for over thirty years! Continuing the cycle, he now treated his own son-in-law (the husband of his eldest daughter) as he himself had been treated (S. Potter 1977).

The story of Chiangmai village fathers-in-law and sons-in-law thus has a familiar ring, with younger men resenting their dependent station and eager to come into their own. Of course, dominant fathers-in-law in Chiangmai, like the fathers and maternal uncles in control I described earlier, were not always old. But when these men were old, sons-in-law, sons, and sister's sons often became all the more impatient for their subordinate days to end.

Grandparents and Grandchildren. These kinds of strains are notably absent from relations between grandparents and grandchildren, although here we can be surer that individuals in the grandparent role are old. Grandparenthood in some societies in fact is an important criterion of old age.

Compared with the struggles and enmity that characterize many relationships between men in adjacent generations, relations between grandparents and grandchildren are thought to be friendly, familiar, and relaxed. It is not only that by the time individuals in nonindustrial societies reach adolescence or adulthood few of their grandparents, if any, are alive. (Grandfathers are less often living than grandmothers, if only because men marry and sire children at a later age than women, often until they are quite old.) The young do not inherit authority and property directly from their grandparents: the old people do not feel threatened by their grandchildren; and grandchildren are not waiting to step into their grandparents' shoes.

While the two may not vie for control of wealth and authority, an element of constraint and hierarchy can enter into their relations. According to Dorrian Apple's (1956) analysis of data from fifty-five societies, relations between the two could be quite formal. Formality between grandparents and grandchildren, she writes, was linked to the association of grandparents with family authority. Among other findings, Apple discovered that relations were formal with both sets of grandparents in societies where grandparents exercised a high degree of authority over the parental generation.[12] Close and warm relations between grandparents and grandchildren, by contrast, were fostered by the disassociation of grandparents from family authority.

Although an idyllic picture of grandparent–grandchild relations thus seems overdrawn, in general, the bond between grandparents "on top" and grandchildren is not a major point of strain. Remember, however, that a grown person's living grandparents are likely to be very old—dependent on the young and in need of custodial care. Problems between grandparents and grandchildren may arise at this stage due to the old people's dependent position, a subject I will discuss in chapter 4.

Old and Young Men in the Community

Not all strains between old and young men occur between close kin or affines. In some societies, there is a general opposition in the local community between old men who

dominate political, economic, and religious affairs and subordinate young men who are hedged in by restrictions that
limit their activities and their ability to get ahead.

Of course, it is difficult to separate "the community" from
close kin in nonindustrial societies, since local communities
are often very small and consist of people who are, by and
large, linked by kinship ties. Yet in the examples I have described so far, strains between old and young arose precisely
because the two had particular—and close—kinship or affinal
relations. We now need to widen our field of vision. At times,
strains between young and old men have to do with the fact
that older men in general hold powers and privileges in the
wider kinship group or community at the expense of younger
men.

The Samburu. Such is the case among the Samburu pastoral nomads of northern Kenya. Paul Spencer (1965) describes the Samburu gerontocracy he observed in the 1950s
in no uncertain terms. Older men maintained a repressive re-
gime to protect their privileges, while younger bachelors were
held in a state of social suspension.

Polygyny was the root of the trouble. During their prolonged bachelorhood young men had to sit on the sidelines
while older men not only controlled family and settlement
affairs but also continued to take additional wives. The number of wives men had increased with age, only declining when
they were very old, that is, past seventy. Much of Spencer's
rich account explores why such profound inequality did not
tear the society apart. For the moment, I want to describe
briefly age-related tensions in Samburu society, saving an
analysis of the factors that alleviated strains between younger
and older men for chapter 5.

What makes the Samburu particularly interesting is that
father–son relations were not a prime source of strain. In many
other African patrilineal societies, older men could accumulate wives because they controlled the cattle needed to marry,
and competition for marriage cattle between fathers and sons
was a major source of difficulty. Not among the Samburu. Older

men, to be sure, did control stock and younger men depended on senior male kin for a livelihood. But the fact that the initial bridewealth payment was small inhibited competition between fathers and sons. In any case, the rules of the age-set system, rather than unequal access to marriage cattle, prevented many young men from marrying until they were over thirty. By the time young men were allowed to marry, they had usually founded their own herds (although their fathers retained ultimate ownership of sons' cattle until death or advanced senility). In addition, bachelors' direct oppressors did not include their fathers.

To better understand how older men maintained control as well as the sources of tension with younger men we need to sketch out the workings of the age-set system. An age set consisted of all men circumcised in youth during a specific period, a new set usually having been formed every twelve to fourteen years. Once initiated—typically at about fifteen—a man advanced up the hierarchy, formally passing through various age grades with other members of his age set.[13] Moran (traditional warriors in the precolonial era) and elders were the two main age grades, but these were further subdivided: junior and senior moran; and junior, firestick, and senior elders.

The main opposition was between young men in the moran age grade and older men in the firestick elder grade. (In the late 1950s, moran ranged in age from their teens to early thirties; firestick elders from their forties to late fifties; and senior elders from their late fifties to about seventy.) Members of alternate age sets had a special—firestick—relationship. Men in the senior set ceremonially brought the junior set into existence. The term "firestick elder" referred to the ceremonial kindling of fire that marked the formation and symbolic birth of the junior set. Firestick elders were the "watchful oppressors" of the moran, their sponsors, patrons, and disciplinarians, and these elders could unleash a powerful curse upon the junior set.

Firestick elders were "the immediate agents of gerontocratic control," but men in this grade did not include fathers

of the moran (Spencer 1976:157). According to the rules of
the age-set system, a man could not be initiated into the alternate age set below that of his father. Instead, the Samburu
insisted that a youth join a set no less than three below that
of his father. With rare exceptions, most youths did just this.
Thus, when a man was in the moran grade, his father was a
senior elder. And senior elders were often the defenders of
the moran. If moran got into trouble, senior elders were likely
to oppose the severe demands firestick elders made on the
moran. But even if senior elders defended moran, they were
elders nonetheless. Young men had to respect all of the elders. And all of the elders, including the senior elders, benefited from the distribution of women. This point is crucial.

The rules of the age-set system enabled older Samburu
men to corner the marriage market by formally delaying the
first marriages of younger men. Young men could not simply
take a wife when they felt ready to do so. All members of an
age set in the moran grade, whatever their age or individual
proclivities, had to wait until specific ceremonies were held
(and they were replaced by a new age set) before they were
permitted to marry.

What these rules meant was that many moran were well
over thirty before they could take a first wife. Not surprisingly, the moran were a frustrated group. Rarely did moran
directly express hostility to elders, but they made no secret
of disliking the restrictions elders imposed on them. The moran
were unable to start building families of their own and were
even constantly losing mistresses to elders, who married these
young women. The elders controlled all significant settlement activities, while the moran were associated with the bush.
In fact, elders were happy to have the moran away from the
settlements—and thus from their wives—much of the time. The
moran, as Spencer sums up, were "the odd men out in the
society": "Physiologically they are of an age to marry, but they
may not do so for many years. They are in a limbo between
boyhood and elderhood, and the elders like to keep them there
outside the competition in marriage and outside the decision
making of the local clan groups" (1965:100).[14]

Even after the ceremony that entitled the moran to wed, marriage still eluded them. The moran were supposed to wait another year or two for their ritual leader to marry first. While some could then marry, others might have several more years to wait because of the shortage of marriageable girls. This delay could be more of a hardship for some than others. The wide age range within age sets (more than ten years) meant that older senior moran tended to be eager to marry and settle down, while younger ones still found the freedom of moran-hood attractive. The moran who could and did want to marry, however, competed for available women not only among themselves but with elders who wanted to marry their second and third wives.

Inability to marry and exclusion from settlement affairs were not the only crosses the moran had to bear. In the name of educating and instilling the moran with a developed sense of respect,[15] elders, particularly firestick elders, criticized, humiliated, and harangued the younger men. At initiation ceremonies, youths had to do what they were told by their elders, no matter how painful or frightening, and bullying by elders continued throughout their bachelor days. At formal and informal gatherings, elders advised and ranted at the moran, accusing them of irresponsibility and lack of real respect. This was especially galling to older moran who wanted to convince the elders they were worthy of advancement. The elders, however, treated the whole age set as an "undifferentiated mob" in their criticisms (Spencer 1965:142). Younger moran may have been the guilty ones but older—restrained— moran were not spared the wrath of the elders.

At harangues, elders picked on defaulters and shamed them before others. And they reminded the moran of their power to withhold their blessing and even to curse. When the firestick elders bestowed their blessings at ceremonies, it was given grudgingly: "It is relentless, and oppressive, as if to terrify the moran, who frequently break down under the ordeal" (Spencer 1976:156).

Not only were firestick elders in charge of disciplining the moran but they arranged the ceremonies that marked young men's advancement. Elders often delayed these ceremonies. After all, keeping the moran wifeless meant that elders had a monopoly on marriage. Elders said, for example, that they had to postpone the ceremonies because drought conditions prevented large gatherings or because the moran had too little sense of respect.

The elders also tried to persuade the moran that they were still too immature for marriage and elderhood. They encouraged young men to hang on as long as possible to the glories of moranhood—the freedom, adventure, and ostentatious display, for example. But, says Spencer, the glamour of moranhood was superficial (1965:144).[16] It was "the plain broken elders" who were the political rulers of the society. Indeed, such common "unelderlike" behavior among the moran as going on stock raids, infighting, and having affairs with elders' wives gave elders further ammunition to stall the advance of the moran to elderhood.

Samburu moran, it is clear, were "pinned down from above" (Spencer 1976:156). Younger men in other East African age-set systems faced the same problem, particularly when formal rules in these systems restricted their first marriages.[17] In many of these age-set societies as well, relations between older men on top and subordinate young men in the general community were strained.

But it would be a mistake to think such strains are limited to age-set societies. Let us move, then, across several continents to the Tiwi of North Australia in the early days of this century.

The Tiwi. As in Samburu society, prolonged bachelorhood was young men's main problem among the Tiwi. The inequitable distribution of wives in this hunting and gathering society created tensions beyond the household unit—in the group of households of about forty to fifty people who temporarily camped together for perhaps several weeks at a time. Indeed, Hart and Pilling say that a dominant theme in Tiwi culture was "the general hostility of all old men to all young unmarried men" (1979:36). Marriage was not regulated, as among the Samburu, by an age-set system.[18] Nevertheless, it was delayed for young men. A powerful old man could have as many as thirteen wives in residence,[19] while young men could not marry before about thirty. And until about forty a man's resident wife was usually an elderly widow.

Social rewards in Tiwi society—"many wives, much leisure, many daughters to bestow, many satellites and henchmen, and much power and influence over other people and tribal affairs" (Hart and Pilling 1979:77)—were beyond young men's reach. Young men in their late teens and early twenties were wifeless. They were also considered boys until they had completed the long initiation process, which began when they were about fourteen or fifteen and lasted until their middle twenties and required them to spend much of their time in the bush.

If young bachelors were completely unimportant in tribal eyes (Hart and Pilling 1979:95), a few old men represented the peak of success. These old men were not at the top simply because they were old (past fifty-five or so). Only *some* old men had large households and many wives, and this was due to their activities in their younger days. Ability and good connections (such as having many sisters or wealthy maternal uncles) enabled them to lay the groundwork for successful old age in their thirties. Aging gave them the chance to enjoy the fruits of their wheeling and dealing.

Having many wives was prestigious in itself. With more food gatherers and preparers, an old successful polygynist's household was also well provided for. He had the leisure to make ceremonial objects and to participate in public life and ceremonies, and he had the wherewithal to give gifts to others and provide feasts. Many wives also meant he had many daughters to promise to other men—a source of political clout. A man with many daughters could attract satellites and have control over other men. That young men in his household supplied meat, game, and fish further enhanced an old man's economic position.

The politics of marriage was a complicated business, and

anthropologists who have studied the Tiwi do not even agree as to how the system worked. All agree, however, that old men dominated the distribution of women as wives. Men even arranged the marriages of women who had not yet been born. Although Tiwi girls did not join their husbands until puberty, female infants were betrothed before (or soon after) birth. Widows were immediately remarried so that unmarried women were unheard of among the Tiwi.

According to Hart and Pilling, a girl's father had the right to promise her to another man, and this clearly gave him a great deal of power. Since men bestowed newborn daughters on men who were at least twenty-five, by the time the daughter joined her husband, at about fourteen, he would be at least forty. Goodale says, however, that the reason men were often so much older than their wives had to do with another form of marriage, in which a man selected a husband for his daughter's unborn daughters (1971:52–54). The arrangement was made between a man, his daughter, and his future son-in-law. The future son-in-law was promised the future daughters of his young mother-in-law. Since the son-in-law was often ten or more years older than the mother-in-law, he would be still older than his promised wife.

Because husbands could be so much older than their wives, women were likely to be widowed once, if not more. Who arranged a widow's remarriage (the deceased husband's brothers, for example, or the widow's own brothers) need not concern us here. What we need to note is that widows could be married to men much younger than themselves. By Hart and Pilling's account, as I mentioned, a man's first wife was generally an elderly widow (1979:14–29). A more noteworthy menage, however, might await him in the future.

A young man wanted to ensure that in his old age he would have many bestowed wives coming into his household and many daughters (or granddaughters) whose marriages he could arrange. In tracing the marriage careers of a number of successful men, Hart and Pilling show how successful young operators in their thirties manipulated rights in kinswomen's marriages and became satellites to much older men. By their late thirties and early forties, these "comers" would begin to receive bestowals. By their late forties, they would have daughters of their own to use in marriage arrangements, and by their fifties they would head large households and be men of influence.

What were the tension points between older and young men in this system? Young "comers" in their thirties and early forties, Hart and Pilling note, were not old men's rivals or competitors (1979:73–77). These younger men were clients of old successful men (sometimes, but not necessarily, their maternal uncles), trying to build up their reputations and making deals and alliances to ensure future bestowals. By the time these men were in their mid and late forties, however, the situation had changed. They were enjoying the fruits of their labors and were no longer content to be old men's clients. With daughters of their own, they wanted to build up their own, not their client's, households and influence, and they competed with old men for younger men's allegiance.

In additon to the rivalry between old successful men and rising men in their mid to late forties, there was the problem of young bachelors preying on old men's wives. Old men were constantly worried that young men, including their sons, were seducing their young wives. "In any Tiwi camp comprising more than two households," Hart and Pilling write, "few weeks went by without an outraged and angry old husband shouting accusations at one of the younger men sitting by another campfire a few yards away" (1979:37). Which young men were the targets of old men's suspicions Hart and Pilling do not say. Perhaps young men in their twenties, who had not yet entered the "marriage business," were prime suspects. Perhaps less successful men in their thirties—those whose futures did not look bright and who were not receiving bestowals from older men—were reckless in their attentions to old men's wives since they had little to lose. Or up-and-coming young men under forty might ogle the wives of old men to whom they were not clients, for they, as yet, did not have young wives in residence. Bachelors, in any case, "had to be satisfied, by and large, with temporary and casual liaisons, and even in these, because of the constant suspicion of the old husbands and the constant spying and scandalmongering of the old wives, they had to be prepared to be often caught and, when caught, to be punished" (Hart and Pilling 1979:80).

Strains Between Old Men and Young Women

The Tiwi case, like the other examples so far, shows why strains often arise between disadvantaged young men and old men at the top of the age hierarchy. What about these old men's relationships with young women?

Certain sources of strain are conspicuously absent in relations between young women and old male kin. Young women in most societies do not as a rule inherit from their fathers or maternal uncles. In their day-to-day activities, young women tend to interact mainly with other women and children, not with old men. At marriage, moreover, authority shifts, at least to some extent, away from a woman's male relatives to her husband.

There are some possible trouble spots, however. On occasion, a woman comes into conflict with senior male relatives over their selection of her husband. If she is unhappily married, they may command or implore her to remain with her husband or make it difficult for her to divorce or leave him. Once married, a woman's allegiance to her husband and affines often conflicts with her willingness or ability to perform certain expected duties toward her senior male relatives.

As for old fathers-in-law, when a woman lives in her father-in-law's household, the old man does not directly supervise her activities. This is usually the mother-in-law's job. Tensions that do arise stem from several factors: the old man's resentment of his daughter-in-law as an intruder who threatens his son's loyalties; the daughter-in-law's fear of an old powerful father-in-law; and her resentment of the old man's control over her husband and his reluctance to grant her husband independence.

Finally, there are relations with old husbands. In many societies it is not unusual for a young woman to be married to an old man. There are various sources of tension between them, but these tend to have more to do with sex, rather than age, inequalities. Age clearly does come into the picture, however, in that old men are often insecure in their ability to hold on to their young wives or to keep them faithful. Young women may have a wandering eye. And old husbands may be jealous of young wives' affairs or flirtations with younger men. While old men, as we just saw in the Tiwi case, commonly place the blame on the young men involved, it is possible that young women, too, will at times come in for a share of their old husband's anger.

Clearly, when old men are at the peak of the age hierarchy, the most pronounced strains and ambivalences arise with younger men, not younger women. What about powerful old women's relations with younger people? Old women in nonindustrial societies, after all, frequently have "more of what there is to have," particularly compared with young women. We must now look to see what happens when old women are the ones at the top.

3
Consequences
of Age Inequality: II

Old Women at the Top

The later years are a time when women in a large number of nonindustrial societies come into their own. Old age offers them the chance to achieve greater freedom, influence, and prestige within as well as beyond the domestic group. Indeed, one writer even speaks of mid and late life "women's liberation" in societies around the world (Gutmann 1977:309). While women's opportunities often expand with age, young women are, for the moment, left behind. They are frequently bound by cumbersome restrictions and at the mercy of old women's, as well as men's, demands and wishes. Not surprisingly, we find that many times relations between old women at the top of the age hierarchy and subordinate young women are subject to strain.

The analysis of age inequalities among women not only rounds out this discussion of old people at the top of the age hierarchy but also adds an important dimension to the study of women in cross-cultural perspective. The anthropological literature on women has mainly been concerned with exploring and evaluating women's power, prestige, rights, privileges, and importance relative to men. Recent writings have critically examined such central questions as the universality of male dominance; cross-cultural variations in patterns of sex-role differentiation and inequality; and the extent to which women in different societies have been able to obtain influence, wealth, and prestige. Recent studies, too, have made clear that women's status is not one but many things and that various aspects of women's status—domestic authority or property ownership, for example—tend to vary independently from one society to another (Whyte 1978; see also Rosaldo 1980).

But it is not just that the status of women in any society is multidimensional. Various aspects of women's status change as women move through the life course. This point is too often ignored in polemical writings on women's status in other cultures.[1] A perspective on age inequality bids us to consider not just how old women fare relative to old men but how they do compared with younger women. Because women in so many societies can aspire to and frequently achieve numerous benefits as they age, many of the deprivations that women suffer may be endured only by younger women, or at least be less severe among the elderly. And while inequalities between men and women, of the same as well as different ages, are obviously of the utmost importance, the investigation of age inequality demonstrates that hierarchical relations among women are also significant. Indeed, men are not the only ones who gain by young women's subordination. Old women in many societies, too, have a strong interest in keeping young women in their place.

Like women generally, old women have been given short shrift in most ethnographic accounts, and much less material is available on them than on old men, particularly concerning tensions with younger people. Nonetheless, certain patterns emerge that help us to understand the impact of age inequalities on old as well as young women's lives. This chapter first examines the sources of old women's privileges and powers in nonindustrial societies and then goes into the kinds of strains that arise with younger people.[2] The final section takes up the question of how old women benefit from and sometimes help to perpetuate young women's subordination.

Bases of Inequality

The opportunities available to old women for authority and achievement may be less extensive than those open to old men, but old women in many nonindustrial societies come out ahead relative to young women. In many places, growing old enables women to participate more freely and actively in the public sphere. Frequently, old women have greater scope than young women for informal influence in community affairs, and, on occasion, they can even aspire to formal political roles outside the household. As they age, women often have increased knowledge and expertise and, at times, more control over material resources. Most important, growing old tends to give women the chance to exert authority over younger people within the domestic group. All these benefits are sources of prestige. Age and seniority, in themselves, also often bring respect and deference from younger people.

In societies where old women are relatively advantaged, not all old women necessarily acquire every single one of these benefits. Some are more successful than others because of such factors as their personality or their good fortune in having many adult sons. And societies where old women are more privileged than young women differ in the assets available to elderly women, especially in the opportunities to exercise authority beyond the household and to accumulate wealth and property. At a minimum, old women are at the top of the age hierarchy when aging offers them the opportunity to acquire considerable domestic authority, to gain prestige in the family and community, and to become more active in the public sphere.

The rest of this section looks more closely at the advantages that come to women as they age, indicating as well how these compare with the benefits available to old men. Although women in many societies have much to gain in their later years, elderly women are simply not eligible to fill, or are less likely to achieve, some of the valued roles and resulting rewards old men acquire.

Community Influence

In the world of politics, old women are much less likely than old men to be found in formal political roles outside the household. It is men, frequently old men, who usually dominate local assemblies, courts, and councils and who are headmen and chiefs, "law makers, judges, and administrators of justice" (Simmons 1945:130).

Nevertheless, old women sometimes do achieve important political positions. There are societies where women, at times old women, step into high-ranking political roles in the lifetimes of powerful brothers, sons, or fathers. On occasion, old women inherit political office directly from other women. And there are cases where they acquire political leadership positions on the basis of their age and a combination of personal qualifications. As ethnographers pay closer attention to women's political roles and as we learn more about female leadership patterns in the precolonial period, it may turn out that women have played a more significant role in the political realm in nonindustrial societies than is commonly supposed. Such research will also, it is hoped, give us a better idea of the extent to which age and seniority have provided women in various societies with the opportunity to become political leaders and wield political influence in their later years.

Already, several accounts show old women in a number of societies wielding considerable political power. We know, for example, that although men dominated intertribal league affairs among the Iroquois in the seventeenth and eighteenth centuries, senior women were important in the political process. It was they who named the men who would assume vacant league titles (Wallace 1971). Among the Ashanti, studied by Fortes in the 1940s, older women played a part in selecting the male head of the localized lineage (1950:255–256). The lineage head and his elders also informally chose a senior woman to serve as his assistant. The senior woman of the royal lineage was the Queen Mother. Before British rule, a Queen Mother had the most to say in selecting a new chief or king, and she held court and decided cases with the full powers of the chief when he was away at war. A few Queen Mothers were even recorded as accompanying an army to war (Rattray 1923:81–85). Although the British did not officially recognize Queen Mothers, these old women maintained important powers in the colonial period—supervising girls' puberty ceremonies, for instance, and commanding great influence in the lineage on the basis of their genealogical authority (Fortes 1950:257). Writing about another West African society, the Abron of the Ivory Coast, as they were in the 1960s and 1970s, Alexander Alland describes an old Queen Mother, a woman of regal bearing "heavy framed, and bent like a horn tree," who because of her great age and status could wear a cloth like a man (1975:100–101). Her influence in village affairs was sometimes stronger than the king's.

In a different part of the world, among the Shahsevan nomadic pastoralists of Iran, women had the chance to acquire leadership roles in their old age (the life stage reached around menopause) that gave them influence in the women's subsociety and in the male sphere as well (Tapper 1978). An *aq birchek* was always an old, postmenopausal woman who typically arrived at this position by accompanying a male relative on a pilgrimage or establishing herself as a ceremonial cook. She was able to join men in conversations on all subjects on more or less equal terms, participating, for example, in their discussions on such key topics as plans for migration. One *aq birchek*, Mashadi Fatima, had great power in her local community, and her wishes were respected in matters concerning men as well as women:

For example, a superb bull camel owned by her sons was dying, and the men wanted to slaughter it in the prescribed manner for meat—to the Shahsevan, camel meat is a rare delicacy. Mashadi Fatima intervened, declaring that this camel was too noble a beast to be eaten. The camel died naturally and was buried near the camp. (Tapper 1978:385)

The examples mentioned so far describe elderly women with influence over men *and* women in community-wide affairs. In many instances, old women's authority beyond the domestic group extends only to younger women. Thus in many societies, elderly women supervise initiation ceremonies for young girls or direct other rituals involving younger women. Old Khanty women, for instance, in pre-Soviet days in Siberia had a dominant role in females-only sacred groves, and they presided over birth and naming rituals that involved young mothers and their children (Balzer 1981).

There are also cases where elderly women have had considerable public authority over younger women in everyday, practical affairs. The titled head of the women in Nupe villages in northern Nigeria was an old woman, that is, one beyond childbearing, of about or over fifty. Elected by married women of the village, she advised women, organized women's work, and arbitrated between them (Nadel 1942:148–149). Among the Afikpo Igbo, older women had authority over younger women as part of the age-set system (Ottenberg 1971:102–112, 243–244). Women in this society joined an age set after they married, in their twenties. Village women in the three sets in the executive age grade (in their late forties and fifties in 1960) called on unmarried girls to perform communal labor and had the authority to fine those who did not show up without a good excuse. As for women in the elders grade, they were given an honorary feast twice a year by women in the executive grade along with £5, which these elders divided among themselves. At the wider village-group level (consisting of twenty-two villages), female elders regulated women's trade, deciding, for example, the price of cassava meal or the number of pots women could sell in a day.

The Afikpo Igbo are one of the few peoples for whom we have good documentation of women's age-set organization. To what extent this is because male ethnographers did not, or could not, learn about them is unclear. Women's age sets do seem less common than men's, and, where found, they are less well developed and less socially significant than men's age sets (see Kertzer and Madison 1981, for a discussion of the various explanations for this situation).

Whatever powers are available in the community to a few old women leaders or, as in the Afikpo Igbo case, to all female elders, it is clear that in many societies older women in general enjoy a fuller participation in public life than young women. Once past menopause, restrictive menstrual customs as well as other taboos no longer apply. There are reports of older women engaging in various activities denied to younger, childbearing women, such as eating with men or beer drinking at public gatherings (see, for example, Simmons 1945:64–66). Women past childbearing among the Bedouin of Cyrenaica (Libya), to take one example, had easier relations with men of the camp than before. Whereas previously they argued with men in the confines of their own domestic units, they now took part in public discussions and voiced opinions that might be backed by other women in the camp (Peters 1978:331). Indeed, in some societies old women are allowed to take a more active role in formal dispute settlement processes in the community. Aged women among the Sakhalin Ainu, for instance, occasionally participated in the "male territory of law," and Ohnuki-Tierney (1974) was told of one instance in the past when an aged woman overturned the verdict in an accidental murder case which had been agreed on by a body of male elders.

It is important to note, too, that old women often gain informal political influence in the community because at this point in their lives they can exert pressure on husbands, brothers, or adult sons. The portrait of Tiwi women in the last chapter made them seem like mere pawns in men's marriage maneuvers, but old Tiwi women with influential senior sons were very powerful—the center of strong influence networks as behind-the-scenes advisors to their sons in marriage dealings (Hart and Pilling 1979:53; see also Goodale 1971:228). A widow whose brothers were no longer alive could actually arrange her own remarriage (Goodale 1971:56–57).

Having her husband's ear could be a source of informal political clout for an old woman in other societies. Among the Tallensi, old women had more equal relations with spouses than young women did. A man often listened to his old wife's opinions and advice. "I have seen a lineage head's senior wife," Fortes tells us, "listen to a group of lineage elders thresh out a domestic squabble and give her opinion without restraint" (1949:98).

Material Resources

When it comes to material resources, old women's control is generally more limited than old men's (Simmons 1945:47–48). This is not to say that old women have no property or no control over economic resources. Much like younger women, old women in many societies have a certain control over such important resources as land, animals, and crops.

But while the literature on women's economic position tells us much about how women manage relative to men, the question of how *old* women do compared to young women is largely unexplored territory. Does aging put elderly women at an advantage in acquiring rights over material resources? How extensive are these rights in different societies? And do such rights give old women significant power over the young? We do know that in some societies elderly women whose husbands have died or become incapacitated control much of the family patrimony during their lifetimes. Aging also sometimes gives older women the chance to accumulate more movable property than younger women. In a number of West African societies, for example, years of trading enabled some older women to have considerable wealth at their command.

Expertise

Like old men, old women in preliterate societies are repositories of wisdom and experience. Indeed, one reason women in many societies can aspire to, and sometimes achieve, certain respected positions outside the household (particularly in the ritual sphere) is that growing old has enabled them to accumulate important knowledge.

Elderly women are commonly valued for their special knowledge in such matters as pregnancy, birth complications, and delivery, and in a number of societies they serve as midwives. Old women's ritual expertise is often admired and at times feared. The very fact of aging frequently gives old women mystical powers that they can use to help and protect as well as, in some cases, to harm. In many societies, ritual specialists who diagnose and cure illnesses often come from the ranks of old women as well as old men, and elderly women sometimes direct or play an important part in certain rituals. A fascinating example comes from the Bimin-Kuskusmin of Papua New Guinea, where women chosen to be *waneng aiyem ser* (female ritual leaders) were "old, postmenopausal, no longer married, sexual androgyne[s]." They played a prominent role in most female *and* male ritual performances, including birth, female naming, male and female initiation, male cult, and death rituals. Their gender was ambiguous, and indeed they appeared in male initiation contexts in the guise of hermaphroditic ancestors (Poole 1981).

Domestic Authority

It is in the domestic arena that women usually achieve their greatest authority and influence. A women's power in the domestic group tends to increase with age, so that by the time she is old she often has considerable control over, and commands respect from, a large number of people. As a woman ages so do her children. When she reaches old age, many of her children, daughters-in-law, and grandchildren may live under her wing.

How much domestic authority an old woman has and who comes under her control varies. Admittedly, old women, unlike old men in many societies, do not hold sway over many spouses, mainly because polygyamy is almost always confined to men. Even in those few societies where polyandry occurs (where women are married to two or more men simultaneously), men still have certain jural rights over their wives (Levine and Sangree 1980:388–391). There are some instances, however, where aging enables women to assume another role typically associated with men: household head. This is a common pattern in a few societies where husbands and wives live all or a good deal of the time in separate residences.

In the case of the Mundurucú of Amazonian Brazil, the oldest woman was the "undisputed director of all the internal affairs of the house," supervising food processing among the women (her own resident daughters and her younger sisters and their daughters), serving as midwife, and dispensing advice on various matters. In the past, households sometimes contained as many as fifty people, including attached males who had moved to the community to join their wives but who slept and spent much of the time in the village men's house (Murphy and Murphy 1974). Among the Abron, too, old women were formal leaders of their households. Men normally remained in their father's house, with men only, while women lived out their lives in women's houses headed by older women. Women past menopause, Alland reports, dominated their households, which typically consisted of their daughters, younger sisters and their daughters, and their own and their sister's uterine granddaughters (1975:185). These elderly household heads planned the marriages of the young women, supervised daily tasks, and raised the younger generation of children.

In some societies where married women live full time with their husbands, those who are widowed or divorced also occasionally end up heading households in their later years. Of course, in most societies official authority in the household usually rests with a male head. Even so, women tend to gain considerable domestic authority as they age.

In societies with patrilineal inheritance and virilocal residence—the most common combination in the nonindustrial world—old women often have informal influence over grown sons in the domestic group and are trusted advisors of their husbands as well. In rural Taiwan, for example, older women who had shown years of good judgment were regularly consulted by their husbands about both major and minor social and economic projects (M. Wolf 1972:74). Older women often play a role in arranging their children's marriages. And they frequently have authority over younger women in the domestic group—unmarried daughters, daughters-in-law, granddaughters, and perhaps junior wives—whose activities they supervise. These younger women owe old women respect and obedience as well as help in domestic work. Depending on such factors as her personality and relationship to the younger women of the domestic group, an old woman's dominance can range from a rather awesome authority to the gentle role of advisor and guide.

Many anthropological reports on patrilineal societies note how a woman only fully comes into her own in her later years, when she has adult sons to provide a support group and younger women to do her bidding. Sarah LeVine's (1978) account of Gusii women illustrates how women gained confidence and became more forthright as they aged. She interviewed women at the bottom of the status hierarchy of married women: those with no married children. Above them in the pecking order were women with married children, and one rung higher were women with grandchildren. Women with grandchildren who had no living senior women in the homestead were on top.[3]

It is not hard to see why Gusii women would look forward to aging. Young married women were "beholden at every turn to the judgment and authority of . . . seniors." They were social dependents in their husbands' homesteads even though they took the major share of responsibility for the daily maintenance of their families. Having adult sons changed all this: a woman now had a position of permanent authority in her husband's lineage (S. LeVine 1978:361). Formally she became an elder when one of her children married, and this status was confirmed by grandparenthood. A woman could become an elder at a relatively young age. If a woman gave birth at seventeen or eighteen, she could have married children by her early thirties, grandchildren by thirty-five. Whatever her chronological age, a female elder now expected help from daughters-in-law and grandchildren. As a female elder she could drink beer at beer parties and be more openly aggressive in public. And she frequently was. Older women were more confident, more assertive, and more outspoken than younger women (S. LeVine 1978:12–13).

If women have more domestic authority with age, is this also true when they become widows?[4] After all, old widows often change residences to join sons or daughters, new husbands, or natal kin. Detailed accounts of old widows, however, are so scanty that we usually know little, if anything, about these women's authority over people and property, about the quality of their relations with kin and non-kin, or about how free they are from male control. Old widows' status seems related to such factors as the descent and inheritance system, residential patterns for postmenopausal women, and rules of remarriage. Although elderly widows in some places can find themselves uncomfortably dependent on others, in many societies these women have considerable domestic authority.

In Chinese society, for example, old widows who stayed put (rather than choosing to live in sisterhoods) could have their "only chance of exercising supreme authority over adults" and of enjoying "the fruits of domestic power." A widow who was the most senior family member alive might, in fact, assume control of the family's estate and affairs in general (Freedman 1966:66–67). Among the Dukawa of northern Nigeria, to illustrate a different residential pattern, healthy postmenopausal widows might return to their father's compound, where, Salamone (1980) reports, they were economically active, outspoken, and consulted in any major decisions in the compound.

Age and Seniority

Putting aside the question of widowhood and domestic authority, there is also the fact that age and seniority—for old widows as well as other old women—may bring increasing prestige and deference from others. Take two West African examples. Among the Tallensi, a widowed woman past childbearing age who lived with her son had, as senior woman of the house, an esteemed place. In Fortes' words, she was "the central pillar of his domestic establishment" (1949:59). The old woman's rooms were larger than those of the other women and in the position of honor. Most of the ancestor medicine shrines that were kept indoors were stored in her rooms (Fortes 1949:58–59).[5]

Among the Gonja, the status accorded an elderly woman approached that of a male elder (E. Goody 1973:163). Old women were respected not only for their wisdom and ritual knowledge but for their seniority as well. By "retiring from marriage"—that is, leaving their husbands and returning to natal kin—older women assured that they were surrounded by respectful juniors.

As a wife in her husband's home, a woman in Gonja society (where descent was traced in both lines and marriage was virilocal) was subordinate to her husband and surrounded by his kin. Unless she was married to a kinsman, constraints of affinity took primacy over considerations of birth order with her husband's kin. Exchanging the role of wife for sister was a big improvement—a major reason why most women rejoined their natal kin (usually a brother) in old age.[6] An old woman living with her natal kin was in a genealogically superior position. By this time in life, most of her surviving kin were her juniors—younger siblings, her own children, and children of her siblings and cousins—who owed her respect and deference on the basis of her seniority. "If I had stayed there," said one elderly woman referring to her husband's home, "they would have expected me to fetch water, carry firewood, and cook for them. But here in my brother's house I can sit in the shade of my room and spin thread for my shroud in peace" (E. Goody 1973:160).

Strains Between Old Women and Young People

If old women are relatively privileged and powerful, does this generate strains with the less disadvantaged, particularly young women? Answering this question is not always easy. The available data on age-related tensions involving old women are, to repeat a familiar theme, sparse compared with what we have for old men. Most marked is the lack of material on the strains that arise between powerful old women and the subordinate young outside the domestic group. We do not know whether serious tensions develop in situations where old women exercise considerable authority over young women in the community, including cases where elderly women are awesome figures at rituals, even, on occasion, administering, supervising, or initiating painful procedures that are inflicted on young women.

What information is at hand on tensions between old women at the top and young people tends to center on strains stemming from old women's domestic authority. This is therefore the focus of the following pages.

Mothers and Children

Far from being described as a breeding ground for tensions, strains, and resentments, the bond between mothers and children is generally characterized in rather idyllic terms: warm, affectionate, loyal, and supportive. That mothers are so often nurturant child-rearers is part of the story, but other factors are also involved.

A woman does not usually have much, if any, economic or jural authority over her sons so that she cannot, for example, disinherit them or delay giving them the resources they need to marry. Young men are waiting to succeed senior men—not their mothers.

Indeed, a woman often identifies with her sons and equates her aspirations with theirs. In the absence of substantial jural and economic authority, a woman typically stresses ties of affection and moral obligation with sons to strengthen the bonds between them. Because women generally do not occupy formal political leadership roles, what informal influence they exert in the community often depends to a large extent on ties to (and the success of) adult sons. In patrilineal, virilocal societies sons provide a woman with a crucial link to and source of support in her new community and insurance against insecurity in her declining years.

For his part, a son is often intensely loyal to and protective of his mother and may form a united front with her to further their common interests. But relations between the two are not always harmonious. There are societies, for example, where men remain in, or move to, households run by widowed mothers who manage the family property. In such cases, a son may find himself constrained by the old woman's authority and ambivalent toward her.

What about relations with daughters? Although there are sometimes problems, especially when mothers play an important role in arranging their daughters' first marriages, we rarely read of serious strains between them. Perhaps this is because adult women in most societies join their husbands' people at marriage and do not live in the same households or communities as their mothers. Then, too, in most societies a woman has little, if any, economic or jural authority over adult daughters. Her personal and domestic property may be inherited by a daughter, but a woman does not generally control rights to key productive resources that pass to daughters at her death. Daughters are usually not seen as a threat from below. Whereas a young man's economic status and influence often hinge on his father's relinquishing of these prerogatives, a daughter's economic status and her ability to influence others is rarely inversely linked to her mother's status (Kertzer and Madison 1981:128).

Absence may make the heart grow fonder and actually contribute to an idealized view of mothers (see S. LeVine 1978). But even in societies where mothers and adult daughters live together, relations between them tend to be portrayed as loyal and cooperative. Mothers and daughters do share a common bond as women, and they have a long history of frequent interaction in domestic tasks. But my suspicion is that sources of amity have been emphasized at the expense of sources of discord.

One hint that strains do develop comes from a report on on the traditional Nayar of Central Kerala, where, according to Gough, a deep undercurrent of rivalry often marked relations between mothers and daughters in matrilineal extended households (1961:346). And Spiro notes that when adult daughters in a Burmese village lived with mothers, their sub-ordination, and desire for autonomy, could present problems (1977:116). In general, if a daughter is subject to her mother's constant directions and orders and if a woman's domestic authority only waxes as her mother's authority wanes, it is likely that some tensions will arise.

Co-Wives

While mother–child relations tend to be warm and affectionate, co-wife relations are more problematic. Granted, there are many cases where an older woman and her younger co-wife get along amicably. Bonds of cooperation often draw them together. Many times, they lighten each others' workload, and the older woman assists her young co-wife before, during, and after childbirth. On occasion, they may even form a united front to wrest demands from their husband. When there is a large age differential between them (and their children), they are less likely to compete over various matters. And residential separation and autonomy in daily affairs tend to mitigate problems between a young woman and an old senior wife. Co-wives usually have their own separate huts and domestic equipment, and in some places they even live in different households.

Nonetheless, relations between an old woman and her younger co-wife are often stormy. An unfortunate woman—who is barren, for instance—may envy her more successful co-wife. Co-wives often compete for their husband's affection as well as for his attention and largesse to their children. The "more the co-wife relationship [in African patrilocal polygynous extended families] involves uncertainty as to the present or future distribution of advantages among the wives and their children," Robert LeVine writes, "the more likely that hostility will result. The hostility reaches a peak where the wives' own efforts play a part in determining how much their sons will inherit from the father" (1965:193).

Then there is the matter of the young woman's subordination to her old co-wife. In some societies, wives in polygynous households are ranked so that an old woman is the senior (or first) wife and the younger woman is clearly defined as junior. Such ranking minimizes competition between the two, but problems can still arise. Younger women defined as junior may know their place, but they do not always like it. In societies where the old senior, or first, wife has authority over junior co-wives, it is not hard to imagine a young woman feeling unjustly oppressed by a dominant old senior wife. Among the Tiwi, the first and oldest wife had jurisdiction over all other wives of the household. She could assign tasks to the younger women and even direct them in the care of their children. "She can sit all day in a camp and send the other wives out hunting," is how one junior wife described an old senior wife (Goodale 1971:228). Though Goodale does not relate tales of hostility or conflict, perhaps some Tiwi woman buckled under the authority of old senior wives who tried to hinder their liaisons with young men and who ruled with an iron hand.

Where the senior wife has no official authority over and is not supposed to control her co-wives, young women usually resent an old senior woman's attempt to dominate. Among the Plateau Tonga of Zambia, co-wives had their own kitchens, fields, and granaries. Although the chief or first wife had certain privileges—for some purposes her ritual status was higher than that of other wives and it was expected that she would have the most influence with her husband—she did not have the right to subordinate other wives to her demands. No wife, including a chief wife, could order a co-wife or a co-wife's children to work in her fields, and a woman shared what she produced with a needy co-wife only if she so desired. If at times a chief wife did try to subordinate her co-wives, she found her actions countered by the claim that they, too, were free women, not slaves to do her bidding (Colson, quoted in Stephens 1963:63–64). A senior wife among the Tallensi had no disciplinary authority over co-wives, though she had a privileged position in the homestead and exercised considerable moral authority over co-wives. Generally, co-wives accepted her advice and guidance. "A wise and tactful senior wife," Fortes tells us, "will keep an eye on the household economy and on the children without seeming to interfere with the liberty of her younger co-wives" (1949:132). Not all senior wives were so benevolent, however, and some, with overbearing dispositions, made life difficult for their juniors (Fortes 1949:133).

Mothers-in-law and Daughters-in-law

Mothers-in-law and daughters-in-law, according to a Sicilian proverb, were quarreling when they first descended from heaven (Chapman 1971:111). This saying would be well appreciated in many other societies.

The most often reported, and probably the most serious, strains between dominant old women and the young are those between mothers-in-law and daughters-in-law. Although in Sicily, as elsewhere, disputes between the two women may only occasionally erupt, tensions frequently simmer beneath the surface. Not surprisingly, antagonism between mothers-in-law and daughters-in-law is most likely to arise when they live in the same domestic group. Although with advanced age and frailty the older woman tends to lose much of her power and eventually becomes dependent on her daughter-in-law, I am concerned here with cases where the mother-in-law is still definitely in charge.

Young women's position as a newcomer to her husband's family's household is part of the problem. Unlike a daughter, she was not reared by her mother-in-law, nor does she feel an obligation to the older woman for services rendered in childhood. Sometimes she even comes from a group regarded as enemies by her husband's kin. That being a stranger can make her life difficult, especially in the first years of marriage, is illustrated by the words of an old Galician man who prayed to the rosary every night surrounded by his children. "For the welfare of everyone in this house except for the daughter-in-law who is an outsider," is how he would end (Lisón-Tolosana 1976:307).

But it is more than being an outsider that leads to friction between the two women. They compete for the son-husband's allegiance and affection, a point that comes out clearly in Margery Wolf's (1970, 1972) study of family life in rural Taiwan.[7] There, a woman's tie with her son was crucial, and she was intent on keeping it strong. It was her son (or sons) whom she could count on in times of crisis and for protection and care in her declining years. The entry of the daughter-in-law put the relationship with her son in jeopardy: the older woman inevitably resented her son's relationship with his wife. One way she expressed this jealousy was to abuse her authority. She might criticize, scold, and sometimes even beat the younger woman. The daughter-in-law, usually without kin in her new community, turned to her husband to speak for and protect her and tried to win him to her side.

It did not matter if the young woman's appeals to her husband went unheeded or if the issue at hand was minor. That such appeals were made at all confirmed the older woman's fears that the daughter-in-law was trying to steal her son away from her. The daughter-in-law's actions seemed to be an attack on all the older woman had worked so hard to build, and she felt justified in her dislike of the daughter-in-law. A vicious circle was thus set up: "The more resentful and jealous the mother-in-law, the more she tyrannizes her son's wife; the more she is victimized, the harder the girl works to pry her husband out of his natal family, an effort that only serves to intensify the older woman's fears and to escalate the conflict."[8] (A. Wolf 1968:869).

In general, mothers-in-law and daughters-in-law in patrilocal extended families are working at cross-purposes—doomed enemies, as Jane Collier puts it (1974:93). While the old woman is trying to keep her household together and her sons with her, the daughter-in-law is often trying to persuade her husband to set up his own household, where she will have more autonomy and control. When the daughter-in-law is slated to take over as mistress of the household when her mother-in-law dies or steps down, she represents a different kind of threat. The younger woman must bide her time, waiting for her mother-in-law to die or hand over control of the household so that she can fully come into her own.[9]

Such a situation has the makings of trouble. In addition,

the mother-in-law's domination is often quite repressive. Submission and toil, Lisón-Tolosana (1976:307) says, are the two words that sum up the daughter-in-law's (the heir's wife) situation in the highlands of Galicia.

In many societies, the mother-in-law not only inducts the daughter-in-law into the woman's life of the household but supervises her work in the home and fields. The image of the new bride as servant to the mother-in-law frequently crops up. An old Pondo man in South Africa called his son's wife "the bell" because "now my wife just sits still and calls when she wants anything, just like a white lady ringing the bell" (Monica Wilson, quoted in Mair 1971:133). In general, the mother-in-law's harsh domination may be a kind of revenge for her own days as a helpless daughter-in-law. Finally she has an adult person she can order about to do her bidding, and she may relish this new power.

How long the mother-in-law's domination makes life difficult for the daughter-in-law varies, however. Often, tensions are most severe in the first year or so of marriage (when the mother-in-law is frequently not yet old). So Robert LeVine argues is the case in most African patrilocal extended families where young women soon attained considerable autonomy in their new homes (1965:194–195). Indeed, he does not consider the mother-in-law–daughter-in-law relationship to be a point of great strain in these families. If tensions were extreme at the beginning stages of the marriage, he says, it might be broken off. As the years passed, the two women usually developed a backlog of common experiences and became used to and friendly with each other. Although a woman might be expected to serve her mother-in-law and relieve the older woman of onerous tasks, several factors tended to prevent her from being "excessively dominated": the young woman had her own hut; she became autonomous in cultivating fields allotted to her and in trading at market; and she had freedom to travel on her own.[10]

Yet a detailed study of childbearing women in the 1970s, written mainly by his wife Sarah LeVine (1978), suggests that Robert LeVine's earlier views were over optimistic, at least for the Gusii. Young Gusii women did have their own huts and allotted fields in their husbands' family homestead. But tensions with mothers-in-law frequently continued past the first years of marriage into the mother-in-law's old age.

Admittedly, not all young Gusii women had difficult relations with their mothers-in-law. Some young women were content with their subordinate role. But antipathy and ambivalence often characterized relations with mothers-in-law well into a marriage. Daughters-in-law were supposed to help their mothers-in-law, and mothers-in-law could be very demanding. Young women were expected to keep their resentments under cover. Obedience and proper respect is what they owed their mothers-in-law.

How typical the Gusii case is of patrilocal extended families in other African societies is an open question. Evidence from other parts of the world, however, indicates that a mother-in-law's control in the household often created strains with daughters-in-law long beyond the first year or two of the young woman's marriage.

Women in an urbanized village of metropolitan New Delhi, for example, could retain a firm grip on the household management well into their later years, often making life a misery for their daughters-in-law (Vatuk 1975, 1980). Mothers-in-law had day-to-day managerial authority in the household, including control of the purse strings. Young women had to ask for money for even routine purchases. Although women were supposed to cede managerial control in their later years, "the symbolic act of 'handing over the keys' to the daughter-in-law is often resisted up to the end" (Vatuk 1975:158). As a rule, a woman did not voluntarily give up responsibility for household organization until she was physically or mentally incapable.

The daughter-in-law's lot was not an easy one. Many were confined to the house most of the time under the supervision of their mothers-in-law. The mother-in-law's work—shopping and dealing with tradesmen and artisans, for example—took her out of the household. The daughter-in-law's duties kept her at home. The young woman was relegated to the heavier, more onerous jobs in the house. She cooked the meals and washed the clothes and utensils. She was expected to serve her mother-in-law—to scrub the old woman's back when she bathed, for example, and massage the old woman's legs. Young women often complained that they were made to press their mother-in-law's legs for hours at night until they dozed off from exhaustion, at which point the old woman demanded that the massaging continue (Vatuk 1975:153). If the old woman fell ill, the daughter-in-law could end up nursing her for months and even years.

Mothers-in-law and Sons-in-law

What makes the mother-in-law—daughter-in-law relationship so difficult is that the two often must spend so much time together. By contrast, not only do mothers-in-law and sons-in-law usually live in different communities (or residences), but their various activities also tend to be quite separate. Even so, in many societies avoidance rules regulate a man's behavior to his mother-in-law, requiring him to show respect toward her in various ways.

In some societies, he is not permitted to eat with her, look her straight in the eye, or mention her name. Where he cannot address her directly, he must communicate with her through a third party. Among the patrilineal Iteso of Kenya, blindness was believed to strike a man and his wife's mother who saw each other. "I have often been walking on the road with an informant," Ivan Karp writes, "when he dived headlong into the bushes to avoid his wife's mother. This avoidance is extended to all women the wife calls mother, but is only strictly adhered to with an actual wife of [his] wife's father" (1978:79–80).

Strict avoidance was possible among the Iteso because the two did not live together. But even in matrilineal societies where mothers-in-law and sons-in-law lived in the same compound and had to avoid each other, the two could manage to follow the rules. Goodwin describes how a man and his mother-in-law among the Western Apache were not supposed to see or speak to each other (1942:251–253). When they talked about each other, they had to use the polite form of the verb. Avoiding each other was made easier by the fact that the two lived in separate dwellings, arranged so that exit and entry were possible without one being seen by the other. A woman who accidentally met her son-in-law immediately put a blanket over her head and turned the other way, and the young man scurried off at once. With the introduction of cars, an ingenious solution enabled women to ride in a son-in-law's car: a blanket was hung between the front and back seats.

Avoidance customs suggest underlying tensions or ambivalence in the mother-in-law–son-in-law relationship. Radcliffe-Brown attributes these tensions to the fact that the mother-in-law, the person most closely connected with the wife before marriage, now has to give way to the son-in-law, who gains control and has sexual rights over the young woman (1950:58). Perhaps, too, as Karp suggests for the Iteso, the relationship is anomalous because the older woman is in a clearly superior position to the young man (1978:102). She is the wife giver, he the wife receiver. She is also in the parental generation. If avoidance did not regulate their relationship, a woman would be in a position to exercise authority over an adult man. Given the generally inferior status of women, this would involve a contradiction.

Avoidance taboos may be strictly maintained well into the mother-in-law's old age. In some patrilineal societies, however, the taboos are relaxed with time as the two become used to each other and, especially with the birth of children, when the wife-daughter's allegiance to her husband and his group become more firmly established.

Conclusion:
Old Women's Dominance
and Young Women's Subordination

This chapter has shown that old women in many nonindustrial societies have the chance to reap numerous rewards. At the same time, younger women are relatively deprived. Indeed, privileged old women stand to gain much by keeping young women in their place. Their power and prestige depend in good part on young women's subordination. It is not just that elderly women on top expect young women to show them the proper respect or that they have the authority to issue orders to certain young women in the household and, at times, in the community. The ability to call on the labor and support of young women (as well as children and frequently young adult men) gives elderly women increased leisure and is one reason they can participate more fully in the public sphere.

Old men at the top of the age hierarchy, needless to say, also profit from young women's unfortunate position for they, too, command respect from and have authority over these women and enjoy the fruits of female dependents' labor. But while we are used to thinking about men (old and young alike) keeping young women down, other women are rarely portrayed as dominant oppressors. Yet old women often have a vested interest, perhaps as strong as men's, in perpetuating a system which victimizes young women.

Old women may, in fact, sometimes try to preserve customs that contribute to young women's unfavorable position. Older women are often the ones to administer and uphold feminine modesty standards, even on occasion against the wishes of male family members and in opposition to government policy (Vatuk 1982:153). Old women in Arab Muslim Sudanese society, to cite a particularly dramatic example, were respected by their sons and had considerable authority over their daughters-in-law. At this stage in life, they approached full membership in their husband's and son's patrilineage and had a keen interest in its welfare and continuity. It was these powerful old women who were the strongest advocates of the excruciating and dangerous (and, it should be noted, outlawed) custom of genital mutilation, performed on young girls and on mothers after the birth of each child to ensure the moral character of women and the honor of the patrilineage (Hayes 1975).

Whether Sudanese girls and young women resented having to submit to these ordeals and the old women who were the chief perpetuators of the practice is an open question. Other cases indicate more clearly that young women's relations with old women at the top, like relations between advantaged old men and deprived young men, are often far from easy. To be sure, many sources of strain between old and young men— old men's ultimate control over the family's economic resources, their extensive jural authority over junior men in the household and community, and their attempts to delay young men's marriages and inheritances—are not a serious problem for old and young *women*. Old women usually do not have the kind of control over material resources or jural authority that old men do. Nor do they seek to monopolize the market in spouses. While strains between dominant old women and subordinate young women may not be as widespread or well documented as those between their male counterparts, they are certainly known to arise, especially between coresident mothers-in-law and daughters-in-law, and they can, at times, be quite serious.

What is clear from the analysis of hierarchical relations among old and young women is that age and sex inequalities are closely connected. Old women are sometimes active agents in upholding or reinforcing social practices that help to keep young women subordinate to men. Age inequalities, moreover, may prevent women from uniting to further their interests as women or from even becoming aware that they have common interests as women. Far from inevitably joining together, old and young women often have widely divergent interests and are sometimes divided by deep strains and cleavages. These comments about the linkages between age and sex inequalities will be developed further in the concluding chapter. For the moment, we need to round out the discussion of inequalities and relations between the generations by turning from privileged and powerful old women and men to those who have experienced serious social losses.

4
Consequences
of Age Inequality: III

Social Losses for the Old

Not all old people are at the top. Often, the old are relatively deprived. This, too, is another form of age inequality.

To speak of old people at the bottom of the system of age inequality, however, can be misleading. It ignores the complexities and inconsistencies of their position. While the elderly (or some of the elderly) may be disadvantaged in many ways, certain prerogatives and rewards may still be theirs. Thus, I prefer to talk about various social losses the old in nonindustrial societies experience rather than referring to old people at the bottom.

This chapter looks at the conditions that lead to losses of prestige, influence, and independence among the elderly. It also examines how such losses affect relations with the young. Marked social losses may precede the state of advanced debility, and in a number of societies the still capable old must relinquish valued economic roles and positions of domestic or community-wide authority. But everywhere the aged who become physically or mentally incapacitated have to depend on younger folks for support and care, even though they do not always formally cede economic, domestic, or other controls. Physical incapacity and the need for custodial care usually lead to social losses for individuals as they become less independent and increasingly marginal in daily affairs.

If experiencing social losses is not bad enough, problems also commonly arise with the young. The loss of valued roles and the need for care often lead to tensions with younger people.[1] The elderly frequently resent their reduced status; the young may only grudgingly support the old. Matters are complicated not only because many of the old once had numerous privileges and powers but because in old age their status is often inconsistent. That is to say, on the basis of age, old people may have limited opportunity to acquire some rewards while they have the edge in accumulating others. The aged who still occupy certain rewarded roles may be especially aggrieved by their losses. In many cases, they expect deference because of their seniority and experience, for example. But young people, mindful of old people's economic or other losses, are not always so ready to accord the old deference.

Of course, the elderly in nonindustrial societies are not all alike. The two preceding chapters pointed out that the old in a society do not all have the same success in getting ahead. Some rewards are out of the question for old women. Among old men, for example, political office may elude those who do not qualify by virtue of descent or seniority. Not only do those with prosperous kin have a clear advantage in many places, but personal qualities and even luck mean that only certain people can make the most of the opportunities aging provides for success.

Nor are all the elderly hit equally hard by social losses. Social losses among the old are most often the result of physical or mental declines that render the elderly incapable of performing certain roles and make them dependent on the young. The extent and seriousness of physical disabilities vary from one old person to another, however. Indeed, some people remain vigorous and productive until a ripe old age. And since mental incapacity is not inevitable, some individuals, despite their advanced years, never experience it at all. Even among the elderly who do suffer pronounced physical or mental declines, some, because of such differences as sex, personality, and wealth in material goods and offspring, are more adversely affected by these declines than others. This differential success, or failure, can, as we shall see, have important implications for relations with the young.

Losing Valued Roles: The Physically and Mentally Competent Old

Just as aging gives individuals in many societies the opportunity to get ahead, so old age (or a particular phase of old age) can be a severe handicap, disqualifying individuals from keeping social rewards and valued roles they have worked hard to obtain. This losing process need not be a direct result of physical incapacity or mental incompetence. And it can be quite a formal affair.

In a number of societies, the competent old, whatever their physical state, have to retire officially from valued positions at a given time. In some age-set societies, for instance, physically capable old men must give up formal leadership roles when their set moves on to the next grade (see, for example, Kertzer and Madison 1981 on the Latuka of Sudan). And in some peasant societies, the elderly formally transfer all, or nearly all, of their economic resources and relinquish headship of the household when their children marry.[2]

We have fairly detailed accounts of this transmission process in a number of peasant societies. Far from being physically or mentally incompetent when they retire from control of resources, the old are often active and alert when they formally cede control of property to the younger generation. While holding on to property until death provides, Jack Goody observes, "both a carrot for the young and a surety for the old" formally transmitting resources before then is risky for the elderly (1976a:118). It can lead to a loss of prestige and influence over the young and affect relations with juniors who officially take over the reins.

The Sherpa

Transferring property before death had a devastating effect on old people's status and social identity in Sherpa society. According to Sherry Ortner, old parents were "more or less abandoned or at least neglected and treated with some callousness" (1978:47).

The first child's marriage was, in a real sense, the beginning of the end. With each child's marriage, the family estate was further reduced. A son had to be given his share of the father's land and ideally a house; a daughter, a quantity of cash, jewels, and utensils. Parents tried in various ways to delay the process, which would end in their "being metaphorically thrown overboard by their children." Often they succeeded— at least up to a point. Many Sherpas did not marry and live with their spouses until quite late, sometimes not until their late thirties.

Eventually the youngest son married, however. It was this son, according to inheritance rules, who received the parental house. He was obliged to feed and care for the old couple out of the last share of their estate. The situation was far from ideal for the old people. They were often reduced to the status of dependents, sometimes almost servants, in their son's household. No wonder old people felt betrayed by their sons, a sentiment expressed in an ancient poem. At first, according to the poem, a son "is as pleasing as a scion of the gods." Inevitably, however:

> He brings home the daughter of some strange man
> and turns outside his kindly father and mother.
> Though his father calls he gives no answer,
> though his mother cries out he speaks never a word.
> At last he becomes a hasty-tempered lodger
> and drives them away with false complaints.
>
> (quoted in Ortner 1978:44)

The youngest son's marriage, however, did not signal the end of the parents' working days. The old couple continued to work as long as they could. If they had turned over all their remaining property to the youngest son, they worked in his fields and received food from him. In some cases, the old people clung to independence for as long as possible by buying or building a small hut for themselves and by retaining a small piece of land to cultivate. When they moved to the new dwelling they took only the bare essentials with them, leaving most of their domestic equipment behind. Some widows or widowers separated themselves even more completely from their sons by becoming religious mendicants.

Rural Ireland

While Sherpa parents' property was gradually whittled away as each child married, in County Clare, Ireland, official control of the family estate was an all-or-nothing proposition (Arensberg and Kimball 1968). The family property, house, stock, and land were passed intact to one son when he married. A man picked the son who would remain on the farm with an eye to which one would "carry on most successfully" (Arensberg and Kimball 1968:63).

Transfers, however, were effected late in a man's life. At the time of Arensberg and Kimball's study in the 1930s, farms were generally turned over to a son when the father passed his seventieth year (1968:120). The old couple's reluctance to renounce their leadership was responsible for late marriage. In 1926, 88 percent of men between twenty-five and thirty and 73 percent between thirty and thirty-five in rural districts of County Clare were still unmarried. "Even at forty-five and fifty," the authors note, "if the old couple have not yet made over the farm, the countryman remains a 'boy' in respect to farm work and the rural vocabulary" (1968:55).

When a match was finally made for the inheriting son, agreements were put into legal form—"the writings"—by a solicitor. The "writings" was usually both marriage settlement and will, spelling out that the father would hand over the farm and all appurtenances to his son in return for the dowry brought in by his son's bride. (The dowry, as well as savings, was used to provide portions for those children who were not settled on the land.) Nor was the old couple's fate after transfer left to chance. The "writings" made provision for the old couple's support. Generally they were given the right to the "grass of a cow," to food, and to the use of the hearth as well as a room in the house: "To take care of possible disputes arising out of the failure of these provisions to work smoothly, certain very hard-headed stipulations are often included, allowing for the conversion of these rights into cash support or a lump sum" (Arensberg and Kimball 1968:111).

The transfer of the farm was a social loss for the old people. The old man might continue to work on the farm, but he no longer directed the farm enterprise or controlled the farm income. The old woman was no longer "woman of the house."

Yet by Arensberg and Kimball's account, old people's position was far from grim after transfer. Old men and women in the family were "objects of respect and a mild sort of veneration on the part of all younger members" (1968:163). The room they lived in, the west room, was the best in the house (Arensberg 1968:107). The chair by the fire—the seat of honor and most comfort—was theirs. Outside the family, they also received respect. Old men regulated the length and subject of conversations as young men hung back and listened. Even in small matters old people had precedence. The better cup of tea, the largest piece of bread, the two eggs instead of one, or the pipeful of tobacco went to the older men (Arensberg and Kimball 1968:170–172). Old men, including those whose sons had succeeded them, were informal community leaders who met regularly in an informal clique at the "old men's house." The old men's clique, Arensberg and Kimball argue, played a decisive role in community life:

[It] is the seat of judgment in the community. It is the clearing house of information and the court of opinion in which the decisions of the community are reached and the traditional knowledge of the peasantry applied and disseminated. From these meetings the men return home to their wives and sons, and the formulations they have reached spread . . . through the community (1968:183).

Why old Irish men in County Clare continued to have so much prestige and influence after the transfer of property is puzzling. Within the family, norms of filial respect were still underpinned by economic realities, however. Despite having ceded their property, old men at the time of Arensberg and Kimball's study had some economic leverage in the household because they received government pensions. Indeed, men usually had to hand over their small farms in order to qualify for pensions. Old-age pensions were an important resource in small farm households. "To have old people in the house is a blessing in these times," said one farmer, "because if you have one, it means ten bob a week and, if you have two, it means a pound a week coming into the house" (Arensberg and Kimball 1968:120).

There is also the question of how much influence old men had after they transferred their farms. Most of the men Arensberg and Kimball describe as important in one community, and who met at the old men's house, had not yet been succeeded by the younger generation. As for the family, there is some evidence that men experienced greater losses after transfer than Arensberg and Kimball's general statements on the privileges and precedence of old age indicate. Young men's deference could be a rather empty formality, for example. One son got on well with his father by seeming to defer to the old man. "Every morning, even after I was married," the younger man said, "I would go to the old man and ask what he thought I should do for the day. . . . I would then go and spend twenty or thirty minutes doing what the old man said, and then go about my own business" (Arensberg and Kimball 1968:121). The transfer of property was not always so smooth, however, and in cases of extreme discord, as I discuss below, the old people could even be forced to leave their son's home.

Basque Villages

A final example from Spain shows yet a different pattern. Here the transfer of the farm was usually partial and the old couple retained other economic assets as well.

In the Basque village of Murelaga, a couple legally trans-

ferred the *baserria*, or farmstead, when their son (or, in a minority of cases, daughter) chosen as the sole heir married
(Douglass 1969). (The *baserria* included the dwelling, household furnishings, agricultural tools, landholdings, and household site on the floor of the village church.) A legal contract
set out the donor's and recipient couple's obligations after
transfer. Among other things the contract outlined, the older
couple received the daughter-in-law's dowry in return for relinquishing control of the *baserria*. The dowry gave them the
means to provide for their other children. (If the younger couple kept the dowry, they had to make dowry payments to the
heir's unmarried siblings.)

Although the older couple transferred the farm, they did
not stop working. Old men continued to take an active role
in agricultural tasks until physically unable to do so. Indeed,
they were valued as agricultural experts. The older couple also
retained authority as the heir's parents—and this authority had
economic backing. The contract frequently stipulated that the
donors kept the right to one-half of the profits of the farm.
Moreover, the older couple still owned a personal estate consisting of cash, for example, property other than the *baserria*,
and control of standing timber, which they could retain until
their deaths, when it was usually divided more or less equally
among all their children.

Formal Transfer of Resources: Tensions

If the transfer of property can alter the balance of power
between the generations, how does it affect their day-to-day
relations?

Some general comments first. Before transfer (when parents could already be defined as old),[3] tensions can arise with
the young over the timing of the transition. The young wait
with bated breath while the old often try to delay giving up
control. Once the property and/or household control have
passed to the younger generation, it is the old couple who may
feel deprived while younger people try to assert their new
status.

The old, to be sure, may be resigned to their lot. Like the

Sherpa old described by Ortner, they may expect little of their children and go off on their own as a way to avoid friction (1978:47). But in other societies old people no longer in charge often have greater expectations and have a hard time adjusting to their new role. The elderly who have transferred their property know what it is like to be on top, and for many the decline in status is a bitter pill to swallow. They lament their loss of authority and may still try to dominate even though formal control is gone.

Accustomed to exercising authority, they may well be irritated if their opinions are ignored. Younger people who are formally in charge of the land and/or household, however, may want to make this clear. Some are clever diplomats and, like the Irish farmer mentioned earlier, seem to defer to their parents' advice while actually making their own decisions. For the sake of harmony and out of respect for the old people, the young may not exert their full authority. But they may resent having to exercise such restraint. Moreover, pleasing the old folks can be difficult. And young people's assertiveness, or disregard of the old people's wishes, can severely strain relations with an old father or mother-in-law.

The rural Irish and Basque examples illustrate some of these points. On the one hand, old people, as parents, were owed respect and obedience. They also retained a degree of economic clout after transfer—from pensions in the Irish case and from control of half the cash profits of the farm and their personal estate in the Basque case. On the other hand, they had ceded formal control of the farm and household and were officially subordinated to the authority of the heir and his spouse.

Although Arensberg and Kimball stress the tensions arising from old men's privileged station and control before transfer and although they emphasize the smooth and gradual nature of the transition, there are hints that tensions arose because handing over the farm weakened old people's position. Relations between father and son after transfer could be rocky, especially when the younger man did not keep up the front of deferring to and seeking the advice of his father (Arensberg and Kimball 1968:121). When old people met, they discussed such topics as young men's failure to help as they should and the "good old days," when young men were more dependent on the old (1968:166). Perhaps such grumbling carried over into their conversations with the young. When tensions reached an unbearable point in the household, younger people seemed to have the upper hand. Turning old people out on the side of the road was not unheard of. If a family found old people too great a burden, "the old may go to the County Home, where the poor and derelict old people are maintained" (Arensberg and Kimball 1968:120).

In Murelaga, conflict between the couple formerly in control and the heir and his wife was, Douglass says, potentially present in any domestic group (1969:135). Both the younger and older couple wanted to assert their authority in the household—the old people as parental authority figures, the young couple as official master and mistress of the house. Usually, disputes did not become so bitter that the household was dissolved. When the younger, or older, couple exercised no restraint in their power struggle, however, drastic results could follow:

The attempt on the part of the younger couple to exert their . . . authority in dictatorial fashion may trigger open conflict leading ultimately to the dismantling of the three-generational grouping. The attempt on the part of the old couple to exert their family authority over the heir to the detriment of the latter's ability to discharge his . . . role may just as quickly lead to a schism within the domestic group.[4] (Douglass 1969:118)

More typically, young and old made accommodations and followed a policy of restraint. Harmonious relations, at least on the surface, were often preserved. The younger folks had to be satisfied with placating their elders—and waiting for the older couple to die before full authority was theirs.[5]

In Murelaga as well as in County Clare, the sharpest intergenerational strains in the household were between mother-in-law and daughter-in-law.[6] Relations after transfer were eased between a man and his son for several reasons. The older couple had chosen and were used to living with their son-heir. Father and son had a common identification with the farm and had worked closely together for years. The heir was also conditioned to occupying a subordinate position to his parents. A daughter-in-law, however, was a stranger to the household. No long history of working together or of filial respect tempered relations with her mother-in-law.

In rural Ireland, according to Arensberg and Kimball, good relations were possible when the younger woman submitted to her mother-in-law and allowed the old woman to feel she was "master mariner" (1968:119). But the daughter-in-law was not always so submissive. On occasion, relations deteriorated to the point where the old woman left her son's house and joined a daughter. People in the community disapproved of such a break, but they felt that the son should take his wife's, rather than his mother's, part (1968:123).

In Murelaga as well, a man's loyalty to his wife was supposed to take precedence over loyalty to his parents. Young men often had a hard time mediating between their wives and mothers since these women were frequently on bad terms. Sometimes, the young man brought in a priest to arbitrate. In extreme cases, he might even emigrate to America or Australia to extricate himself from the situation (Douglass 1969:135).

Tensions, of course, usually did not erupt into serious open struggles, a topic that foreshadows the fuller and more general analysis of the next chapter. In Murelaga and County Clare, young women generally did not want to alienate mothers-in-law, on whom they relied for help with child rearing and other household tasks. In Murelaga, both younger and older people—men as well as women—had an interest in maintaining amicable relations and holding the household together. The older couple, unable to perform strenuous farm tasks, was economically dependent on the younger people. The younger pair were often partly financially dependent on the donor couple, who controlled half the farm income. The younger couple also wanted to avoid the heavy financial drain that partition would bring. The old people would be a greater burden on the household cash reserves if they moved out. Finally, consideration for what the neighbors thought encouraged young people to fulfill their obligations to the older couple: young folks wanted to avoid public gossip and scandal.

Just as young people's economic dependence on the old couple was a factor reducing the likelihood of bitter quarrels in Murelaga, so in County Clare young people's dependence on old women's (and old men's) pensions had the same effect. "Before the old-age pension," one countrywoman said, "the young woman and the old woman [would be] slashing each other with tongs, the doors broke, and it would be two dwellings in the house, like, but since the old-age pension, there are no rows and, if there are, then they make it up with the old people for the ten bob a week" (Arensberg and Kimball 1968:121).

The Physically and Mentally Incapacitated Old

Among the villagers of County Clare and Murelaga, old men and women were frequently still quite physically active and mentally alert when they officially stepped down as household heads and farm managers or, in the Sherpa case, after they had witnessed the breakup of the family estate.

In many societies, however, people only begin to experience significant social losses when, and if, they become seriously disabled physically or mentally.[7] At this point, they can no longer attend to their own daily existence and they need custodial care. Sometimes this state is clearly demarcated so that we are talking about a distinct life stage. The "last scene of all" marked by "second childishness and mere oblivion" is how Shakespeare (As You Like It) described the seventh age of man. Whether or not the physically or mentally incapacitated old are distinguished by the natives, ethnographers, or even poets, such incapacity and increased dependence, as we shall see, usually bring problems. Indeed, according to Amoss and Harrell, the incompetent aged are everywhere regarded as a burden (1981:4).

Physical or mental incompetence does not, to be sure, necessarily mean that the old must officially give up valued roles. An old man among the Tallensi, Fortes tells us, could be blind, deaf, and mentally incompetent and have relinquished the management of household affairs to his sons, "but he is still the head of the family and lineage, the hub of their unity, and the intermediary between them and their ancestors. However infirm an old man may be of body or understanding he is regularly told of everything that happens in the house, and his consent is always obtained before anything is done in his name, as everything that pertains to the family and lineage must be" (1949:181). Nor does physical incapacity inevitably lead to retirement from political office. Jack Goody relates seeing a divisional chief among the Gonja "scarcely able to speak, being carried into his courtroom to take part in the decision-making process. His judgment, delivered to the assembled audience by the spokesman, appeared to be that official's interpretation of 'the sense of the meeting.' Nonetheless, it was seen as coming from the lips of the chief rather than of his advisers" (1976a:127). While the disabled old do little or no physical labor, they may still occupy supervisory positions and be respected for their expertise. Even those who suffer serious mental impairments may be thought to have ritual powers.

All this said, it is still true that the physically or mentally incapacitated old, whatever their formal powers, tend to retreat to the sidelines and become increasingly marginal in everyday affairs.[8] Simmons argues that, where ample details are available, deference seems to decline "when individuals become physically and mentally incompetent and socially useless in actual or imaginary terms" (1945:62). In general, the incompetent old must, in addition, depend on others for their very livelihood and care. It is this change that I want to emphasize here. How does their need for support affect relations with the young? What kinds of tensions can arise?

Relations with the Young: Two Stereotypes

Two stereotypes usually come to mind about relations between the incapacitated old and younger caretakers in the nonindustrial world. In one view, the old are subject to cruel treatment: they are abandoned and left to die. At the other extreme, there is an idyllic picture of the young faithfully carrying out their caretaking duties.

As with most stereotypes, there is some truth in them. Two recent cross-cultural studies indicate, in fact, that abandoning or killing the aged is more common than we might think. Glascock and Feinman (1981:23–28) uncovered twenty-six instances of killing and sixteen of abandoning the elderly in forty-two societies. And Maxwell and Silverman (1981) found evidence of younger people abandoning and/or killing the aged in twenty of the ninety-five societies in their sample (see also Simmons 1945:225–228, 235–240).

But if the helpless elderly have been abandoned and left to die in some societies when they became too great a burden, this is far from universal. This brings us to the second stereotype about tender care of the aged. Many studies of the elderly show children, kin, or neighbors looking after the physically incapacitated aged up until the end. This is even true in some hunting and gathering societies, where, it might be thought, catering to the needs of the helpless old would endanger the very existence of the family or band. Richard Lee says, for example, that geronticide was extremely rare among the !Kung San of Botswana (1968:36). The blind and crippled aged—long past their productive years—were fed and cared for by children and grandchildren and were respected for their technical and ritual skills.

In general, children tend to be under strong moral obligation to provide for aged parents. They often feel affection toward elderly parents as well as a debt for services parents rendered in earlier years. In many societies, moreover, the son or daughter who looks after the old couple is rewarded with special treatment in the division of property. If these sentiments and the promise of economic benefit are not enough, various negative sanctions are often applied against children who shirk filial duties[9]—as well as against others who refuse to help the needy old. Indeed, the burden of supporting the aged is sometimes spread throughout the community. Communal food sharing and food distributions, for instance, are common in some societies (see J. Goody 1976a:121–122; Simmons 1945:20–26). Where the sharing ethic is strong, those generous to the aged may be honored and applauded. And in some societies, the elderly are assured of certain foods at communal gatherings or other occasions because these foods are taboo to younger people (Simmons 1945:26–31).

Sources of Strain

But to stop here is to give a distorted and incomplete view of relations between the frail old and their young caretakers in nonindustrial societies. Abandoning the old can be less cruel than we might suppose; caring for them less idyllic. Thus, a number of questions arise. How do young folks feel about looking after the aged? Do the young always carry out their caretaking duties willingly and with devotion? Do the aged have reason to feel hostile to their young caretakers? Do they resent the young who will, or do, abandon or even eventually kill them?

Abandonment and Killing. The subject of the quality of relations and sources of strain between the incapacitated aged and young has received little attention, and we have to tease out clues and hints from various ethnographic accounts.

There is a particular dearth of material on the strains immediately preceding or accompanying the killing or abandonment of the aged. One could argue that this is because such strains are so rare. Indeed, we read of the aged accepting, or at least not actively resisting, their fate (Glascock and Feinman 1981:28). In some societies, it is reported, the decrepit old were only abandoned upon their request. Tonkinson tells us that Mardudjara hunters and gatherers of Australia fed the incompetent old and tried to spare them the difficulties of moving too often (1978:83). Sometimes, however, frequent movement could not be helped, and the old, feeling they simply could not manage, asked to be left behind to die. In some societies, being buried alive was considered an honorable way to go. In "ancient times" among the Yakut of Siberia, extremely decrepit old people generally begged their children or other relatives to bury them. Before being led into the wood and thrust into a previously prepared hole, they were honored at a three-day feast (Simmons 1945:237; see also Holmes 1972:84–86, on Samoa). And cultural attitudes toward death might soften the blow or make the aged indifferent to dying. The elderly among the Eskimo of northern Canada in the precontact period, Guemple (1980) argues, were willing, and sometimes even pleaded, to be abandoned when they became weak or ill because they did not believe they would really die. Their name substance—"the essential ingredient of a human being which includes the personality, special skills, and basic character"—would live on, entering the body of a newborn child.

Despite this evidence, it seems likely that the aged were not always so resigned to their death. In some places and in some instances they had mixed, if not downright hostile, feelings toward their young "executioners" (see de Beauvoir 1973:83–87). It is possible that abandoning or killing the old could, on occasion, be an index, or a culmination, of strained relations with the young.

Custodial Care. Even in societies where the old are, at times, abandoned or killed, they are often looked after for a long period during their "helpless" years. In general, there are several possible sources of tension and conflict between old and young in this custodial period.

The young may resent having to meet their caretaking obligations and only fill them grudgingly—sometimes not at all. The old often have a hard time adjusting to their reduced circumstances, resenting their young usurpers and complaining of neglect and ill treatment. These resentments and complaints are, to some extent, matters of individual variation and personal dislikes. But tensions and strains also have deeper structural roots.

First let us explore the situation from the perspective of the aged. Why should they feel resentful? Their physical state often has much to do with their bitterness. To become worn out and unable to work was distressing for the Gwembe Tonga, to take one example. The very old, Colson and Scudder say, "resent physical processes of aging within their own bodies and project their resentment on younger people who flourish while they suffer" (1981:128).

It is not only that the aged may envy the young for their physical vigor. The powers and privileges the aged once enjoyed are now the prerogative of younger adults. As the frail elderly become increasingly marginal in the community and household and as they experience other social losses, they frequently resent the young who have stepped in to replace them.

Another source of resentment among the aged stems from their dependent station. The issue of old people's dependence, however, is a complicated one that deserves some discussion.

We tend to think it is "natural" for the aged to wish to maintain their independence. Yet, by our standards, the old in many nonindustrial societies have relatively little difficulty coming to terms with their increased dependence on others. Far from recoiling at the thought of asking close relatives for favors and help, they often demand such support as a right.

In our own society, the elderly, as various surveys show, generally want to be financially and residentially independent. They are even reluctant to request financial assistance from children when needed (Hess and Waring 1978:259–260). But not all cultures put such a strong emphasis on self-sufficiency and economic independence as ours does. The elderly in nonindustrial societies tend to expect support from children, and cultural norms usually decree that it is their due. Among the Igbo of Nigeria, Shelton observes that old privileged men could demand care as a publicly acknowledged right "without any sense of guilt, ego damage, or loss of face" (1968:241). The person who failed to give such care was the guilty party, subject to scorn and ridicule.

Nor is dependence as closely associated with old age as it is in our own society. Where government does not provide social welfare benefits and where services cannot be hired when needed, individuals must rely on kin and other associates throughout their lives in times of emergency, disaster, or danger. Sally Falk Moore writes that it would be erroneous to say that individuals in nonindustrial societies have a dependent childhood, a completely independent adulthood, followed by a dependent old age. "Such a sequence," she argues, "exaggerates the independence of adulthood" (1978:69). Individuals must depend on, and cultivate and maintain, a large array of social relationships as a resource throughout their lives.

Children are a major human resource in nonindustrial societies, and the elderly have usually long relied on them in both good times and bad. Thus, the dramatic role reversals of later life we hear so much about here are less of a problem in the nonindustrial world. In middle-class America, material exchanges between parents and children tend to be one way, with parents the main givers. A startling shift may occur in late old age if parents, especially in times of serious illness or debility, have to turn, in an "unparent-like way," to adult children for support.[10] Asking children for help is not a new development in nonindustrial societies. Adult children have usually contributed to their parents' material support for much of their lives.

But old people's increased dependence can lead to problems. One difficulty in many places is that the old often feel, or are regarded as, useless when support and assistance become one-way. Those who become incapacitated have greater needs and are more dependent than before. Used to providing services in exchange for those they got, their ability to contribute to the subsistence of the group wanes and they now have little, if anything, to offer in return. "You are old, you can do nothing, you are no good for anything any more," Hopi women told their very aged mothers (Simmons 1945:59). Old Hopi women might well take such remarks to heart. In general, old people's sense of worthlessness can increase their frustrations, which they may take out on the very people who support them.

Of course, the frail old do not feel useless everywhere. In some societies they are seen as making a contribution—if they are religious specialists or political advisors, for example, or property owners letting others use what they have. Then, too, the old, as well as the young, commonly take a longer-range view of the situation and feel that the old deserve to be repaid for the services they provided to the young in the past.

Even where the old are comfortable on the receiving end, however, their need for support can create difficulties. The main problem arising from old people's increased dependence is that they often feel abused or neglected. They may believe the young are not supporting them properly or treating them with the respect they deserve. In many cases, such complaints are well founded. The neglect and poor treatment of the frail old in many societies gives them good cause to grumble.[11]

Except for those elderly men who maintained a degree of control in their homesteads, very old men and women among the Gwembe Tonga whose "feet will not carry them beyond" the homestead any more "are the first to suffer when conditions are hard. Sleeping alone without adequate covering, they shiver at night throughout the cold season. Restricted in their movements, they must endure the dust which sweeps through barren villages during the height of the dry season when others retreat to more sheltered areas" (Colson and Scudder 1981:128).[12] Given these conditions, it is not surprising that many of the very old again showed the "greed and quick anger of childhood"—openly envying the good things they saw others having. Young children might bear some of the brunt of these old people's frustrations, with the very old bursting into angry rages when the youngsters raided their possessions (Colson and Scudder 1981:129).

Life for the disabled Hopi aged sounds even more trying. As long as they controlled property rights, held special ceremonial offices, or were powerful medicine men, the aged were respected. But "the feebler and more useless they become, the more relatives grab what they have, neglect them, and sometimes harshly scold them, even permitting children to play rude jokes on them." Sons might refuse to support their fathers, telling them, "You have had your day, you are going to die pretty soon." Aged Hopi were heard to remark, "We always looked forward to old age, but see how we suffer" (Simmons 1945:59, 234).

Even the elderly who are relatively well looked after may feel they are not being supported properly. Where the old retain economic, political, or ritual authority, this authority gives added cogency to their demands for better treatment. Complaining, moreover, can be a conscious or unconscious strategy to ensure or maximize support—to accentuate the negative with positive consequences as Kerns puts it (1980:124). Public compalints may prod the young into fulfilling their duties and ensure that aid and attention are forthcoming.

If the old have grounds for dissatisfaction, so have the young. Consider their point of view. Many of course are willing and devoted caretakers. But there are reasons why they sometimes perform their duties with mixed, and perhaps even hostile, feelings.

While the elderly recipients may feel they are not getting enough, the young givers may, as Simić (1978b:102–103) observes in the Yugoslav case, "feel they are being leveled excessively." However diligent they are in caring for the aged, fulfilling these duties can be a legitimate but heavy burden that saps their limited resources, physical strength, and sympathies (Amoss and Harrell 1981:4; Colson and Scudder 1981:128).

The disabled old man or woman in the house is an easy target for tired and overworked young people's frustrations, especially if the old person cannot do anything useful to reduce the young person's load. Young people are usually expected to maintain an air of deference to the old, particularly old parents or close kin, but the cranky, demanding, or complaining behavior of the aged can try their patience. "Even old women sometimes lose their kindness," a Kikuyu man said, "demanding and destroying the peace of the homestead" (Cox and Mberia 1977:9). That young people can feel pressured by what they think are unreasonable demands is illustrated by another example. One old woman among the Tallensi, "half sunk in the hebetude of senility," complained endlessly of the neglect of her daughters-in-law. The younger women often quarreled with her because they regarded her demands on their firewood, labor, and food supply as exorbitant (Fortes 1949:95).

Young people's inability to meet all the demands of the elderly can, often unwittingly, add fuel to the fire by contributing to old people's sense of neglect. Many times the young are hard put to give the old the kind of attention they demand or expect. Even with the best intentions, young folks are often simply too busy with productive or other tasks to attend to an old parent's every need. Environmental factors beyond young people's control—drought, for example, or low food reserves—sometimes require decisions that increase the frustrations of the elderly. A poor harvest among the Gwembe Tonga, for example, could necessitate moving the very old— who were no longer essential workers—to relatives in distant and more prosperous regions "to reduce the number of bellies dependent on homestead granaries" (Colson and Scudder 1981:128).

The young, too, may be torn between obligations to dependent old parents and to their own children. Changes in recent times can accentuate this problem as land becomes scarcer and consumer needs escalate (see chapter 7). The young have less to spare for the old while the elderly make increased cash demands. "It is a difficult job to look after them," one Kikuyu man said about his aged parents. "They are often as unreasonable as children. They forget what it is like to have nine children and little land" (Cox and Mberia 1977:9).

What I have said so far describes why tensions can arise between the aged and younger adults in adjacent generations. Can the same sorts of strains develop when very young grandchildren attend to old people's needs? After all, this is a common situation in many societies. Young girls or boys may even be specifically assigned to minister to a grandparent's wants. An old Chagga woman, for example, not only expected to be looked after by her youngest son and his wife (who ultimately inherited her husband's *kihamba*, or grove).

She could also claim a young grandchild, who slept in her hut and served as companion and domestic helper (Moore 1977:67–69). In Gonja society, a young boy or girl was delegated to care for his or her aged grandparents (E. Goody 1973:179).

We know little about the kind of strains that arise between incapacitated grandparents and their grandchildren. Relations between the two, as I noted in the last chapter, tend to be eased because grandchildren do not inherit directly from grandparents. But, I imagine, tensions of the sort described in the preceding pages can develop, particularly when the old people are difficult and demanding. Reports on the Navaho, for instance, indicate that grandchildren had ambivalent feelings toward their grandparents. Grandparents, on the one hand, were affectionate and indulgent toward the youngsters. But grandchildren felt some resentment at being assigned to care for an aged grandparent and at the restrictions on their freedom that such care involved. Having to cut wood and haul water for incapacitated grandparents, for example, and having to accompany them on journeys cut into the time they could spend with other children (Kluckhohn 1967:105–106; see also Leighton and Kluckhohn 1947:102).

Differentiation Among the Very Old

Having outlined the basic sources of strain between the frail old and the young, we now need to narrow our scope of vision. As I have repeatedly emphasized, old people are not the same. Nor do they all have strained relations—or relations that are strained to the same degree—with younger caretakers.

Personality, Material Wealth, and Other Differences. Obviously, personality differences affect the tone of relationships. Some of the aged are irascible, others good-tempered. Young people who are dilatory in meeting their obligations or do so without warmth or generosity may simply dislike the older person they are supporting. Then there is the history of the relationship between the dependent old person and

younger provider. In some instances the two have always got-
ten along well; in others, they have long been at odds and the
old person's increased dependence may open or exacerbate
old wounds.

Additional factors can make life more or less difficult for
the incapacitated aged and thus influence relations with the
young. The elderly bring with them certain advantages or disadvantages accumulated over a lifetime. Some have more material wealth than others. Very old men with little land and
few cattle, for example, cannot lure the young to care for them
with promises of bountiful inheritances as can their more
successful counterparts. The extent of old people's political
influence or family authority also affects how they will be
supported. Physical health, too, can make a difference. Individuals who remain relatively vigorous up until the end place
less of a burden on the young than those who have suffered
from serious incapacitating illness for most, or all, of their later
years.

Gender Distinctions. Gender distinctions also influence
the quality of relations between the incapacitated old and their
younger caretakers. Whereas men often depend heavily on jural
and economic authority to back up claims to support from
children, women usually rely more on their children's sense
of moral obligation and affection. As those who raise and care
for children, women often have stronger ties of affection to
children and grandchildren than men do. Indeed, these ties
of affection may be nurtured with an eye to old-age support.

Admittedly, children's affection does not ensure smooth
relations with dependent mothers. Fortes tells us, for example, that among the Tallensi sons kept old mothers in their
homes out of affection and duty (1949:175). But some sons
complained that these women became too egoistic, thinking
only of their comfort and of having enough to eat and cursing
those who crossed them. Then, too, when a woman lives with
a son, her daughter-in-law is likely to bear the brunt of the
burden. Little love may be lost between the two women. Yet
a son usually makes sure that his wife cares for his old mother,

as Margery Wolf notes for rural Taiwan. There, sons publicly fulfilled their filial obligations to old fathers, but they generally did their duty and not much more. Sons were ambivalent toward fathers who had been aloof, authoritarian figures for most of the younger men's lives. By contrast, relations with mothers were warm and affectionate. If a woman had trained her son well, his affection saw to it that his wife cared for her "with a gentleness that an old man might never experience" (1970:51).

If affection sometimes guarantees old women loving care from children, the fact that women can be useful well into their later years also minimizes strains with younger caretakers. In some societies, incapacitated old men are viewed as useless when they are no longer able to do productive work. Quite frail old women, however, frequently continue to perform useful child-rearing duties and other relatively light domestic chores. Thus, Margery Wolf describes how in rural Taiwan fragile old women of eighty or more, until completely bedridden, still performed domestic tasks that even a "revengeful daughter-in-law" found valuable (1970:51; 1972:227). Although slow, the old woman could help in such ways as washing vegetables for dinner or rocking babies to sleep. Such tasks were inappropriate for old men, who were considered drones in busy farm families once they could do no "male" farm work.

The Childless or Sonless. The above discussion assumes that the elderly have children to look after them. Not all are so fortunate. The state of childlessness or, in some societies, sonlessness is a "biologically based feature of individual biography" (Moore 1978:73) that influences not only old people's well-being but their relations with the young. This becomes especially crucial for the physically or mentally incapacitated.

The childless or sonless old are forced to depend upon more distant kin for support. The aged usually have less close bonds of affection and obligation with more distant kin; have provided these relatives with fewer services in the past; and do not have the same kind of moral, jural, or economic authority over them.

To be sure, family arrangements are flexible in many societies so that couples unable to bear children can rear youngsters who will support them in old age. Formal adoption is found in many European and Asian societies , and fostering, which involves no permanent change of identity, is common in Africa (J. Goody 1976b:84). In societies where daughters are supposed to leave home at marriage, couples who only bear daughters can sometimes arrange an uxorilocal marriage for a daughter so that they can keep her—and their son-in-law—around for old-age support (see, for example, Shahrani 1981:180; M. Wolf 1972).[13]

Yet the best laid plans do not always succeed. Foster or adopted—as well as natural—children sometimes predecease, or for other reasons are unable to care for, aged parents. This is not to discount the role of spouses. Since men are typically older than their spouses and, in some societies, polygynous, they frequently have younger wives still living with them when they need care.[14] Even then, however, sons (or sons-in-law) may be essential for such productive tasks as herding, farming, or hunting. Indeed, in many nonindustrial societies it is a son's duty, often a particular son such as the youngest, to care for his parents. Whether or not the elderly turn to sons or daughters (and sons-in-law) for support, the concern here is with cases where the incapacitated old lack the expected caretaking child or children. Such people are likely to have a difficult time.

Consider the evidence from a number of societies. Elderly !Kung hunters and gatherers with no surviving spouse or children—an estimated 5 percent of old men and 20 percent of old women—were less likely to receive adequate food and care than their more fortunate counterparts (Biesele and Howell 1981:86–87). Among the Kirghiz herders of Afghanistan, the glories of old age eluded the childless, who were apt to suffer from lack of proper care and attention. Aged couples with grown sons in this patrilineal society could count on all of them for help, and they knew that their youngest or only son, and his wife and children, would remain to look after them in their household (in exchange for inheriting the tent, family herd, and camping grounds when the father died). Even couples who only had daughters could bring a son-in-law into the household. A few unfortunates, however, ended up without any natural or adopted children in their old age. In the period 1972–1974 two of the 333 Kirghiz households consisted of elderly couples on their own. In both cases, their children were no longer alive, one couple having lost all nine children before the children reached the age of nine. The other couple, a sixty-year-old man and his fifty-five-year-old wife, complained that they did not have adequate labor and were at the mercy of kinsmen when they moved camp (Shahrani 1981:181–183).

To reach late old age and have no adult sons was an unfortunate state in many African farming and pastoral societies.[15] Among the Tallensi, a man's own sons or, second-best, proxy sons were his chief economic asset (Fortes 1949:216–217).[16] A son was morally bound to look after and farm for his father. "Yet how can I leave him since he is almost blind and cannot farm for himself?" asked one man who had just bitterly quarreled with his father. "Can you just abandon your father? Is it not he who begot you?" (Fortes 1970:177). More than filial piety was involved in a son's meeting his obligations. Old men, no matter how incapacitated, still exercised authority over sons. Indeed, sons had an interest in the patrimonial land still in their father's keeping.

Old men among the Tallensi without adult sons had to turn to others for economic assistance, and it was not as readily forthcoming. A major problem was their inability to get regular, full-time help with farm work. Because they had to rely on sporadic assistance from kin and neighbors, they were unlikely to have more than a "minimum of food and other necessaries." When they became incapacitated and could no longer farm at all, kin gave them shelter and food. Refusing gifts of food to needy kin was, in fact, viewed as an offense against the ancestors. But people were not bound to be overgenerous to kin living with them who did not contribute to the common pool. Fortes mentions a childless old man who eked out a poor existence by "scrounging a bit of food or a basket of millet . . . or an old garment" from kinsmen and friends (1949:216).

If sonless old men could be at a disadvantage, so could sonless old women. Among the Tallensi, an old woman's strongest guarantee of economic support was her own son. Since women did not own land, the stress, Fortes says, was on a son's duty (felt to be in part a privilege) to care for her (1949:216–220). Among the Gusii, an old woman needed at least one son who could care for her and whose wives would work for her. Sonlessness, Robert LeVine says, was a disaster second only to barrenness (1980:94).[17]

Having sons ensured old Samburu women a place of honor—as well as respect and care—in any of their homesteads (Spencer 1965:224). A woman without sons tended, by contrast, to be viewed as "a necessary liability" (Spencer 1965:225). She saw her allotted herds gradually taken over by her husband's heirs until she was dependent on them. She could return to her natal kin or, if she had a daughter, join her. But she was an outsider in her son-in-law's settlement, and her position depended solely on her relationship to her daughter.

Lack of sons to count on for old-age support is not only a matter of biological destiny. When parents reach old age, sons may be alive and well but living far away. The younger men may be working in towns, for example. Sometimes sons are not around because they have quarreled with their parents. Sally Falk Moore (1978) tells of Siara, a Chagga man who was in his mid-seventies when she knew him. When Moore first met him, Siara lived with his wife and teenaged granddaughter, although later the granddaughter was sent away to school by her uncle. However, Siara had no living sons nearby to rely on in old age. His first-born son had died. His eldest living son, a Catholic priest, only came home on holidays. According to Chagga custom, the youngest son, Danieli, should have stayed at home, looking after his old parents and caring for their needs. In return, he would ultimately inherit their

garden and whatever was attached to it. Relations between
Siara and Danieli had long been marked by serious conflict,
however. The roots of this conflict are unclear, but difficulties were already evident years before when Danieli married
for the first time. Siara then gave Danieli a *kihamba* (grove)
far from his own—an indication he did not want Danieli
around. (Customarily, the youngest son would build a house
in his father's *kihamba*.) In the late 1950s, Danieli left the
community. At the time of the study in 1974, he lived far away
and had not even been home to see his father in fourteen years.

Childlessness or sonlessness, it is clear, can be a real
problem for the incapacitated aged. How do these conditions
affect relations with the young on whom the old depend for
support? From the scanty evidence available, it appears that
strains may well occur. Indeed, the kinds of tensions described earlier between the disabled old and young tend to be
compounded when no children are around to provide care.

The basic dilemma is that the childless or sonless old must
rely on kin whose obligations to them are, in the scheme of
things, relatively weak. Not that they are totally isolated or
alone. In small-scale communities, even the elderly living on
their own usually have considerable contact with kin and
neighbors in the community, most of whom they have probably known since childhood. In the Chagga case, hardly any
of the elderly were alone in their homesteads and all had relatives in the area whose responsibility it was to look after them
(Moore 1978:33). This sense of responsibility varied in strength,
however. Those who lacked sons with families nearby had to
depend on kin whose interest in them was "secondary rather
than primary in the Chagga hierarchy of intensity of relationship and obligation" (Moore 1978:73).

Because young people usually feel less bound to support
distant kin or neighbors, help tends to be regarded as a more
onerous burden. Indeed, many of the young are already supporting their frail elderly parents. Since the young may not
give distant kin or neighbors the best of care, my guess is that
these childless or sonless old people frequently resort to a
strategy of complaining to ensure support. They must often

ask kin and neighbors for help that the elderly living with children get more readily. This may put them in the role of constantly asking from people who resent giving, a situation that can generate strains. And compared to relations between aged parents and children, such mitigating factors as ties of affection and bonds of reciprocity are usually less strong.

As we will see in chapter 6, old people who depend on distant kin or neighbors for food and other support are even prone to witchcraft accusations in some societies. But strains engendered by the need for support need not have such dire consequences. Among the Black Caribs of Belize, old people could legitimately expect support from children, spouses, or, to a lesser extent, siblings.[18] Frequent requests for help from more distant kin, however, could be labeled begging. Old people who made too many demands or became too dependent on assistance from those who were not children or spouses aroused resentment, Kerns says, and invited ridicule (1980:119). There were usually one or two such people in a village. One sixty-year-old childless widow, for instance, had married into the village where she lived. With no close kin around, she had to depend for food on the generosity of neighbors who resented having to help her.

The situation of this Black Carib woman was, of course, worse than that of most of her age peers. Yet the elderly I have portrayed in this chapter are all, in many ways, on the losing end. Having relinquished valued roles and rewards and/or been forced by physical or mental disability into increased reliance on the young, they tend to lose prestige, influence, and/or independence. Relations with the young who have taken over and on whom they depend for care may be quite difficult. This chapter has begun to explore the quality of relations between old and young in such cases, with an emphasis on the kinds of strains that can develop. Clearly, more in-depth research is needed to round out our understanding of these relations and to provide a fuller picture of how the disadvantaged old feel about their situation.

5
Age Conflict
and Accommodation

The three preceding chapters have explored how age inequalities in nonindustrial societies produce strains and tensions between old and young. On occasion, these strains lead
to open and sometimes violent conflict. Usually, however, serious open conflict is averted. This chapter looks at both sides
of the picture: the kinds of conflicts that develop as well as
the forces that lead to accommodation between old and young.

Open conflict, as many theorists observe, is a normal part
of social life, and the chapter begins by investigating the many
ways that open conflict between old and young is manifested.
The study of social inequality, however, must identify not only
the roots and forms of conflict but also the sources of accommodation between the advantaged and deprived. Why, in other
words, does a system of inequality—and relations between
unequals—continue to exist in the face of marked strains and
even profound discontent among the disadvantaged? Thus, the
second, and major, part of the chapter analyzes the factors that
prevent or mitigate sharp open conflicts between old and young
in nonindustrial societies.

In discussing conflict-reducing factors, the chapter is
concerned with two levels of analysis: conflicts in the society
and community as a whole, as well as conflicts in interper-

sonal relations and the family. In the first instance, the issue is why, despite dramatic inequalities and tensions between old and young in nonindustrial societies, the disadvantaged old or disadvantaged young have not struggled to transform the age hierarchy that consigns them to a lowly status. This question is especially pertinent in the case of age-set societies where the underdogs have, in Marxian terms, a high degree of consciousness—common group identification, fellow feeling, and often an awareness that their interests are opposed to those of other age strata—and should be ripe for revolt.

But the issue of organized struggle is not the only important one. It is also crucial to consider why interpersonal antagonism and hostility between old and young is so often suppressed or latent. To put it another way, why is it that most of the time strains between young and old lie beneath the surface of fairly stable ongoing relations?

The examination of conflict and accommodation between old and young, then, starts out with forms of open conflict, moves on to bases of accommodation, and concludes with some comments about potential for conflict in stratification systems generally.

Open Conflict

Numerous examples in chapters 2, 3, and 4 have already shown how strains between old and young can lead to open conflict. One indication that such strains exist is the very fact that open conflict sometimes occurs. Societal norms, to be sure, usually dictate that the young should respect the old, which they frequently do. Yet inequality and competition between old and young mean that the potential for open conflict is ever present. For various reasons—having to do with the structure of social relations as well as individual circumstances and personalities—younger people do not always obey and defer to the old. Nor do the old always exercise proper restraint in their demands or behave in a "just" manner toward the young. One result of "unfair" behavior by individuals in the advantaged age strata and grievances among the disadvantaged age strata is open conflict.

Open conflict, as I pointed out in the Introduction, does not simply refer here to the existence of divergent interests or opposition but to "interpersonal behavior consciously directed toward injuring a person (or group) or interfering with his attainment of goals" (R. LeVine 1961:5). Overt conflict or aggressive behavior occurs in various culturally patterned forms: physical aggression; public verbal dispute; indirect public aggression; breach of expectation; and avoidance and separation (LeVine 1961:5–6).

The following pages give some examples of these types of open conflict. Why tense relations between old and young lead to open flare-ups in some situations and not others is a question beyond the scope of this study. Nor am I concerned with why strains between old and young are expressed in one form of conflict rather than another. I simply want to give an idea of the wide variety of ways that tensions between old and young can be expressed in overt conflict.

Physical Aggression

The most serious form of overt conflict is physical aggression, and in most societies there are severe sanctions to prevent its occurrence. Nonetheless, it does happen. Indeed, in some societies direct interpersonal violence is an approved way to retaliate for physical assault or to react to other kinds of wrongs. Physical aggression covers a wide range of behavior, for example, homicide, brawls, and dueling, as well as property destruction and theft of valued goods (R. LeVine 1961:6).

Quarrels between old and young can result in one party physically attacking the other. Despite community disapproval, the young are sometimes the assailants. In a dispute between a Kgatla man, Lekwalo, and his father, the son severely injured the old man. The father had the last word, however. Lekwalo was sentenced by the chief "to receive eight cuts in the Government gaol" (Schapera 1971:245). Rigby tells about the troubles between a twenty-three-year-old Gogo man and his fifty-seven-year-old father (1969:329–336). The son struck his father in the course of a dispute about who owned the building poles the young man wanted to use for his new homestead.

In extreme cases, tensions and hostilities can result in homicide. Among the Gisu of Uganda, parricide occurred even though it was a sin against the ancestors. In her analysis of ninety homicides by Gisu men that took place during the years 1948–1954, Jean La Fontaine (1960, 1967) found thirty-two cases where a man had murdered a male agnate. Where the exact relationship was known, eleven fathers and father's brothers were killed. Three of the five brothers killed were elder brothers who had some authority over the murderer.

The most likely time for a son to turn to such violent action against his father was in his mid-twenties to early thirties; of the eight parricides whose ages were recorded, six were between the ages of twenty-four and thirty-two. By this time, young men had been initiated and thus had the right to full adult male privileges. Although they had already set up their own households, they still depended on their fathers for the economic resources to establish their position in society. An old and still vigorous man was reluctant to relinquish the herds and land that assured him high status and political power in the community (La Fontaine 1960:109). While older men complained of ungrateful sons who never stopped asking for economic help, younger men complained that they were not getting all the land and cattle from their fathers that was their due (La Fontaine 1967:253).

Sons, however, had no approved way to force their fathers to give in to their demands. They could appeal to ideals of justice, saying that an older man was not a "good father" if he failed to provide land and cattle. But a young man could not sue his father. Nor did intervention by senior agnates or lineage heads in arbitrating disputes always resolve the difficulties. A young man might resort to physical force as the only way to oppose a determined father (La Fontaine 1967:257). On occasion, parricide was the result.[1]

Other Forms of Overt Conflict

Tensions between old and young, of course, usually give rise to less drastic forms of open conflict than murder. Where relations between old and young are strained, the possibility for public verbal disputes is extremely likely. Public verbal disputes include public insult and accusation of wrongdoing, debate, and litigation (R. LeVine 1961:6).

The seriousness of such disputes between old and young varies, of course. The parties may patch up the dispute quickly. Or quarreling may be a constant feature of their relations. A few mothers-in-law and daughters-in-law habitually shrieked at each other, Edel reports for the Chiga (1957:61). Disputes sometimes even disrupt relationships altogether, as in the case of the Chagga man I mentioned in chapter 4 who had not seen his son for fourteen years.

When severe sanctions deter young or old from becoming embroiled in public verbal disputes, they may be especially likely to resort to more private means to express their antagonism. Rather than facing the "enemy" in direct encounters, they may, for example, engage in malicious gossip. Or, as I discuss more fully in the next chapter, they may openly vent their anger and aggression through privately whispered witchcraft suspicions.

The failure to perform acts that are valuable to other people or groups and that they have come, on the basis of past performance, to expect is another form of open conflict. Individuals, for instance, may refuse to participate in cooperative efforts or they may withhold goods in economic transactions (R. LeVine 1961:6). Refusing to obey elders' commands is a well-known ploy of the young, who may deliberately and persistently refuse to do as they are told.

Refusal to comply with orders may be more than an individual strategy. Among the Afikpo Igbo, it was an aggressive tactic younger men used against elders (men approximately fifty-five or older). Such passive resistance was admittedly rare because, Ottenberg says, few issues generated enough heat to unite younger men (1971:175–176). Yet in 1948, in one village, younger men did refuse to cooperate in elders' schemes. The elders in this village decreed that every male had to take the long and difficult form of initiation normally reserved for eldest sons. The reason for this order, they said, was that initiation ceremonies were less impressive than they had been. Some younger men felt, however, that the higher initiation fees—which the more rigorous ceremony would bring in—were uppermost in elders' minds. The first year of the new rule, one young man refused to put his son through and was fined by the elders. The next year many others refused, including middle-aged parents who did not want to pay the higher fees. In the face of such strong opposition, the elders backed down. It simply became too difficult for them to collect fines and administer the ruling.

The final form of aggression is avoidance and separation. As I will discuss below, avoidance and separation may reduce the possibility that open conflict will occur in the first place. But as Robert LeVine (1961) points out, such actions as erecting fences between neighbors or emigrating from the community are also ways to express aggression openly.

The Effects of Open Conflict

As one might expect, open conflict often worsens relations between old and young and deepens age-related cleavages. Open conflict, after all, rarely eliminates the underlying age inequalities that led to aggression in the first place. The next time conflict erupts, it may be far more drastic. And there may not be a next time. For open conflict sometimes completely ruptures relations between particular old and young people.

But, as theorists in the Simmelian tradition make clear, open conflict also has positive social functions (see Coser 1956; Simmel 1955). Brief eruptions of hostile behavior can reduce the possibility of more serious and prolonged rifts between old and young by offering momentary relief for the sufferers. Once some hostility is let out, the aggrieved party (or parties) may be more amenable to return to the previous state of affairs. If people vent their anger, it is less likely to accumulate and lead to more extreme cleavages or blow-ups. Indeed, openly expressing frustration toward a particular "enemy" releases hostility that might otherwise find an outlet in community- or society-wide age struggles.

It is also possible that open conflict will reduce the strains that initially caused the conflict. This happens when individuals, as a result of the conflict, modify their behavior in ways that ease tensions between them.

This talk about age-related tensions leads us back to the issues raised at the outset of the chapter. Remember, open conflict between old and young who have strained relations is not inevitable. Nor is it always serious and disruptive. The functions of conflict that I just mentioned are only a very small part of the story. What other factors make for peace—however uneasy—between old and young? Although tensions between individual old and young folks may be rife, why is there usually no open state of war between them? Why may open discord be relatively rare? And why don't the young (or, for that matter, the old) unite to change a system that puts them at a disadvantage even when they are conscious of their lowly position?

Conflict-Reducing Factors

Many factors help to prevent or contain serious open conflict between old and young, in particular interpersonal relationships as well as in the community or society. They do this by reducing age-related tensions or, when such tensions are marked, by forestalling the outbreak of sharp, bitter struggles. Of course, not all the conflict-reducing factors I discuss below are found in every society. Various combinations occur in different places.

Whatever the combination, however, the inevitability of aging everywhere seems to play a role in reducing age-related conflict, and it is therefore a good place to begin.

The Inevitability of Aging

Growing old is a fact of life. As age stratification theorists put it, age mobility is universal, inevitable, and unidirectional. This special feature of the aging process can lessen the motivation to engage in open conflict, both between particular old and young people as well as between groups of old and young in a community or society.

Because age mobility is inevitable, age stratification differs from other types of stratification. Despite a good deal of social mobility in industrial societies, the majority of lower-class individuals are born and remain in the lower strata all their lives. Except for highly unusual cases, such as transsexuals, women remain women, and blacks remain black. The young, however, do not remain young. Inevitably, they move through the life course from one age stratum to another. By the same token the old have tasted the glories, or suffered the frustrations, of previous life stages.

The inevitability of aging prevents or mutes conflicts between old and young in a variety of ways (A. Foner 1974, 1975; Riley, Johnson, and A. Foner 1972:443–444). For one thing, young people's discontent with their current position may be reduced by expectations of future gains. After all, how great is the incentive to struggle over the distribution of valued rewards when the future holds promise of improvement (A. Foner 1974:192)? If young people only live long enough, they will enjoy many of the postponed rewards. Sons who chafe under their father's domination, for example, know that one day they, too, will be fathers. Daughters-in-law may console themselves with the hope of becoming mothers-in-law. Growing old usually brings increased ritual as well as domestic authority, to say nothing of the other privileges associated with old age in many places.

Obviously not all expectations are always met, if only because some young folks die before reaching old age. Nor will all the survivors have the same success. But if young people perceive that there is a reasonable chance of obtaining rewarded roles in later life (and if they continue to think that these roles are desirable), hopes for a brighter future tend to reduce dissatisfaction with their current position. Indeed, Terray argues that the sharpness of elder–youth conflicts in lineage-based societies is reduced because normally "at least some youths . . . become elders, and every elder was once a youth" (1975:96). Young men's legitimate hope of becoming elders is, in his view, one factor preventing youths from developing into a "class for themselves"—a group conscious of itself as a class that organizes and struggles together to build a society where it is not exploited.[2]

That the young will grow old, and are thus oriented to future roles, may also make them more tolerant of, and perhaps even induce them to adopt, older people's views—what Anne Foner calls a type of anticipatory socialization or false consciousness (1974:192). Sympathy for or acceptance of older people's views can, in fact, dissipate the sense of group solidarity or "we-ness" among the young.

Even if they remain hostile to the views of the old, the inevitability of aging can reduce young people's motivation to struggle openly against the elderly in still other ways. Thinking ahead to a time when they will be older, the young may avoid behavior that would endanger future rewards. If the old control the gateways to positions of prestige, wealth, and security, the young may not want to anger these gatekeepers.[3]

Just as the young want to safeguard their future, so the still capable old want to protect theirs. And this can make life easier for the young. Old people on top, for example, may temper their behavior and accede to young folks' demands to ensure that they will be well looked after in their more dependent years. Thus, a man may provide his sons with land and wives and help them establish successful households in order to guarantee that they will be able to support him when he is no longer productive (see, for example, Gray 1964:243–244).

The inevitability of aging also tends to blunt the dissatisfaction of the disadvantaged old and to reduce their willingness to engage in open protest. Having known the pleasures of younger days often, it is true, makes the elderly all the more bitter about their present difficulties. But because they were once young, they sometimes empathize with young people's problems.

Good treatment from the young obviously lessens the discontent of the frail elderly, and one reason they may receive it is that their caretakers have an eye to their own old age. In looking after the aged, younger caretakers may be consciously setting an example for their own children so that they will not be abandoned in the future (Hess and Waring 1978:256). Even when the old are not well cared for, their hostility to the young may be reduced if they believe that improvements await them in the future—in the hereafter. And the elderly's knowledge that they will only become more incapacitated with time, and will die soon anyway, weakens the incentive to struggle against the young to improve their lot. Indeed, the physical declines of aging mean that the neglected or abused frail old lack the sheer energy for active and effective protest.

Legitimation of Inequalities

Another factor in keeping the peace between old and young is the legitimation of inequalities. The potential for bitter struggles at both the societal and interpersonal levels is diminished when old and young accept the legitimacy of the unequal distribution of rewards and valued roles according to age (Riley, Johnson, and A. Foner 1972:443).

To what extent people become persuaded of the justice or inevitability of a system of inequality—and their place in it—is a question of longstanding debate in stratification theory. Not all individuals, it is clear, are equally consenting in their acceptance of a system of stratification that places them at a disadvantage. Acceptance of a system of inequality includes consent obtained under duress, passive acceptance, lukewarm adherence, or shared conviction. While some of the underdogs deeply believe in the legitimacy of the system of inequality, others may be only half-convinced. Still others may question the very premises of inequality and be latently opposed or even openly hostile to the system (Godelier 1978:767).

Yet with regard to age inequalities in nonindustrial societies, a good number of the subordinate young or deprived old probably come to believe that the way highly rewarded roles are allocated according to age is "natural" and right.

Inequalities of opportunities and rewards, Riley and her associates observe, "are often legitimated through societal definitions of age-related needs, or through societal evaluation of the past, present, or potential contributions of the respective age strata" (1972:443). Young folks may feel that the old deserve their powerful and prestigious roles because they have, for example, accumulated wisdom, experience, and ritual expertise.

The old, by the same token, may believe that their incapacity does not entitle them to fill the same roles or reap the same rewards as younger, more able people. So Goodwin reports for the Western Apache (1942:512–517). Once past their physical or mental prime, the aged were second-class citizens who were "less likely to receive the best." Their blankets were usually the most ragged; their portions of food the least desirable. According to Goodwin, the elderly did not show dissatisfaction with their lot. They accepted the premise that they did not deserve what younger family members had because they were less valuable economically to the family. Often they were proud to give things to younger relatives. When they received the same attentions as the young, they felt uncomfortable and ashamed. As I pointed out in the last chapter, the incapacitated aged in other societies might even accept as right and proper that they should be abandoned and left to die when they became too great a burden.

How do people come to accept the legitimacy of age inequalities? As numerous ethnographic accounts show, individuals learn societal rules, values, and modes of conduct in childhood as part of the socialization process. Socialization to values that underlie the legitimacy of age inequalities and age-related norms does not occur just in childhood, however. These values as well as appropriate role patterns are reinforced and affirmed in countless ways throughout an individual's lifetime.

Adolescents and adults as well as children in many societies, for example, are continually reminded of the superiority of the old and their right to respect and care in stories, folk tales, and myths as well as in everyday conversations and anecdotes. Simmons relates how stories told in nonindustrial societies, often by old people themselves, commonly glorify the elderly and explain why they possess ritual powers and other privileges (1945:66–74).

Acceptance of age inequalities and age-appropriate behavoir is also reinforced through ceremonials and rituals. Initiation rituals are a prime example, sometimes involving such traumatic and painful experiences as whipping, scarification, ridicule, and severe hazing of young initiates by their elders. However severe or mild the treatment of the initiates, these rituals typically impress on them the powerful force of older people's authority and the fact that elders deserve to be in control.[4]

Other ceremonies provide the opportunity to indoctrinate the young with values that support older people's authority and explain juniors' inferior position. Recall the Samburu, where the firestick elders dominated young bachelors in the moran age grade. At public harangues, elders "brainwashed" moran into accepting their prolonged position of marginality and powerlessness (Spencer 1965:140–143).

It was in the elders' interests to forestall the entry of the moran into the marriage market. One way to do this was to persuade the moran that they were still immature and had no right to expect promotion. The elders harangued the moran at the various ceremonies that marked the stages in the development of the moran. They said that the moran were not worthy of elderhood because they "were a thoroughly bad and irresponsible lot and almost incapable of improvement" (Spencer 1965:142).

Whether or not such haranguing was a conscious strategy of the elders to delay the promotion of the moran does not matter here. What does matter is that haranguing was successful. The moran, Spencer says, were convinced that the accusations against them were sincere and valid. They said, among themselves, that the elders' charges were true and that the only way to gain a sense of respect was to attend, and even ask for more, harangues.

The moran, however, had mixed feelings toward firestick elders—a combination of fear, respect, and resentment. Among the Samburu, as in other societies, the legitimation of age inequalities was not so successful or complete that it could, in itself, prevent serious community-wide struggles. Other factors enter into the picture.

Social Bonds

One such factor is that there are social bonds between certain of the young and old. These ties tend to inhibit serious societal or community-wide age cleavages. Struggles of young men united against all old men, for example, would pit young people against their old patrons and protectors. Indeed, the young may perceive that the best way to advance their interests is to cultivate and reinforce ties to the influential old.

Even in age-set societies, where the high degree of solidarity among age-mates could conceivably provide a springboard for united action against elders, young men have important links to elders. Apart from age-set bonds and loyalties, there are ties to the family. These family bonds are crucial for a young man's well-being. Young men depend on senior kin for obtaining productive resources and wives. Affines, as well as senior kin, are a potential source of support in times of need and in dispute (Baxter and Almagor 1978:11). Of course, relations between young men and senior kin or affines may be far from easygoing, and young men may be motivated to cooperate with them more out of fear of reprisals than good will. Still, young men who go to certain seniors for help generally will not want to put bonds with these older men at risk.

In addition to ties to senior kin and affines, there are other bonds between old and young men in several age-set societies: they belong to age sets that are linked. Sometimes alternate sets have a particularly close relationship (Stewart 1977:125–127). Among the Samburu, there was a different pattern. A special relationship obtained between moran and older men three sets above the moran (senior elders). Most senior elders had moran sons, since a boy was supposed to wait to be initiated into an age set at least three below that of his father. Unlike firestick elders, who were responsible for disciplining and controlling the moran, senior elders were likely to stand up for unruly moran and oppose harsher punishments proposed by firestick elders. For example, after an incident in which moran set out to—and did—attack junior elders, the senior elders urged the firestick elders to go easy in punishing the moran (Spencer 1965:150, 159). Spencer argues, in fact, that the rules of the age-set system protected father–son relations by separating the role of firestick elder and father (1965:135; 1976:166). Young men's frustrations and resentments were directed against firestick elders, who imposed the restrictions on them, rather than against their fathers.

In societies without age sets, various ties between old and young men also check extreme polarization along age lines. Young men, for example, often ally themselves with old patrons to pave the way for influential positions in later life, as we saw among the pre-mission Tiwi. Where young men have severely strained relations with certain old relatives—with fathers, for example, in patrilineal societies—these strains do not necessarily spill over into relations with other old men. Young men may actually look to some old men for solace and support. It is not unusual in patrilineal societies for a man's mother's brother to defend him and provide aid and a place of refuge in times of trouble. This ability to maneuver, in Terray's view, gives young men in lineage-based societies an edge over workers in capitalist societies (1972:172). A worker who leaves one employer has no choice but to work for another employer who will exploit him in much the same way. But a young man in a lineage-based society may be able to leave an elder who has not provided him with land or bridewealth for one who will.

Apart from alliances with old patrons and close bonds to certain senior kin, ties based on class, caste, or ethnicity also operate to prevent all-out struggles of young against old. On occasion, people of all ages may be drawn together in common cause on the basis of their caste or class interests, for example. In peasant communities that are closely integrated into nation-states and nationwide class systems, situations doubtless arise when individuals' concerns as peasants take precedence over age divisions. Alternatively, the young (or old) themselves are unlikely to build solidarity and join together to further their common age interests when deep class, ethnic, or caste cleavages divide them.

If ties between old and young can restrain deep age cleavages in the community or society, within the domestic family bonds between old and young can operate in a similar way. Here, however, the very people who have strained relations are often, at the same time, drawn together by bonds of affection and common identification.

A kind of love–hate relationship frequently develops between young and old within the domestic group. Fortes' (1949) splendid discussion of fathers and sons among the Tallensi captures the complex and multifaceted nature of relations between them. A man's relationship with his father in Tale society was characterized not only by strains of latent antagonism but also by affection, respect, mutual identification, and a sense of dependence (Fortes 1949:181). Tale sons chafed under their father's authority; fathers, meanwhile, felt threatened as their sons advanced in status. But young men were proud of their fathers. Identification between them was strong, growing out of the intimacies and cooperation of everyday life. Old men even delegated sons to act for them in political matters, and sons could represent their fathers in jural affairs. Sons were the fulfillment of a father's life. To become an ancestor, a man had to have sons, and the Tallensi said that a man who died sonless had wasted his life (Fortes 1970:187).

When parents become incapacitated and need support among the Tallensi as well as in other societies, ties of affection between parents and children and their mutual loyalty can counterbalance tensions and reduce the likelihood of open conflict. The ethnographic literature is filled with examples of children caring for elderly parents with loving concern. That the frail old and their children are bound by a kind of balanced reciprocity can also reduce the likelihood of conflict between them. Looking after parents is often seen, at least partly, as a quid pro quo for services they rendered in the past. The young generally feel indebted to aged parents for care, gifts, and provisions their parents provided in earlier years. "When we were children," explain the Siuai of the Solomon Islands (Melanesia), "they fed and cared for us well; and now that they are aged we repay by giving food to them. For, if we did not, they would surely starve" (Oliver 1955:209).

As for the aged, identification with and affection for their children may dampen dissatisfaction with their social losses. This is a point Arlie Hochschild makes in her study of lower-class women in a California housing project, but it may be relevant to the old in nonindustrial societies as well (1973:97–111). Old women in the California project saw their children as extensions of themselves, sometimes even ascribing children's successes to themselves. Such identification made the old women feel they were "haves" when they were actually "have-nots" and built up solidarity with their children in the face of potential envy and rivalry.

Avoidance, Formality, and Physical Separation of Old and Young

While social bonds drawing young and old together can minimize open conflict between them, the same is true of social rules that lead to physical separation and social distance. Absence may not make the heart grow fonder, but serious struggles between old and young are less likely to occur when they have relatively few opportunities to interact. If quarrels do break out, separation allows tempers to cool and reduces the risk that conflict will escalate. Even when old and young see each other frequently, strict rules that regulate their behavior lessen the possibility of open conflict.

Avoidance and Formal Relations. Avoidance prohibitions reduce the likelihood of open conflict between certain old and young people by limiting their contact and by setting up explicit rules as to how they can—or cannot—act with each other. Sometimes stringent avoidance rules obtain, as I indicated in chapter 3 could be the case between a man and his mother-in-law. In some places, a man is not even supposed to see his mother-in-law or mention her name. Frequently, avoidance rules are, by necessity, less rigorous, especially when the individuals involved live close by.

Among the Nayars of Central Kerala before British conquest, avoidance prohibitions structured behavior between a man and his mother's brothers. A boy or man could not touch his mother's brother. Nor could he sit before his uncle except at mealtimes, when he sat down last and rose as soon as the uncle's meal was finished. He could not speak first to his uncle, and before he entered the senior's presence he removed his upper clothing as a sign of respect. When summoned for a long interview, he stood half hidden behind a pillar, holding his hand before his mouth lest his breath reach his uncle. He was not to chew betel leaves, smoke, spit, or use any but the most serious and respectful language in the presence of his mother's brother. These taboos were most strict in the relationship with the *karanavan*, or oldest male member and managing head of the matrilineal property-owning group and household. It was for this reason, Gough tells us, that a *karanavan* spent much of his time among his own age-mates, in a separate part of the homestead (1961:349).

Of course, even the most stringent avoidance taboos do not always prevent open conflict. An elderly Mescalero Apache painted an ideal picture of avoidance taboos (Opler 1979:391). He explained that a husband should obey and show respect to his wife's relatives by adhering to customary avoidances and polite forms. It was later discovered that this same man, when younger, had violated the avoidance taboos by seeing his mother-in-law. In fact, he had come close to scalping her! In another case, bitter antagonism between a woman and her son-in-law, buried for years under avoidance rules, burst out in a hand-to-hand fight between them.

Even where no avoidance rules are in force, relations between old and young may be highly formalized. Not only does formal behavior accentuate the social and emotional distance between people, but the required etiquette precludes expressions of aggression or hostility (R. LeVine 1965:203). We read about how the young are expected to behave respectfully to old people in numerous societies. In Turkish villages, sons, whatever their age, were not to answer their father back or speak publicly in his presence without invitation. To smoke or refer to sexual matters in front of their father was strictly taboo (Stirling 1965:101, 223).

In many societies, honorific terms of address are used when talking to elders. Formal greeting behavior is common, often requiring the young to stoop or bend before seniors or in some cases to touch the elders' feet. And, needless to say, the young are typically expected to speak seriously and courteously to elders in authority.

Spatial Separation. The effects of spatial separation of age strata are complex. If young men spend much of their time with each other, apart from older people, one would think that this would spur united efforts to further their interests. Age segregation, we know, can promote "an awareness of mutual deprivation, nourish a sense of 'we-ness,' and facilitate group formation" (A. Foner 1975:151). In age-set societies, young men actually belong to formal groups of age peers that have common tasks and activities. A strong sense of equality tends to develop among them, particularly when they have not yet begun to acquire or compete among themselves for such rewards as cattle and wives (see Almagor 1978a). Yet, even if physical segregation of young men enhances their sense of group solidarity or consciousness, it also limits the opportunities for open conflict with older people to develop.

The Nyakyusa of Tanzania carried physical segregation between old and young men to an extreme by separating them in different age villages (Wilson 1951, 1977). In the 1934–1938 period, when age villages still flourished, there were serious strains between fathers and sons. Senior men (over fifty) continued to marry young wives, while their sons, in their twenties, were forced, by lack of marriage cattle, to remain bachelors. In fact, in 1935, one chief, Mwaipopo, well over seventy, had just married his forty-first wife, while his younger sons in their late twenties were still unmarried and repeatedly charged with seduction (Wilson 1977:87).[5]

The Nyakyusa device for dealing with generation conflict, as Monica Wilson puts it, was to separate fathers and sons (1977:85). When boys were about ten or eleven, they left their parents' huts to live on land allocated by their fathers, at the edge of the men's villages. A new village was usually closed when the oldest boys were about seventeen or eighteen, and younger brothers then had to build elsewhere. Although boys of an age village continued to hoe for their fathers until they were married, they slept and spent their spare time in the age village, enjoying the "good company" of their age-mates. And before they had wives to prepare their food, they ate, in the company of their age peers, at the house of each one's mother in turn. When the "coming out" ceremony was held, once in each generation, the villages of young men were formally established on their own land as older men moved aside to make room for their sons.

In other societies, physical separation of old and young men who had tense relations was less drastic. Rather than live in another village with their age peers, young men in some societies lived in the same village as older men but in a separate section or compound. And in some places young men lived in separate settlements with their age-mates—but only part of the time. The rest of the time they stayed in household groups with older men. Spencer describes the Samburu moran as being kept "at bay in the bush," spending much of their time with each other, away from elders, in areas some distance from the settlements (1965:100).[6] Tiwi young men, from about fourteen to their early twenties, spent long periods secluded in the bush as part of a long drawn-out initiation process. In the bush, they lived a monastic existence under the supervision of older men of about forty.[7]

Emigration. The types of physical separation I have spoken of so far involve groups of young men who have no choice but to live apart from older men. Emigration, however, is often a voluntary and individual action.

Like other forms of spatial separation, emigration sometimes eases tensions between old and young. Even when emigration is a direct result of open conflict, the parties to the dispute continue their "state of war" at a distance. Emigration is a way to tone down, and sometimes avoid, open conflict.

Emigration is not something new in nonindustrial societies. Urbanization and industrial development, it is true, have opened up new "escape routes" for discontented young men. But in nomadic societies or farming societies with abundant land, young men could often move to a different community or pioneer a new area to escape the domination of their fathers or other senior men.

In patrilineal societies, for example, younger men might leave their community to join maternal kin or to attach themselves to unrelated influential and wealthy patrons. Older men's authority to keep sons at home varied. Sometimes serious struggles, even involving witchcraft accusations, preceded a son's efforts to move away. Once they emigrated, however, young men established a certain independence from their father's control. Gulliver reports that among the Arusha, before good land became scarce, elder married sons achieved considerable autonomy by pioneering new farms at a distance from their fathers (1964:211–212). However authoritarian a man's father, when his son lived in a different local community, it was more difficult for the older man to interfere.

Compensations for Disadvantages

In addition to decreasing the frequency of interaction between old and young, physical separation can lessen the *motivation* to engage in bitter struggles. It does this by providing individuals with certain compensations for their disadvantaged position and thus with less reason to rebel. As I just pointed out for Arusha elder sons, physical separation can give younger people considerable autonomy from seniors. In cases where the young are together for long periods, they often create a world of their own, and this can make life less difficult for them.

Thus we find that young men who spend a lot of time with each other, apart from the watchful eyes of the old, can behave in ways that would be inappropriate in front of older people. Young men, as a group, also often provide each other with mutual help and protection. A subculture may develop among the young that promotes values and aims different from those of older people. Even where the young are without rewards and honor in the society as a whole, they may gain prestige among each other.

The Samburu moran, off together in the bush much of the time, are a good example of some of these processes. Although elders harangued and lectured them about their irresponsibility and immaturity, moran had a certain degree of freedom. The elders did not interfere too closely with the lives led by the moran and allowed them to pursue their own affairs within limits (Spencer 1965:144). The moran adhered to a set of values and aims expected of moran. Whereas elders admired prudence, tolerance, controlled debate, and dependability, honor among the moran was won by shows of physical bravery and courage. A moran would be ashamed if his parents learned of his adulterous affairs. He might even be harangued by elders in front of other moran for his crime. But he achieved distinction among his peers for seducing married women.

Young men of County Clare were not formally organized into graded age sets, but they spent their leisure time in informal cliques. These cliques provided some compensation for their lowly state—a refuge, as it were, from a world dominated by old men. Here, as among the Samburu moran, young men had their own valuations of themselves in which youth and strength outweighed age and wisdom. The young men gambled, played games, and were involved in sports and contests.[8]

But there are compensations that are not related to age-group solidarity and physical separation from the old that can offset some of young people's frustrations.

As the discussion of the inevitability of aging made clear, young people often take comfort in thinking about the rewards the future holds. Other compensations are in the here and now. Where young men are subordinate to their father's jural and ritual authority, they may achieve a certain autonomy in some spheres. In many societies, they receive part, sometimes all, of their property inheritance while their father is still alive. Even when they live near their father, they often run their own households without too much interference.

There are compensations for prolonged bachelorhood as well. Samburu moran had unmarried girls as mistresses, although they kept losing these mistresses as elders married them. Among the Lele, bachelors of an age set shared a common wife in the past (Douglas 1963a).

Despite numerous disabilities young men suffer in many societies, they frequently have qualities that are admired, perhaps even envied, by older men. One is young men's physical vigor. Among the Samburu, it was also their dashing appearance. Powerless and wifeless moran, particularly younger ones, were attracted to the privileges of moranhood. This not only included the fellowship, freedom, and fearlessness I mentioned above but also their clothing and decorations. Spencer tells us of "their long braided hair covered in red ochre, their decorated bead ornaments, and their colorful loin cloths" which contrasted sharply to the relatively drab and unobtrusive apparel of boys and elders (1965:102; see also Spencer 1965:138, 143–144). In a number of societies, including the precolonial Samburu, young men received honor from the old as well as the young for their bravery and skill in warfare and raids.

Although young men may have no power in the society as a whole, there may be some compensation when they can exert authority over others still younger, and worse off, than they are—over younger brothers, for instance (see, for example, Jackson 1977:167–168, on the Kuranko of Sierra Leone).

As for the disadvantaged old, religion may provide some solace for their frustrations. The loss of privileges and domestic or political power may be at least partly offset by gains in ritual powers and the assumption of important roles in religious ceremonies. And religious beliefs and rituals can offer them a sense of worth as well as give meaning to their misfortunes.

The Nyungne ritual among the Sherpa was particularly appealing to the aged, who, it will be recalled, had much to complain of (Ortner 1978:53–60). Not only were they physically in decline but they had given up their property and were often ill treated by their children. In this ritual, however, the aged became "haves." The ritual emphasized abstention from food and conversation and was believed to bring merit to the participants. The very traits old people had—such as asexuality and propertylessness—enabled them to realize salvation and transcendance. Indeed, the ritual endowed their unfortunate position with positive meaning. It moved "the participants to an experience of 'autonomy'—of personal separateness experienced not negatively as abandonment but positively as independence and dignified self-reliance" (Ortner 1978:52–53). And it offered the old a satisfying refuge, enabling them to achieve some distance, if not full detachment, from strains with their children.

Safety Valves

"Safety valves" can also make life more bearable for the disadvantaged by allowing them to express, albeit obliquely, at least some of their hostility.

Rather than express hostility directly against the person or group that is the source of frustration, safety-valve institutions, as Lewis Coser writes, "serve to divert feelings of hostility onto substitute objects (or . . . provide substitute means for such diversion), or . . . function as channels for cathartic release" (1956:164). In other words, they drain off hostile and aggressive sentiments—away from their original object—and thus play a role in "preventing otherwise proba- ble conflict" between old and young or "reducing its disrup- tive effects" (Coser 1956:48).

Although the disadvantaged young are rarely permitted to vent their anger directly against the privileged and pow- erful old, they may be able to displace their aggression onto other targets. Getting this hostility out of their systems can re- duce the likelihood of serious struggles with the old.

In some societies, for example, young men's hostility to- ward their fathers or other older men in the community is channeled into legitimate struggles against other groups in warfare and raids. And the young may release much of their anger and frustration in quarrels with their fellow "sufferers" rather than against the privileged and powerful.

But substitute objects need not be involved. Certain ac- tivities fulfill safety-valve functions simply by offering a way to release hostility (see Coser 1956:41). To return again to the Samburu, one way the moran released some of their nervous energy, frustration, and tension was in shaking. Shivering and shaking were regarded as signs of manliness, and they oc- curred in such stressful situations as when the moran were being "outdanced" in front of their mistresses by other moran and when they could not give way to their aggressive im- pulses (Spencer 1965:262–265). The frustrations of the moran were also deflected into "obstinate, unpredictable, and some- times fiery . . . behaviour." Moran were given to periods of restlessness and irresponsibility. Losing a mistress could throw them into a state of disgust, and they might even leave home suddenly. "It is said," Spencer writes, "that sometimes a group of moran behave like mad bleating goats. They jabber, they quarrel and they brood; no one takes any notice of what oth- ers are trying to say; if one man tries to strike another then others may not intervene to prevent a fight. It is a condition of dysphoria known to the Samburu as *nshakera* or goat-mad- ness" (1965:162–163).

There are also cases where "safety valves" permit the expression of hostility against the old (or young)—but indirectly and at times even unwittingly (Coser 1956:43). As Freud notes, wit is one example of this technique:

Wit permits us to make our enemy ridiculous through that which we could not utter loudly or consciously on account of existing hindrances. . . . Wit is used with special preference as a weapon of attack or criticism of superiors who claim to be in authority. Wit then serves as a resistance against such authority and as an escape from its pressures. (quoted in Coser 1956:43)

Folk tales, myths, stories, and songs may also offer a way for the young to express hostility toward the old indirectly. A rural Taiwanese legend told of the murder and cannibalism of powerful old men by sons or grandsons. Indeed, reluctance to tell the story may indicate that it hit an all too responsive chord; younger people preferred not to admit the existence of these deeply felt desires (Ahern 1973:206–207). In some other places, privileged elders are caricatured in folk tales or stories as stupid or unjust (see, for example, Beidelman 1980:30).

Stories, songs, and satire about the old are often reserved for times when the young are with each other. Young Irish men of County Clare joked and derided elderly men as "old blatherers" and "old fools" when they got together (Arensberg and Kimball 1968:167–168). Stories that the Samburu moran told among themselves emphasized the physical incapacity, greed, or selfishness of elders, weaknesses that the moran despised (Spencer 1965:146). The Samburu moran had another oblique aggressive strategy against the elders that had to do with their songs. They deliberately baffled the elders by introducing new words and giving new meanings and implications to familiar words. In one case, the elders were unsure how the moran were using a song. They did not know if the song was being used to arrange secret trysts in the bush with their young wives or whether the moran were simply singing it "out of gleeful defiance of the elders because of its dubious associations" (Spencer 1965:147).

In some societies, hostility toward elders is occasionally allowed expression in institutionalized ways. As part of the

traditional "coming out" ceremony among the Nyakyusa—
which marked an old chief's retirement and celebrated young
men's entry into public life—young men had the right to seize
cattle and food from old men's villages "as if there were war"
(Wilson 1959:54; see also A. Foner and Kertzer 1978:1090, on
mock battles among Meru age sets).

Another kind of ritual of rebellion, in which young people were permitted to display normally forbidden aggressive
behavior toward elders, is found among the Afikpo Igbo of
Nigeria. At certain village feasts or during public plays of the
secret society, young men lampooned the elders in song:

The young and middle-aged men dress up in costume, often masked,
and sing topical songs they have composed, sometimes presenting
skits as well. They may name specific elders and are free to criticize
their seniors in a way that they could never do at public meetings.
For example, they may ridicule the elders for "eating all the village
food," that is, for always demanding more food at village festivals,
for wasting proceeds of the village palm grove by dividing it among
themselves, for quarreling with one another, for taking a long time
to reach a decision on an important matter, or for making foolish
decisions. They also make fun of elders who are greedy about palm
wine, who quarrel a lot, and those who may have family troubles.
(Ottenberg 1971:176)

The elders in the audience were not supposed to show hostility toward these young satirists. If young men publicly criticized the elders like this at an elders' meeting, however, the
youths would be told to keep quiet or else they would be fined.

Whatever their nature, safety valves seldom drain off all
of young people's hostile sentiments to the old. To the extent
that they do allow the young to let off steam, however, they
reduce the pressure for modifying the age inequalities that
generated tensions and hostilities in the first place. In this
sense, they contribute to the maintenance of the status quo.
This issue will come up again when I discuss the functions
of witchcraft beliefs and accusations in the next chapter. For
the moment, let us move on to other factors that can forestall
open conflict between old and young.

Social Sanctions

When anthropologists discuss why people comply with social rules, they emphasize the role of negative social sanctions or the consequences that follow from breaches of approved behavior. Negative social sanctions operate to prevent or reduce open conflict between old and young at all levels through the fear of punishment.[9] No matter how disgruntled or tempted to break the rules, individuals often refrain from provocative, aggressive, or otherwise socially unacceptable behavior to avoid painful consequences. If disputes do occur, various sanctions can bring pressure for rapprochement.

Economic Sanctions. One important sanction is the fear that economic cooperation will be withdrawn. With this in mind, young and old often fulfill expected duties and hold back their aggressive impulses. Thus, even where old men control productive resources, they may exercise restraint and meet their obligations lest young men withdraw their labor power and move to other communities. For their part, the young may toe the line because they depend on older men for economic resources.

The threat of disinheritance may loom large in young people's decision to curb their protests and anger against seniors. The fear of being cut out of wills, or the hope of being generously provided for, are familiar themes to Western audiences. In the Kangra hills of northwest India, to take a non-Western example, cases where men had disinherited their sons achieved a certain amount of notoriety. By the 1960s, many men were making wills, and recalcitrant sons could find themselves excluded from their share of their father's estate (Parry 1979:162, 171).

In nonliterate societies, there are obviously no written wills. In these societies, inheritance rules operate with varying degrees of flexibility. Where older men have some freedom in disposing of their property and in choosing their successors, they may command obedience and deference by dangling the prospect of inheritance before the young.

Among the Gurage of Ethiopia, for example, an eldest son

expected to inherit most of his father's land, but he only came into this much-desired inheritance if his father thought he had been an ideal son. And an ideal son did not try to override his father's authority (Shack 1966:117). A Chagga father also had the right to disinherit sons if they did not treat him with the proper deference. A seriously disrespectful son could be refused the position of successor as well as provision of land (Moore 1977:34; Moore 1975:126–127).

Even when old men do not, or cannot, completely disinherit their heirs, they sometimes can deny a wayward junior certain benefits. Among the Lakalai of New Britain, the lion's share of the father's property went to a dutiful child; a rebellious child got only the minimum that was in keeping with the father's duties (Chowning and Goodenough 1973:127).

Mystical Sanctions. Aside from control of economic resources, the old may have another card up their sleeves. In many societies, they are believed to have legitimate mystical power to harm.[10] Often, mystical agents are thought to act quite independently but are, so to speak, on old people's side in that they punish the erring young. The key point is that young people frequently fulfill their obligations to, and try to avoid open conflict with, seniors to ensure they do not become targets of mystical attack.

In the Western world we are, of course, acquainted with the notion of divine retribution. Similar beliefs are found outside of Western society. In many places, mistreatment of the aged or disobedience to parents is believed to bring punishment from a god or gods in this life or the next.

In many African societies and elsewhere, ancestor beliefs support the power of the old. Deceased ancestors are believed capable of harming living descendants who act in immoral ways.[11] Young people may be reluctant to risk the wrath of dead ancestors that is thought to follow rebellious or improper behavior. The ancestors may punish those who murder a relative, to take a most heinous offense. Or they may injure individuals who fail to support needy kinsmen or who fail to show respect to elders, to mention two others. Ancestors can cause all manner of disasters, from disease, death, and infertility to crop failure and drought.

Take the case of Pa Nukuomanu on the Pacific island of Tikopia. In the late 1920s, when Raymond Firth was in the field, Pa Nukuomanu suffered from an infection that broke into open lesions on his arm and leg (1963:164–165). The illness, people said, was due to his having struck his mother in an angry fit many years before. His mother did not die at that time but wept bitterly. After her death, she was said to have announced her son's crime to her ancestors. Her ancestors grew angry and bade her "return to men to work sickness on your son." So, it was believed, the mother's spirit did.

Living elders' closeness to ancestors, due to their genealogical seniority, sometimes gives them a direct role in the affliction process. Among the Nyakyusa, a senior living kinsman who was legitimately angry could, it was believed, act in concert with the shades (dead ancestors) to bring injury or misfortune to a junior offender. Such anger was justified if, for example, a son seduced his father's wife or failed to give his father a share of his earnings. "It is really we who get angry," said one old man, "but the shades help a little because they are always with us" (Wilson 1957:179). An angry father "muttered over the fire" or "murmured and mumbled to himself," and the shades would hear. He might not even mutter or murmur since the shades could "see what is within a man" (Wilson 1957:218). If the oracle showed that the anger of senior living and dead relatives was responsible for a misfortune, a ritual of reconciliation was necessary to undo the effects of the elder's anger. This ritual further brought the younger man to heel. He had to beg the elder's pardon, and the senior kinsman confessed his anger.

Another kind of mystical sanction, sometimes connected to ancestor beliefs, is cursing. In many societies, the old have the power to curse the young, or at least certain of the young (usually children or other close junior kin). The old person verbally expresses the wish that some specified or unspecified misfortune befalls the offending junior, often through the instrumentality of some nonhuman power (Beattie 1964:237).

Perhaps, as Jack Goody suggests, old people's physical weakness makes their curses and blessings especially powerful (1976a:128). He argues that the ability to change the world by words alone is often seen as a characteristic of those who cannot change it by other means. Even words may be unnecessary. Among the Tallensi, if a parent simply felt resentment against a child, this was equivalent to a curse that could cause illness or other harm (Fortes 1949:175). Or certain actions may constitute a curse. A Gisu father's most powerful curse against his son consisted of deliberately showing his genitals to his son. This curse was thought to destroy the victim, his family, and his possessions (La Fontaine 1967:251).

Cursing is usually not done lightly. Frequently, it is a measure of last resort, reserved for cases where juniors are "unforgivably defiant" (see, for example, Fortes 1949:175; Winter 1956:69–70).

Even if the old only resort to cursing in extreme situations, the possibility of being cursed often keeps the young in line. In Kangra district, northwest India, sons thought twice about breaking away from their father's household, in part because the old man could well invoke the ancestral curse against them (Parry 1979:162). Threatening to curse was a powerful sanction at the command of Samburu elders. A young Samburu man who offended the elders could find that an elder had announced he would curse the bride-to-be if he, the young man, went through with the proposed marriage. This curse, combined with the young man's offense, would have dire effects on her and her children. Needless to say, a man with a curse hanging over him found it hard to marry (Spencer 1965:193–196, 205).

Other Sanctions. Important as mystical sanctions are, other sanctions can also prevent or contain open conflict between young and old by holding them to their duties and making clear that wrongdoers will suffer for their crimes.

In peasant societies as well as in communities influenced by colonial and new national governments, individuals who break the peace come up against official law enforcement agencies such as the military or the police. They run the risk of being hauled before courts whose decisions are backed up by the apparatus of the state and organized force.

In many nonindustrial societies, punishment is meted out by groups that do not have the power of coercive force. These include local tribunals or assemblies of elders. Their decisions may be backed by diffuse (or unorganized) sanctions expressing public opinion (Beattie 1964:171). Young folks who commit a "crime" in some societies, for instance, know that they will be called before a group of community elders, where they will be lectured and fined. Failure to pay the fine, they also know, will bring public criticism and perhaps supernatural punishment as well.

But punishment is not always the province of groups that formally gather to administer justice. In a small, closely knit community, where people live together in continuing face-to-face contact, public opinion matters very much to an individual. The fear of being exposed to ridicule, humiliation, or disgust are powerful sanctions inducing old and young to behave properly no matter how much they resent doing so. In many groups, ostracism is the most dreaded sanction, although it varies in severity, ranging from exclusion from certain activities while still living in the community to being expelled altogether.

Lest it be thought that sanctions only motivate individuals to behave in accepted ways for fear of negative reprisals, a word should be said about positive sanctions. Approved behavior is, after all, often rewarded. The desire for prestige and the good opinion of one's neighbors and relatives may be important incentives underlying a person's actions. In some societies, prestige is won by generosity and sharing, so that supporting the aged brings social honor (see, for example, Fowler 1982 on the Arapahoe). Likewise, an "admirable man," esteemed in the community, may be one who respects his elders and "knows his place." On the whole, however, the desire to avoid unpleasant consequences seems to be a more important incentive to approved behavior than the quest for rewards (Beattie 1964:170).

Conclusion

Systems of age inequality, like other stratification systems, constitute, by their very nature, delicate balances. They tend, on the one hand, to be plagued by tensions between the "haves" and "have-nots," and it is hardly unusual for these tensions to erupt into open conflict. Yet there are, on the other hand, forces that inhibit open conflict between individuals as well as groups in different locations in the age hierarchy.

In nonindustrial societies, overt conflict between old and young breaks out primarily in the family and in interpersonal relations. Even so, factors that make open revolts of disadvantaged age strata in the community or society highly unlikely also prevent or mitigate serious open conflicts at the interpersonal level.

For one thing, several factors reduce the motivation of the less privileged to engage in open conflict. The subordinate young look forward to improving their position as they age. Then, too, like the disadvantaged old, they often believe that the way highly rewarded roles are allocated according to age is right and proper. Many times, in addition, there are compensations that make life more bearable for the disadvantaged. Individuals who have tense relations may also be drawn together by ties of identification and affection. And young people are not likely to become involved in all-out struggles against the old when this means fighting against elders with whom they have close personal bonds.

Even if the motivation to struggle against the dominant old is there, avoidance, formality of social relations, and physical separation limit the chances for open conflict to erupt. Moreover, the fear of punishment, in the form of various social sanctions, often induces old and young to refrain from aggressive or conflict-producing behavior. And safety-valve institutions reduce the likelihood of serious conflict by allowing the young to displace the hostility they feel toward the old onto other targets.

This chapter has shown how these factors operate in nonindustrial societies. Many of the very same forces also play a role in modern industrial societies, muting conflict between strata not only in the age system but in the class system as well.

Class theorists have long sought to understand why class warfare and the ultimate victory of the working class, as analyzed by Marx, have not occurred in the advanced capitalist societies. With regard to the United States, they have focused on a number of factors they believe account for the low levels of class consciousness and absence of revolutionary class action. These include occupational mobility and the belief that there is plenty of opportunity, both factors that lead people to think that there is a kind of equality in the society; absolute improvements in standard of living without a change in class position; ethnic, religious, and geographic identities that take precedence over class loyalties; legitimizing values and beliefs such as those stressing individual responsibility and that getting ahead in the class system depends on hard work and individual ability; and the threat of violence from the state. Age stratification theorists have found that some of these same factors are relevant in explaining the relative infrequency of organized age conflicts in the United States (A. Foner 1974, 1975, 1979; Riley and A. Foner 1972).

What we find, then, is that a number of similar underlying factors operate to reduce society-wide class or age conflicts in this country as well as conflict between old and young at all levels in nonindustrial societies. For example, opportunities for upward mobility in the class system and inevitable mobility through the age system weaken ties with peers within strata and lessen the motivation to initiate open conflicts (A. Foner 1979:236). In all three cases, widely accepted legitimizing values and beliefs support the existing system of inequality. In addition, just as there are compensations in nonindustrial societies that reduce the dissatisfactions of the disadvantaged old or young, so, too, in industrial societies benefits or improvements bind deprived strata to the status quo. And while diffuse sanctions are more critical in compelling people to toe the line in nonindustrial societies, sanctions are by no means unimportant in analyzing the low levels of age or class conflict in the industrial world. Indeed, the threat of violence and physical compulsion from the police-military force are of paramount importance in preventing revolts of the underdogs.

There are, of course, institutional arrangements which reduce age conflict that are unique to nonindustrial societies. Formal avoidance prohibitions, for instance, clearly do not prevent age or class conflicts in industrial countries. Nor are witchcraft beliefs and practices relevant in the study of inequality and conflict in modern industrial societies. In many nonindustrial societies, as the next chapter will show, witchcraft beliefs and accusations are closely related to inequalities between old and young, and, we shall see, these beliefs do on occasion help to mute or forestall bitter age conflict.

6
The Old Person as Witch

Witchcraft, in a number of societies, is associated with the elderly. Old people are often believed to have the power to cause misfortune illicitly through mystical means. When disaster strikes, it is they who are frequently blamed.

The analysis of witchcraft further illuminates the nature of inequality, tensions, and conflict between old and young in nonindustrial societies. People are likely to imagine that others are witches if, among other things, there are underlying strains in their relations. Young people often wind up believing in the witchcraft powers of the elderly as a result of tensions generated by the unequal distribution of powers and privileges between them.

The case studies in this chapter give us the opportunity to look at the strains and ambivalent feelings observed in earlier chapters from a slightly different angle. The chapter also shows how witchcraft accusations and suspicions operate as forms of open conflict between old and young. And while witchcraft beliefs and practices can heighten intergenerational tensions and conflicts, they sometimes play a role in preventing serious conflict and bringing pressure for accommodation between old and young, a topic I consider in the concluding section.

Two preliminary points before setting out. When I talk about witches I refer to all mystical evildoers whose believed activities are deemed antisocial or illegitimate. I do not distinguish sorcerers from witches. I am not, in other words, concerned with whether mystical evildoers are thought to harm by virtue of internal psychic powers (witches) or by means of spells, charms and potions, or other external techniques (sorcerers).[1] Rather I want to explore why old people, however they are believed to work their mystical evil, are thought of, in Evans-Pritchard's (1937) words, as "enemies of men."

The second matter is a methodological one. I have had to rely on a small number of cases, mainly from Africa, in this chapter. Few studies provide detailed information about beliefs in old witches as well as material on the status of the old or on the nature of age relations. A study, for example, that simply mentioned in passing that old people were one category of the accused and gave no information on old people's position or their relations with the young was of little use here. Even detailed accounts of witchcraft and age relations are not without problems, and several anthropologists have raised questions about the validity of many witchcraft studies. I discuss these criticisms in detail in the appendix. Without minimizing the problems of much of the data I have had to rely on or my inability to say how typical the examples I use are, I feel we can broaden our understanding of age inequalities and relations between young and old by looking at the in-depth material available—from reports about fantasies of old witches to extended case studies and numerical analyses of accusations.

Witchcraft Beliefs
and Age-Related Tensions

Younger people's hostility or ambivalence toward the elderly, or at least toward certain of the elderly, finds expression in beliefs about old people's witchcraft powers in a number of societies.

Younger people's resentment of the old stems from two familiar situations, though there are variations on these two themes. In the first case, younger people find their subordination to the powerful and privileged old grating. Picturing old people as witches expresses this hostility. Actual accusations, and sometimes even loudly voiced suspicions, may be a means to lessen, or escape from, their influence.

The other situation is where younger adults are expected to support the old. The young may feel especially put upon when they must support distant kin to whom they feel no intense obligations or old people who perform no valued tasks. For their part, the dependent elderly are often only too aware of this reluctance and resentment. They may inwardly seethe with anger, and perhaps openly complain, when they feel decent treatment is not forthcoming. One way juniors openly express their resentment is by viewing the old as witches. Accusations can legitimate cutting off aid to an old person.

The young, in short, may resent elders whom they are bound to support, honor, and obey. Perhaps ambivalence is a better word than resentment for it captures young people's complex and often contradictory feelings toward the old—hostility mixed with respect, for example. Then, too, the young are often caught between how they should feel about the old and how they do feel. As Philip Mayer comments about witchcraft accusations generally, "The demand for a positive sentiment and the inability to provide it—are equally essential to the picture [of witches and their accusers]. Painful tension arises because one individual cannot feel towards another as society expects him to feel. . . . If in fact one cannot get on well with him or her, the situation may become tense" (1970:55).

But it is not just how young people feel. It is how they are permitted to behave. Young folks tend to be severely constrained in the ways they can express antagonism to the old. How much deference is required of the young varies, but generally they are supposed to show respect to the old. As a rule, they cannot take older people to court, for instance. And physically injuring an old person is usually considered a heinous offense.

Accusing old men or women of mystical evildoing may, however, be an acceptable way to express hostility and bid for community support. Younger people, moreover, can feel blameless for harboring ill will toward the elderly man or woman. Resentment is justified in their own as well as others' eyes if the old person is believed to be a witch. The old person may of course behave in a manner befitting a witch. But anger and envy may also be projected onto the old people who aroused these feelings in the first place.

Obviously old people are not thought to be witches wherever ambivalent feelings and tensions mark intergenerational relations. Witchcraft beliefs are not present in every society. Even where witchcraft beliefs exist, the old are sometimes the ones accusing juniors. And, as the previous chapter showed, strains between old and young in a society are often openly expressed in other ways, having nothing to do with witchcraft.

But this is not an examination of why old people are thought to be witches in some societies and not in others.[2] Rather, the pages that follow examine the way tensions resulting from inequalities between old and young find an outlet in stereotypes about, and sometimes even accusations of, old witches.

The Witch as a Powerful Old Man

In our own society, the word "witch" conjures up an image of an old woman. *Roget's International Thesaurus* lists "old woman" as a synonym for "witch," and *Webster's New World Dictionary* includes "an ugly and ill-tempered old woman" as one definition. Yet in a number of societies old men, often those in positions of authority, are thought to be witches. Men who have legitimate authority to bring mystical harm upon wrongdoers are, in fact, sometimes believed capable of abusing their powers for evil ends.

Old men in many societies, as chapter 2 made clear, predominate in positions of authority. It is they, for example, who head the homestead or village segment, control important property rights, sit in judgment in quarrels and disputes, and carry the mantle of ritual authority. While they ought to be respected and obeyed, they are also frequently envied and resented. Such resentment may be aggravated if old men monopolize other privileges that are denied younger men such as having many wives. As young men mature, they want to establish their independence from dominant old men whose control they often find stifling.

Thinking of powerful old men as witches, or potential witches, is one way young folks in some societies can express their hostility or ambivalence toward these old men. Accusations can validate younger men's claims to autonomy. After all, they are morally righteous while the old man, they sincerely believe, is evil. Even when the accuser is another older man, younger men who resent the accused witch's authority may be only too ready to believe the allegation.

The Lugbara: Old Men Accused

We can see many of these processes at work among the Lugbara of Uganda. When the Lugbara described witches, they almost always pictured old men (Middleton 1963:262). Old men in authority in fact were often suspected or accused— and in many cases by young men.

Young men in this patrilineal society were supposed to respect and "fear" their seniors. Not surprisingly, young men harbored considerable hostility toward senior men who had a great deal of authority over them. Antagonism at certain times found expression in witchcraft beliefs. Although old men had legitimate mystical power on their side, they could be accused of causing harm for immoral purposes. Young men's allegations that older men were witches, however, tended to fall on deaf ears. It was when the alleged witch was an elder and the accuser another senior man that the accusation tended to be widely accepted. This was most likely to occur at a particular stage in the cycle of development of the family cluster.

The local family cluster of agnatic kin was the arena for witchcraft accusations. These clusters consisted of about fifteen to sixty people, typically including a number of adult men and their wives and children (sons and unmarried daughters). The elder who controlled and represented the cluster was supposed to be the eldest son of his predecessor. His main responsibility was the control and allocation of arable land, and his authority was backed up by his ability to call on the dead to cause sickness to the living.

Men whose fathers had died as well as elders were believed able to invoke the ancestors to bring sickness to junior kin and dependents. Causing sickness in this way was perfectly legitimate. Indeed, men wanted to be thought of as righteous invokers of the dead for this validated their claims to authority. Those who invoked the dead were living guardians of the moral order with the power—and an obligation— to punish sinners. An elder might be righteously indignant because his authority as elder had been flouted. Other senior men might be outraged by disobedient and disrespectful juniors. One of the worst offenses leading to invocation of the dead was striking or fighting with an older kinsman. A man did not acknowledge that he had invoked ("thought words in his heart") until the offender became sick and the oracles pointed out his role. In line with the structure of authority, elders were judged to be invokers in most cases. Given the way such judgments were arrived at, this is hardly surprising. Since elders commonly put cases to the oracles, they actually suggested themselves as responsible.

Senior men could also pervert their powers for evil purposes, however. *Ole ro*, to cause sickness by indignation, referred not only to invoking the dead but also to bewitching. Whether indignation was justified was all a matter of interpretation. While a man claimed he justifiably caused sickness by invoking the dead, public opinion and oracular statements might disagree. He could be judged to have caused sickness without justification. In other words, he had bewitched. Senior men who abused their authority were believed to cause sickness for selfish ends rather than to protect their dependents and maintain community peace. A man was usually not openly accused. Instead, accusations were made behind his back by saying, for instance, that he was "strong" or that he "walked at night."

One type of accusation was leveled by sons against their real, or more usually, classificatory fathers. As young men matured and married—and wanted greater independence and higher status—they often buckled under senior men's dominance. To enforce their authority, senior kinsmen invoked the dead against juniors. Married young men with children, however, often felt that the older men were abusing their powers and that their indignation was not justified.[3] Thus, one informant explained how a man with a wife and children "will get shame" if his father claimed to have invoked the dead against him: "Will not his wife's brother laugh at him and say, 'See, our sister's husband is only a child!'? Then that son will refuse those words of his father, and will close his heart against him . . . and think that his father has forgotten the words of blood (kinship), and think his father to be a witch" (Middleton 1960:227). Such accusations against older men were not accepted by the wider group, however. The authority of older men over the young was too firm, and they had generational seniority clearly on their side. The verdict: sickness was caused by invocation of the dead.

With time, however, witchcraft accusations might be accepted. At later stages in the family cluster's developmental cycle, invocation of the dead—and witchcraft—were frequently in the air. Now it was men of the same generation who were accusing each other. A senior man claimed that the elder, whose authority he wished to escape, was a witch.

The elder at this point had serious rivals for power. Other senior men now headed fairly large family groups within the cluster. These groups (wives, children, and perhaps brothers) might even be the same size as the family group of the elder himself. Once it was accepted that a man had authority over a large family group, he was regarded as equal in generation to the elder in most situations of authority in the cluster. Like the elder, he was probably an old man. Yet he was still not the elder's equal in all matters. He was impatient to break away from the elder's domination and to be recognized as an independent elder. There was added incentive to achieve independence. Natural population growth within the cluster meant that by this time there was simply not enough land to satisfy everyone's needs.

Competition for authority was played out in a mystical idiom. The would-be elder waged his struggle by trying to show that he, not the elder, had invoked the dead against his dependents. The elder did not sit idly by, watching his authority challenged. He invoked the dead more frequently to explain why his dependents fell ill. As conflicts escalated, the elder and his rivals also invoked the dead to explain illness which befell each other's dependents. If they could show that the dead had heard their invocation against a rival's dependents, they showed that the dead trusted in them and not their rival.

Such frequent invocation posed problems. An elder who invoked often, particularly against his competitor's dependents, was likely to be accused of witchcraft by his rival. As the elder's authority "is taken from him by his rivals, especially when he is either aged or unpopular, he tends to invoke more and more often. Clearly a vicious cycle may be set up if he invokes for insufficient reasons, and he will further lose popularity and show that he is losing his sense of responsibility" (Middleton 1960:226). If, in the end, he was widely believed to be a witch, his authority was seriously undermined. The fear of being thought a witch, however, might stop the elder from abusing his powers of invocation, and it was usually only when the elder died that the family cluster split into two or more groups.

Accusations, then, arose when elders or other senior men were believed to overstep the bounds of their legitimate powers. In an attempt to uphold and buttress their authority, they invoked the dead. But those wishing to discredit the invoker's authority and free themselves from his control believed he had practiced witchcraft. Thus, young men often said that senior male kin were using witchcraft against them. It was a measure of senior men's authority over the young that witch-craft accusations against them were only taken seriously in the local group when leveled by other seniors. When young men alleged that old men were witches, these charges were dismissed. We can assume, however, that when a senior rival implied that the elder was a witch, many younger men believed the charge.

Witchcraft Potential

An analysis of accusations can show how individuals use witchcraft beliefs in the quest for power as well as autonomy. But we also need to consider how people conceive of witches and witchcraft powers quite apart from instances of allegation. After all, important old men among the Lugbara, as in a number of other societies, are believed to have witchcraft potential whether or not they are accused in specific cases (see also, for example, E. Goody 1970, 1973; Wilson 1951). The belief that men who have the mystical power to punish individuals for the good of the community are also capable of harming for immoral, selfish purposes both reflects and provides an idiom for expressing ambivalence toward men in authority. Powerful men may be respected, admired, and depended on, but they are often resented, envied, and even feared as well.

The Tiv of central Nigeria nicely illustrate the way witchcraft beliefs express ambivalence toward powerful old men (Bohannan and Bohannan 1953; Bohannan 1960, 1965). In this patrilineal society, influential elders by day were said to be witches by night. Elders (usually men of about forty-five or older) were believed to have a substance that grew on their hearts, *tsav*, which gave them power over other people. *Tsav* could be used not only to protect the community but to bewitch. Men could have *tsav* before they were old, and all influential as well as talented and skilled men were believed to possess it. But once a man was old he was assumed to have *tsav*. How else, it was reasoned, could he have withstood the *tsav* of others for so long? Beliefs about *tsav* thus explained why some men lived longer than others. Since men of greatest influence were usually old men, the beliefs also reflected the realities of power relations in Tiv society.

On the positive side, Tiv felt assured that elders had mystical power to guard them against dangerous forces. Sometimes men with *tsav* even had to sacrifice a human being for the community's welfare. But men with *tsav* could also kill for personal benefit. Powerful men, no matter how respected or well liked, were thus never fully trusted. They were potentially evil killers. *Tsav* was a metaphor for expressing power relations in Tiv society. As Paul Bohannan aptly puts it: power corrupts (1960:332).

From the perspective of relations between old and young, we can also say that beliefs about *tsav* expressed tensions arising from age inequalities. Traditionally, influential elders held no formal political offices. But as compound heads they had jural, ritual, and economic authority over dependents (including wives, sons, and unmarried daughters), and outside the compound they officiated at important rituals, arbitrated disputes, and were informal political leaders. Younger men thus came under influential elders' sway. To say that an old man had *tsav* was at once to recognize his claims to deference and obedience and also to express resentment and fear of his powers.

The Witch Imagined: Dependent Old Men

Old age, of course, is often associated with social losses. When the physical declines of advanced age set in, elderly men find themselves more and more in need of the support of younger adults. On occasion, witchcraft beliefs are related to this dependent position of old men.

The Navaho

Among the Navaho, witchcraft beliefs expressed younger people's ambivalence toward old men's burdensome dependence—and quite indirectly.

Clyde Kluckhohn (1967) based his analysis of Navaho witchcraft on witch tales and gossip told him by numerous informants. Although a high proportion of the witches in these stories and anecdotes lived in distant communities, Kluckhohn argues that this can still tell us about the "seamy side" of relationships with the old close by. Witchcraft tales and gossip as well as generalized fantasies and stereotypes about witches provided an indirect way for the young to express resentment against the old.

The vast majority of the witches in the stories and anecdotes Kluckhohn analyzed were old (1967:59).[4] The very old were in fact considered potentially dangerous individuals who were likely to be suspected. They had little prestige or influence and were frequently neglected. Physically weak and often in ill health, the very old were hangers-on in households, usually an economic burden to younger relatives who felt duty-bound to care for them.

In such a situation, as we saw in chapter 4, relations between the aged and their younger caretakers could be strained. Kluckhohn describes how younger people often resented the burden of looking after old relatives. One suspects that the aged, for their part, were bitter if they received only grudging support. Their complaints could further irritate the young.

Imagining the very old, in general, as potentially malevolent gave shape to young people's ambivalence toward the old they had to support. Gossip about unrelated and, still better, distant old witches was a safe way for the young to release some of their hostility toward old relatives at home.

The Lele

Among the Lele of the Kasai in the former Belgian Congo, witchcraft beliefs also had much to do with old men's dependence on the young. The Lele case, however, is a complex one that does not fit neatly into the category of witches as dependent old men. After all, the most noteworthy thing about old men's status in traditional Lele society was not their dependence but the many advantages they had. Witchcraft beliefs, I will show, were not unrelated to young men's resentment of old men's privileged position. But, according to Mary Douglas, these privileges were precarious. It is the negative side of old age that she emphasizes in her analysis of traditional Lele witchcraft beliefs (Douglas 1963a, 1963b). The stereotype of witches as angry and jealous old men, she argues, reflected real weaknesses in old men's position. Despite their massive privileges, they could not exercise much authority over and they were economically dependent on young men. Thus old men might well be angry and resentful—the very image of witches.

Before looking at the sources of old men's disappointment and their dependence on the young, consider the things that old men could be pleased about—and that gave young men grounds for discontent. Old men had a definite edge in acquiring wives, cult privileges, and wealth in raffia cloth.

While old men averaged two to three wives each, younger men usually could not marry until their mid-thirties. Because old men reserved women of marriageable age for themselves, they could head large compounds, be served by female labor in the fields, have many daughters, and get some service for specified tasks from sons-in-law (Douglas 1963a:5).[5] "The principle of seniority," Douglas writes, "was able to be applied right through the society, even to the upper age groups, because the most important rights were over women acquired by parenthood and grandparenthood. Thus the delayed maturity of young men was the corollary of the delayed retirement of old men" (1963a:5). Entry into valued cults was also restricted to married and therefore older men.

Old men's position was bolstered by their control of raffia cloth. Fatherhood, cult membership, and the practice of a specialist craft or rituals gave older men sources of raffia. Older men, to give two examples, received payments from young men entering cults and marrying their daughters. While older men were constantly receiving raffia cloths, young men constantly needed them to pay the high marriage fees, for instance, or to enter cults they could join as newly married men. Because young men could not weave enough cloths for their needs, they had to ask, and thus became indebted to, older men for raffia. Even when European money entered the Lele economy, the traditional system was maintained because Congo francs could not, as a rule, be substituted for raffia, and raffia could not be bought.

That old men had the lion's share of valued rewards was obviously a potential source of strain with the young. Indeed, Douglas speaks of the "barely veiled hostility" that marked relations between old and young men (1963a:223). One way antagonism to older men was expressed was in the idiom of witchcraft. On occasion, old men were accused and sometimes even exiled as witches.

An old man might find himself acquiring the reputation of a fully committed witch, responsible for every death in the village—consumed with envy, malice, and spite and killing to satisfy his craving for flesh. If hostilities built up against an old man, he could not, like a young man, easily move to another village. Other villages did not want more old men who added little manpower and disturbed the seniority pattern by expecting a place at the top of the status hierarchy. An old man could thus find himself stuck in a village where he was surrounded by a wall of hostility—and eventually accused of witchcraft. In the old days, he had the chance to clear his name by taking the poison ordeal. If he survived the ordeal, he was innocent. When the poison ordeal was outlawed, he ran the risk of being exiled as a witch.

Old men in fact were not the only ones accused. However, when the Lele thought about witches in the abstract, they thought of witches as old men. To imagine witches as old men, I suggest, was to acknowledge old men's potential for evil and thus gave concrete form to young men's resentment of old men's privileges.[6] Also, as Douglas argues, the general image of a witch was an old man because important diviners were old (1963b:130). Lele diviners were thought capable of using their techniques for immoral as well as moral purposes. Although diviners could use their powers to combat witchcraft—and official diviners were expected to protect the village from foreign witchcraft and, if need be, to use their witchcraft powers on behalf of the village—diviners could also pervert these powers for evil ends.

But the general image of a witch, remember, was not just an old man but one who was disappointed and jealous of the young. Witchcraft beliefs thus reflect another side of old men's position: their dependence on young men. What was the nature of this dependence, and why did the Lele talk about witches as angry old men who were filled with resentment?

Here I will take a somewhat different tack than I have so far. In my general scheme for analyzing witchcraft beliefs, and in my discussion of the Lele to this point, I have emphasized how these beliefs expressed young people's hostility. What Douglas stresses, however, is how the Lele view of the witch was related to old, not young, men's resentments (1963b:130). The image of the witch was an accurate description of how many old men felt. Many old men were disappointed and resentful when they reached the long-anticipated prime of life. All their lives they had deferred to seniors, looking forward to the day when they would be on top. Once there, however, they found that their situation was precarious. For all the deference they received and for all their privileges, they could not command the obedience or support of junior clansmen. Instead, they had to be wary of offending young men, whose support they badly needed. They might well feel envy and malice toward young men they could not control.

In many ways old men were at a disadvantage in the economic system: they were uncomfortably dependent on young men's physical labor. As their physical abilities declined, they were forced to rely on young men for clearing the forest, drawing wine, and bringing home meat. They could not demand these services for they controlled no valuable fixed assets that they could dangle before the young as eventual inheritances.[7] As Douglas writes, "There were no possessions, land, equipment or trees so valuable as a man's work" (1963a:32). Refusing to contribute to a young man's raffia needs was not an effective sanction for young men could usually get raffia from other old men (Douglas 1963a:103). Nor did old men use their influence in allocating wives to bind young clansmen more securely: old men kept younger women to themselves and their own generation (Douglas 1963a:118). Old men did not have special claims on any particular sister's sons. And a son-in-law's services for such tasks as clearing land or house building, though crucial, were brief and irregular (Douglas 1963a:119).

Some old men, who had a harder time than others, best fit the image of the neglected and angry old witch: "Those who have had no daughters, or whose children have not survived, or whose wives have run away, taking their children with them, or who for any reason are unable to command the goods and services of sons-in-law, these old men find that the deference of junior clansmen is a somewhat empty formality" (Douglas 1963b:131). Such unfortunate old men had especially good cause to be disappointed. Having to depend on young folks whose obligations to them were relatively weak perhaps also made them more demanding.

The image of the old disappointed witch was, then, by Douglas' account, directly related to old men's dependence on young men's "brawn and muscle." It was because of this dependence that young men could effectively use the threat of accusation against senior antagonists as a "counter-weapon of control" (Douglas 1963a:223–224). Thus, here young men's resentments do come into play.

Old men knew that if they pressed their claims too far, young men were likely to accuse them of witchcraft or propose to leave the village as victims of witchcraft. And old men wanted to make sure to have young men to help them out. Old men were, as a rule, undemanding—never or rarely commanding. They tended to wear "a deprecatory and self-effacing manner, possibly a defence against the general belief that they were potential dangerous characters" (Douglas 1963a:223).

By "putting the whip into the hands of the young" (Douglas 1963a:7), witchcraft beliefs, it could be argued, also provided young men with some compensation for their inferior position in a social system that reserved so many advantages for old men. A few well-aimed accusations, Douglas writes, could easily destroy old men who abused their powers (1963b:131). And since old men were undemanding for fear of being accused of witchcraft, this gave young men one less thing to complain about—and freedom from control.

The discussion of how witchcraft beliefs among the Lele strengthened young men's hand and limited old men's powers raises questions I will return to later in the chapter. What is clear is that the Lele example shows some of the complex ways that witchcraft beliefs and practices are related to age inequalities and age relations. Other complications—and dimensions of witchcraft beliefs—come into play when we consider old women as witches.

The Old Woman as Witch: Dominating Old Women

Much of what I have said to explain why younger people imagine old men to be mystical evildoers holds true for their beliefs about old women witches as well. Yet, as we shall see, when old women are associated with witchcraft this may well reflect aspects of their social position and social relationships that old men do not share.

Let us start with old women at the top. As chapter 3 showed, women's powers tend to increase as they grow old. Within the domestic group, old women frequently become a force to reckon with. By the time a woman reaches menopause, she can delegate tasks to younger women of the household, and she often commands the close allegiance of sons as well. With increasing age, women may acquire considerable ritual powers, and in some places the economic resources under their control expand. Old women commonly take a more active role in public life than younger women and gain influence (albeit often from behind the scenes) in community affairs.

Thus, when women grow old they can, in many societies, more easily make demands on others and be heeded. Particularly if widowed, they may be relatively free of senior men's control—an ambiguous state in places where women are supposed to be subject to male authority. In any case, old women's seniority, combined with domestic and sometimes ritual and economic power, means that the young are obliged to respect them and comply with their demands. Young people often fulfill these obligations with mixed feelings, having affection for old women who raised them but chafing under dominating old women they are bound to obey and to whom they are beholden. Antagonism and ambivalence can find an outlet in beliefs about old female witches.[8]

The Old Mother-in-Law as Witch: The Gusii

In light of these comments, what better candidate for a witch than an old mother-in-law? The Gusii of Kenya would heartily agree (S. LeVine 1978:23–96). Although suspicions rose and fell in intensity over time, young women in this patrilineal, patrilocal society commonly thought their mothers-in-law had the potential for malevolence. In times of personal crises, a young woman could well turn her anxieties and frustrations onto her mother-in-law.

The complex and intertwined factors that led many daughters-in-law to suspect their mothers-in-law of mystical evildoing are brought out in the case of Suzanna Bosibori. During the period I discuss here (1974–1976), Suzanna, a woman in her mid-twenties, had been living in her husband's home for about six years. Her husband, Ongaki, was away from home much of the time, looking for work after he had been fired from his teaching job. Kemunto, Suzanna's mother-in-law, was, however, ever present. Suzanna and her children had their own hut, but Kemunto, a woman of about sixty whose "face was wrinkled with a thousand tiny lines," was a dominant figure in the compound.

Not long after Suzanna gave birth to her first son, she became convinced that Kemunto was trying to kill her through witchcraft. Perhaps these fears were linked to her feeling trapped in marriage and in her husband's home. Now that she had a son, she was more firmly bound to her husband's clan. The expected marriage of, and payment of cattle for, Ongaki's sister would bind Suzanna further since then bridewealth payments would be made for her. But why was Kemunto the focus of Suzanna's anxiety? Why did Suzanna think her mother-in-law was making her ill?

Suzanna had much pent-up hostility toward her dominating mother-in-law. The two women saw each other constantly, but Suzanna was always in a subordinate role. Kemunto expected Suzanna to help her with daily tasks and to respect her. No matter how imperious or demanding Kemunto was—and she was often an irritating presence to Suzanna—Suzanna was supposed to obey the old woman, to control her anger, and to keep her criticisms to herself.

It was not just that Kemunto ordered Suzanna to do her bidding in seemingly minor chores—cutting her toenails, to mention one task Suzanna found annoying. Kemunto kept a tight hold on the homestead's land, something both Suzanna and Ongaki deeply resented. Kemunto refused to divide the plot her husband had left his sons, even though three of these sons, including Ongaki, were landless. The old woman would not allow her sons any say in how the land was to be used. Neither Suzanna nor Ongaki could rent or sell the small bit of land he would eventually inherit or even plant what they wanted on it. Kemunto was boss. Kemunto may have been jealous of her son's allegiance to Suzanna on the land question as well as on other matters. Indeed, Suzanna said that Kemunto was bewitching her because "she fears Ongaki loves me more than her" (S. LeVine 1978:67).

Suzanna's suspicions of Kemunto's malevolence were buttressed by the fact that Kemunto, like many older Gusii women, was associated with the practice of divination. Diviners, spirit mediums between the living and their ancestral elders, were thought capable of using their powers for evil as well as for good. Kemunto, Suzanna knew, had once been a diviner. And Kemunto was aging and ill. She was the sort of person, in other words, the Gusii generally suspected of witchcraft—a sick old woman who harbored feelings of rage toward younger people who neglected her. Possibly, too, Suzanna felt guilty that she was not as dutiful a daughter-in-law as she should have been and thought Kemunto, in her anger, was retaliating through witchcraft.

The diviner whom Suzanna consulted confirmed her worst fears. Kemunto, the diviner said, was bewitching Suzanna. Suzanna did not keep her suspicions to herself. She told many of her friends as well as her husband. Each person she called on offered sympathy. In portraying herself as a sufferer and pitiable victim, she was able to bask in the attention and support she received from those she loved. Ongaki even came home from town, "risking his life in the face of his mother's jealousy and rage to be with her" (S. LeVine 1978:71).

Being able to rally support in this matter gave Suzanna a feeling of self-confidence and satisfaction she did not normally enjoy in her dependent role as daughter-in-law and wife. But all was not easy. Suzanna still had to live in the same homestead with Kemunto; and Suzanna was worried that her mother-in-law would kill her. For about a month after Suzanna went to the diviner, the atmosphere in the homestead was chilling. Suzanna was incapacitated by anxiety and hardly did any farm work.

Tensions gradually subsided, however, and the two women cooperated once again. Perhaps this was partly because Suzanna's anxiety at being trapped in marriage was allayed now that Ongaki's sister's marriage prospects fell through. This meant that bridewealth would not be paid for Suzanna so soon and she would thus remain in limbo, in the condition of not-yet-paid-for wife. That suspicions could arise again, however, albeit in less serious form, is indicated by the fact that when Suzanna's eye infection returned briefly she got medicine from a witch smeller to protect herself against Kemunto's witchcraft.

Suzanna was not alone in believing Kemunto to be a witch. Ongaki, who had good reason to resent his mother's economic control, joined forces with Suzanna against his mother during the period of terror I described. In general, young men as well as young women may have ambivalent feelings toward dominating old women that can find expression in witchcraft beliefs. In the case of men, it is not simply that they are constrained by old women's control. An example from southern Spain will show that dominating old women may be resented, and their position deemed anomalous, because they are women, with power over men.[9]

Witch Fantasies in Andalusia

Say the word "witch" in Andalusia, Spain, and what came to mind was an old predatory woman riding astride her broomstick (Pitt-Rivers 1977:44, 80–83). This image or fantasy expressed ambivalence and anxiety about old women's position in the social order. (Note that in this Spanish case we are talking of fantasies about old witches and not accusations of particular old women.)

Old Andalusian women's position was anomalous in several respects. For one thing, they eluded the constraints of men. Although young women were in their proper—subservient—place, under the domination of husbands and fathers, old widowed women were free from male control. In other settings, as well as in Andalusia, anxiety about old women not directly subject to male domination found expression in witch fantasies about old women (see, for example, Beidelman 1980:31). In Andalusia, such women were thought to be sexually aggressive and dangerous.

Another anomaly was that old women became in a sense "surrogate males" (Pitt-Rivers 1977:81). They could no longer bear children, obviously a key female role. At the same time, old women assumed male roles. Many old women began to take charge of family affairs when their husbands' physical strength began to wane. Once widowed—and most women ended up life as widows because they tended to live longer than men and were usually several years younger than their spouses—old women were formally released from male domination. For the first time, they had full legal and economic responsibility as well as greater influence in the household (Pitt-Rivers 1954:89).[10] Authoritarian Spanish widows became in Pitt-Rivers' words, "like certain hen birds of the pheasant family who in old age put on the plumage of the cock" (1977:80). The symbolism of the old witch on a broomstick thus fits neatly into place in Pitt-Rivers' analysis. The broomstick, normally a symbol of a woman's domestic role, became "the most impressively male symbol imaginable" once the widow sat astride it (Pitt-Rivers 1977:82).

Old women thus made young men uneasy because they reversed the rightful state of affairs. Not only were they free of male control and "malelike" in their social roles; they also had increased authority over younger men.

While widows generally greeted their new independence and authority with enthusiasm, younger men in particular might be less jubilant. Young men often resented old women's dominance, and this resentment fed into beliefs about old women witches.

Men resented having to work for old women, something they frequently did. The word "widow" was common in business enterprises in Andalusia, and some old women owned agricultural properties. Male workers commonly believed that women were not competent to run these properties. As for the position of sons in family businesses controlled by their mothers, an old widow might be "tougher in business than ever her husband was and keeps all the male members of her family trembling" (Pitt-Rivers 1977:80). Despite the affection and deep attachment that bound young men to their mothers, sons might well resent having to obey these domineering old women. Picturing witches as malevolent old women with masculine characteristics gave expression to young men's ambivalence and hostility toward dominating old women in their lives—old women who inverted the social order in reality and subverted it in fantasy.

The Old Woman as Witch: The Dependent Old

Not all widows in nonindustrial societies have as much economic control or autonomy of senior men as they do in Andalusia. Indeed, old women are often far from independent.

Their very dependence on younger people for economic support may lead them to be accused of witchcraft.

Of course, many children look after old mothers with warmth and devotion. But some children, as we saw in chapter 4, resent these caretaking duties. And not all old women have sons or daughters on hand to help them out. Old women tend to have an especially hard time when they must rely on distant relatives and neighbors for support.

There may be little an unfortunate old woman can do to improve her lot except complain or quietly seethe, hoping to arouse the guilt or fear of the young. In this she may well succeed. Those who are expected to provide for the old woman may feel a mixture of resentment and guilt toward her, and in some societies, they may fear that the neglected old woman will retaliate through mystical means.

English Villages

This sequence of events is not unlike what typically happened in sixteenth- and seventeenth-century English villages (Macfarlane 1970; Thomas 1971). Available evidence indicates that suspected witches were often poor old women, and many were widows.[11] These women were thought to have the mystical power to kill or injure people or animals by such means as touching their victims, pronouncing curses, or using technical aids.

This is not the place for a discussion of the rise and fall of witchcraft prosecutions in sixteenth- and seventeenth-century England, a subject Keith Thomas (1971) explores in his enormously detailed account. Suffice it to say that the beginning of the witch craze in England had much to do with changes brought about by Protestant Reformers. The Reformation took away rituals that the English medieval church had provided as protection against witches. Villagers now took recourse in the newly approved method of legal prosecution. In the sixteenth and seventeenth centuries, witchcraft was a statutory offense in England, and hundreds of people were brought to trial and convicted of witchcraft.

Once witch trials multiplied, old women, as dependent

members of the community, were likely targets. Social and economic changes made them especially demanding of their fellows. As customary sources of support dried up, old women (particularly widows) were increasingly dependent on neighborly aid. And neighbors were more and more loathe to provide such support. As Thomas sums up: "The great bulk of witchcraft accusations . . . reflected the conflict between neighbourly conduct required by the ethical code of the old village community and the increasingly individualized forms of behaviour which accompanied the economic changes of the sixteenth and seventeenth centuries" (1971:561).

Before the sixteenth century, there had been a kind of "built-in system of poor relief" for widows and the elderly. A widow had the right to inherit part of her late husband's holding; if she could not cultivate the land herself, she could give it to a younger member, who, in turn, would guarantee her maintenance. Other traditional privileges such as permission to sleep in the church also helped the poor.

Social and economic changes in the sixteenth and seventeenth centuries made life more difficult for old women. With the decline of the manorial system, they had less access to land. To make things worse, such economic factors as the rise in prices, the development of agricultural specialization, and the growth of towns and commercial values ushered in a decline in old traditions of mutual charity. More and more, relatively well-off villagers had to decide whether to use their resources to give support to the old and poor or to invest in improvements to keep up with their neighbors (Macfarlane 1970:205).

Increasingly they yielded to the impulse to say no to needy old women—a decision that was backed up by the introduction of a national Poor Law in the sixteenth century that began to institutionalize public charity. But it took a while before welfare for the indigent was completely assumed by public bodies. In the meantime, norms as to how to treat the dependent old were unclear. While the state, for example, banned indiscriminate begging, begging was permitted in a parish if approved by the overseers of the poor. Many local authorities forbade villagers to give alms at the door, but clergymen still sermonized on the moral duty of charity. In many places, loans of food and equipment from neighbors were still a vital means of support for the old.

Attitudes to the elderly poor were clearly ambivalent. Villagers recognized that it was their Christian duty to give alms to old women who had no other means of support. But they resented burdensome dependents. "The conflict between resentment and a sense of obligation produced the ambivalence which made it possible for men to turn begging women brusquely from the door, and yet suffer torments of conscience after having done so. . . . The tensions which produced witchcraft prosecution at the popular level . . . were the tensions of a society which no longer held a clear view as to how or by whom its dependent members should be maintained" (Thomas 1971:564). The householder, in short, felt guilty at turning the alms seeker away and transferred the guilt back to the needy old woman. Blaming the victim is what we would call it today.

Typically, an old woman came to the door to beg or borrow food, drink, or a loan of some household utensil from a more prosperous neighbor. She was turned away. When the refuser was struck by a misfortune, he or she blamed the needy woman for mystical retaliation. Susan Cook, a woman of about fifty, was refused support and told that "she was a young woman and able to work for her living." She was then accused of bewitching some livestock of her refuser (Macfarlane 1970:164). Margaret Harkett, a sixty-year-old widow, was executed in 1585:

She had picked a basketful of peas in a neighbour's field without permission. Asked to return them, she flung them down in anger; since when, no peas would grow in the field. . . . A neighbour refused her a horse; all his horses died. Another paid her less for a pair of shoes than she asked; later he died. A gentleman told his servants to refuse her buttermilk; after which they were unable to make butter or cheese. (Thomas 1971:556)

The link between refusing the old woman and suffering misfortune was often not hard to find. The old woman was frequently heard to mumble a curse or threat against the supposed victim after being turned away. "An evil death to light upon her," said one believed witch to her victim (Thomas 1971:511). Another threatened "this shall be forty pounds loss to thee," after which her victim's animals died (Thomas 1971:557). Whether or not the rejected woman uttered a curse, the person stricken believed the old woman guilty. And so in many cases did other villagers and the courts of law. It was the old dependent woman who was judged immoral. The householder was blameless.

Central Africa

Blaming dependent old women for misfortune has also been reported in more recent times for two Central African societies. Among both the Ndembu and Luvale, old women who were a burden to the young could find themselves accused of witchcraft.

An analysis of thirty-five cases of witchcraft accusations among the Luvale showed that twenty-six of the accused were women—and almost invariably old women (White 1961:60–67). In most cases, too, the witch was alleged to have attacked a person in the generation immediately junior to her.[12]

In this matrilineal society, a woman joined her husband at marriage and spent much of her life among his kin. But when widowed or divorced and too old to remarry, women usually returned to their own relatives. Once there, old women were sometimes accused of witchcraft. Perhaps having lived so many years away from home made such women liable to suspicion. Luvale witches were thought to be "hidden and involuntary destroyers" who secretly met to eat the flesh of individuals their familiars killed. According to White, witches were viewed with horror not only because of their evil qualities but because they put loyalties to the group of witches above loyalties to the matrilineal kin group.

More important, witchcraft accusations against old women reflected tensions that arose from old women's ambiguous structural position in the community. Old women expected to exercise authority over and receive support from members of the generation junior to themselves. But providing such support was an onerous burden to juniors, one they could not always meet. They were under pressure to provide for their own children or nieces and nephews (White 1961:66). Old women, I suspect, resented the grudging support of juniors, and they may have been frustrated by the lack of authority and deference they felt was their due. It is not surprising that younger people believed these burdensome, and perhaps contentious, old women were mystical evildoers. Indeed, accusing them of witchcraft was a way to justify withholding support.

Whether all or only certain types of old Luvale women were prone to accusation is not clear. Among the nearby Ndembu (Turner 1957:151–152), it was old women without immediate male kin but who were classificatory matrilineal relatives of the village headman who were frequently considered to be witches.[13]

Like the Luvale, the Ndembu are matrilineal. Here, too, women joined their husbands at marriage. Once past menopause, widowed or divorced women usually returned to live permanently with their male matrilineal kin. Since old women were often widows and since divorce was common, old women generally lived with close maternal relatives, including, most importantly, their children (Turner 1957:62–63). Women without sons or brothers, however, were in a weak position. Without close male relatives, they had no one to obtain meat for them, and they had to depend on the uncertain generosity of more remote kin. Such support was not always forthcoming.

Neglected old women were constantly grumbling about the lack of meat, suspicious behavior in a society where witches were believed to lust for meat. Witches were thought to congregate in the bush with their familiars, where they ate the bodies of their victims. One old woman Turner knew was supposed to have bewitched her classificatory daughter (her sister's daughter) because she was angry at the young woman's refusal to give her meat.

Accusing old unfortunate women of witchcraft eliminated them from the scene. In the past, Turner says, they were burned to death. By the 1950s, they were often driven from the village.

Old women who lived with such close kin as sons and brothers were not immune from suspicion. They, too, were generally an economic burden to the community. But they were, by Turner's account, never banished from the village as accused witches. Perhaps they had less reason to complain because sons and brothers were under strong obligation to provide for them. Perhaps, too, the fact that these women could invoke the support of close male kin in the village acted as a deterrent to accusations. Indeed, in the Luvale and English examples as well as among the Ndembu, old widowed or divorced women may have been victimized because they could not easily garner male support to back up their claims to innocence.[14]

The Effects of Witchcraft Beliefs and Practices

The discussion so far has considered how tensions between old and young feed into and help to shape witchcraft beliefs. Witchcraft beliefs and practices themselves can also go on to alter age relations in a wide variety of ways. Two questions arise: Do beliefs and practices concerning old witches strengthen or weaken the position of the old? Do they reduce or intensify intergenerational strains and conflicts?

Old People's Position

As one might expect, beliefs about the witchcraft powers of the elderly often have negative consequences for them.

Whether the old "witch" is in a dependent or powerful position, witchcraft accusations can make things worse for the convicted old person. Indeed, old "witches" are sometimes killed for their supposed crimes. Being driven out of the community for witchcraft is also hardly an enviable situation for a dependent old person who may have a difficult time finding acceptance elsewhere. And, needless to say, a powerful old accused man who is thrown out of office or ostracized suffers a dramatic loss of influence and prestige.

Witchcraft suspicions, though less drastic than direct accusations, can also weaken the position of the elderly. For one thing, they can justify ill treatment of the dependent aged. Villagers in Tudor and Stuart England, for example, could feel that they were right to withhold alms from old women who were thought to be witches. Moreover, the fear of being accused may even induce the dependent old to adopt an obsequious manner toward more successful, younger people, "bowing and scraping" before those whom they rely on for aid. In the case of the privileged old, the fear of being accused can act as a brake on their powers.

It is possible, however, that the fear of old people's witchcraft powers can work to their benefit. Young folks may fulfill their obligations to the elderly to avoid an old person's mystical revenge. In fact, both the dependent and influential old sometimes manipulate people's witchcraft fears to strengthen their own position.

We thus read about the dependent old who encourage beliefs in their witchcraft powers as a way to induce others to be generous. In seventeenth century England, John Device, for one, was so afraid of being bewitched by the old woman, Anne Chattox, that he agreed to pay her "a yearly dole of meal, on condition that she hurt neither him nor his goods; on his death-bed he was convinced that he had been bewitched because the latest instalment had been left unpaid" (Thomas 1971:565). Among the Kpelle, old women without children to support them or those needing to draw on wider ties played on younger people's fears of their witchcraft powers to get enough to eat (Bledsoe 1980:115–117; see also Basso 1969:51, 62, and Kluckhohn 1967:119).

As for the influential old, they may deliberately imply that they are witches to enhance their commanding role. Among the Kaguru of Tanzania, many powerful leaders hinted at their reputed strength as witches to justify why they need not obey the rules but could demand conformity from others. One paramount chief had been notorious for witchcraft boasts and threats, which he used to seduce other men's wives (Beidelman 1963:76, 97)! In Laura Bohannan's (Elinore S. Bowen) fictionalized account of Tiv life, Yabo, a senior man, played on beliefs in his witchcraft powers to enhance his stature and make people afraid of him. "Yabo had been accused," she writes, "because he was feared. Now he embraced that accusation that he might be still more feared" (1964:204).

Although accusations can have unfortunate consequences for the particular elders accused, they may strengthen the position of elders in general. Accusing or even suspecting an influential old person of witchcraft, it can be argued, deflects aggressive impulses away from the system of age inequality that allows the old to monopolize powers and privileges—often the cause of young folks' resentment in the first place. Instead of challenging a system that permits older people to have an unequal share of valued rewards, particular elders are blamed for mystical evildoing. "It is the perversity of an individual and not the discord between structures that is assigned the blame," as Terray writes (1975:111).

I have focused on the "old person as witch" in this chapter, but it should be noted that accusations of young men by old men can also uphold old men's powers. One way existing office holders consolidated their position among the Cewa of Central Africa, according to Mary Douglas' interpretation, was by accusing young rivals of witchcraft (1963b:125–126). Among the Taita of Kenya, some junior male household heads even claimed that elders deliberately created beliefs in evil spirits and medicines to keep juniors in line by threats of witchcraft accusations (Harris 1978:65–66).

Relations Between Young and Old

The analysis of the effects of witchcraft beliefs and practices on old people's position has inevitably touched on relations between young and old. We now need to look more closely at witchcraft and intergenerational relations in light of some of the questions raised in the preceding chapter on conflict and accommodation. Witchcraft accusations and suspicions are, of course, a form of overt conflict. But can accusations and suspicions of old witches exacerbate tensions and conflicts between old and young? Conversely, can fantasies about old witches and beliefs in old people's witchcraft powers prevent or mitigate bitter age conflict?

Reducing Conflict. First consider how witchcraft beliefs help to avert or reduce conflict between old and young at both the interpersonal and community level. They can do this in two familiar ways: by operating (1) as negative social sanctions and (2) as safety valves for young people's hostility.

Like other mystical sanctions, witchcraft beliefs frequently inspire fear in the hearts of potential "criminals" and discourage behavior that could generate or intensify open conflict. Old people may modify their "witchlike" behavior, and tread softly in their dealings with the young, lest they be suspected or accused. Meanwhile, young folks may be properly deferential for fear of being bewitched.

Among the Suku of Zaire, Kopytoff tells us, junior men often were careful not to disobey an elder in case he was a witch—and avenged himself by witchcraft (1965:469–470). Elders, for their part, could find themselves accused of causing death in the lineage and forced to undergo the poison ordeal if they abused their authority. Although poison was thought to act only on witches, "unpopular elders have at times been killed under the guise of such a test."

Witchcraft beliefs can also reduce the likelihood of overt conflict between old and young by providing an alternate outlet for young people's hostility. Holding a generalized image of the witch as old or thinking that old people have witchcraft powers—without actually accusing particular old kin or neighbors—can offer a release for some of the animosity that arises in daily relations with the elderly.

The safety-valve analogy has been elaborated by Clyde Kluckhohn (1967) in his study of Navaho witchcraft. Witchcraft tales and gossip about distant and unrelated witches, he argues, were a safe way for the Navaho to express ambivalent feelings about their own old relatives and affines. By displacing aggression, these stories insulated close relations from disruptive conflict and thus helped to preserve them:

Instead of saying all the bitter things one has felt against one's stingy and repressive father-in-law (which would threaten one's own economic security as well as bring down upon one's head unpleasant social disapproval), one can obtain some relief by venting one's spleen against a totally unrelated witch in the community. This displaced aggression does not expose one to punishment so long as one is discreet in the choice of the intimates to whom one talks. And if one rages against a witch who isn't even in the locality but who lives over the mountain a safe hundred miles away one is perfectly assured against reprisals. (Kluckhohn 1967:96)

Even guarded gossip about the witchcraft powers of one's own relatives, Kluckhohn suggests, was a useful safety valve. It channeled antagonisms that might otherwise have accumulated and disrupted close relationships.

As for accusations, in general, even they can serve as safety valves. When one or two elders in a community are accused, this may allow the young to let off steam and spare other old people, or old people as a group, the wrath of juniors. Indeed, by providing a few old scapegoats for young folks' aggression, accusations reduce the possibility that the young will engage in struggles to make basic changes in the system of age inequality.

The safety-valve model can also be applied to the case of the Kamcape witch-cleansing cult that flourished among the Fipa of Tanzania in the early 1960s (Willis 1970a, 1970b). The rituals associated with the cult, it could be argued, allowed subordinate youths to express some of their pent-up hostility and, in this sense, could have forestalled more sustained open conflict against the old.

The Kamcape movement claimed to rid a community of witchcraft. The feature of the cult that concerns us here is the operations where alleged witches were forced to submit to being branded with deep razor or knife cuts on their foreheads and having "medicine" rubbed into the incisions.[15] It was believed that if they reverted to witchcraft, the medicine

would kill them. Although the whole community participated in the witch-cleansing rituals, the most active participants were those with the least status in Fipa society: young
men and women. Those degraded were the most dominant,
prestigious, and economically privileged: male elders. Quite
a number of elders might be branded; in one village of about
fifty, seven old men were accused and branded during a
Kamcape operation.

Branding the elders and administering antiwitchcraft
medicines were done in the name of restoring peace to the
community. The elders were viewed as responsible for the
village's harmony and integrity. Once they were ritually and
magically rendered harmless, the community, it was thought,
would be rid of witchcraft and the elders could resume their
privileged place in the community.

The reversal of roles at the Kamcape operations, in fact,
lasted but for an hour or two. Although the operations contained, says Willis, "in germ the idea of society remade"
(1970b:197), the age hierarchy was restored to normal. After
the operations, the alleged witches became respected elders
again and the young reverted to their former subordinate status. Indeed, by allowing young people to abuse old men they
usually had to respect and obey, the operations may have made
their normal low status more bearable.

Accentuating Tensions and Conflicts. The argument that
Kamcape operations provided a safety valve for young people's resentments of the old may of course be overdrawn. That
Fipa young men and women took charge and degraded their
elders, albeit for only a few hours, perhaps gave them a hint
of their potential power for action. And even if the Kamcape
operations—like witchcraft beliefs in other societies—reduced the likelihood of open flare-ups between old and young,
they did not eliminate the underlying sources of tension and
animosity toward the old. As long as basic age inequalities
continued, tensions would undoubtedly arise. In general, insofar as witchcraft beliefs and practices prop up the existing
system of age inequality, they preserve, rather than ease, tense

relationships between old and young. Witchcraft beliefs, as Nadel noted, are but a palliative for deeper structural strains:

The concrete hostilities are 'canalized,' in the sense that they are directed against a few scapegoats rather than against more numerous victims. . . . Each persecution of witches no doubt relieves the tensions and stresses in a cathartic manner; but the relief is itself creative of new difficulties; equally, it is short-lived, for witchcraft cases go on happening all the time. (1970:279)

But allowing inequalities and tensions between old and young to continue is one thing; accentuating these tensions is another. As the quote from Nadel indicates, witchcraft accusations often create new difficulties—and aggravate hostilities between particular old and young people.

Even a generalized fear of old witches, rather than accusations, allows some of younger people's resentment to surface and can add to stresses in relations with the old. "Some people like Ned or this old man here (about seventy years), Navahos are kind of afraid of people that age," said one Navaho. "They say they might be a witch, and if you don't feed them they will go off and work against you some way. One of your children will get it or women will get it" (Leighton and Kluckhohn 1947:91). Clearly this was an uneasy state of affairs. Moreover, those who cultivate a reputation as witches to ensure support are playing with fire, for more hostility, as well as support, may result.

As for accusations, they allow individuals to express hostilities they are not supposed to feel but can justify feeling if the disliked person is guilty of the most serious offense. Witchcraft accusations thus legitimate expressing hostility toward the elderly, and they may unleash all sorts of anger, frustrations, and resentments that had previously been dormant. As J. R. Crawford observes, accusations can give free rein to "emotions of hate and terror . . . moments of rationality and irrationality" and even brutality (1967:161). They can also seriously escalate the conflict that gave rise to the charge in the first place by providing a way to marshal the support of the whole community against the supposed witch.

Witchcraft accusations can, in fact, lead to and facilitate the rupture of relationships between certain old people and their juniors. This obviously was the case in England and Central Africa, where dependent old female witches were sometimes executed or exiled for their believed crimes. In other societies, accusations at times gave young men an acceptable reason for breaking away from dominant seniors (see, for example, Rigby 1969:329–339). Ultimately, one might argue, tense relationships are eased by separation. Before the breaking point, however, open hostilities can reach fever pitch and tensions can clearly mount.

In line with this discussion it is worth noting that accusations may only lead to a temporary rupture in social relations. Even old people who are driven out as witches are sometimes reintegrated into the community. An old Ndembu woman who had been banished as a witch, for instance, was actually encouraged to rejoin the community at a later date. When her daughter and granddaughter returned from abroad, she was seen as a desirable addition to the entourage of a man trying to become village headman (Turner 1957:152–153). Among the Lele during the early 1950s, villages that adopted the Kabenga-Benga antiwitchcraft cult readmitted accused witches who had been exiled. It was thought that once initiated into the cult, these men would die if they used their witchcraft powers again. One old diviner had been chased out of his village and forced to live in the forest because no other village would have him. He was allowed back several years later, when his village adopted the Kabenga-Benga cult (Douglas 1963b).[16]

Whether old witches who return home—among the Lele or elsewhere—will live happily ever after is unclear. The returnees may be reformed and their social situation altered after exile so that they live peacefully with their neighbors and kin. But it is also possible that suspicions will arise again, perhaps because they are forced by circumstances to return to behavior patterns (such as begging for food) that generate resentment.

So far in this book I have largely ignored the question of how social change affects inequalities and relations between old and young. This is not because I consider it unimportant. Until now, however, my objective has been to analyze the structure of age inequalities and age relations. In the next chapter I single out the processes of change for intensive analysis.

7
Social Change:
Age Inequality,
Tensions, and Conflict

Inequalities between old and young, and the strains that characterize their relations, are not fixed or static. They can undergo significant change. Certainly, nonindustrial societies have experienced dramatic changes in the past hundred years or so. New technologies, new economic arrangements, new governmental institutions, and new secular and religious ideologies have come on the scene. These changes have often had a profound effect on the status of the old and the quality of relations with younger people.

The impact of change on the status of the old is, however, not as simple as much of the anthropology and aging literature would lead us to believe. The picture that emerges from these writings shows the elderly in the changing nonindustrial world steadily losing their privileges and influence as younger people continue to gain. In these times of change, the young question traditional values and the authority of elders. The generation gap widens, and tensions between old and young increase.

Available evidence raises questions about this pessimistic prognosis. Social changes of the past century have not inevitably eroded old people's power and prestige. Nor have they inevitably worsened relations between old and young.

The view that the overall status of the aged deteriorates as urbanization and industrialization proceed is associated with the modernization model. This model looms large in the literature, implicitly or explicitly guiding much of what has been written about changing age relations in nonindustrial societies. It has limitations for the study of aging, however, and I will take a little time to explain the criticisms historians in particular have leveled against it. I then turn to the ethnographic data. By exploring case material from ethnographic accounts we can begin to appreciate the complex ways that change has affected inequalities and relations between old and young in nonindustrial societies.

The Modernization Model

Much like "conventional wisdom," the modernization model sees "traditional" society as a better place for the old than the modern Western world. According to one extreme variant of the model, modernization ushered in a decline and fall from a previous golden age for the old:

In all historical societies before the Industrial Revolution, almost without exception, the aging enjoyed a favorable position. Their economic security and their social status were assured by their role and place in the extended family. The extended family was often an economic unit of production, frequently a household unit, and always a cohesive unit of social relations and of reciprocal services between the generations. But the balance of prerogatives of property, power, and decision making belonged to the aging. This Golden Age of living for older persons was disturbed and undermined by the Industrial Revolution. . . . Urbanization not only weakened family relations and undermined the extended family as an economic unit but also made it more difficult for children to support their needy aged parents. More and more, the parents lost the economic independence guaranteed by ownership of a farm or shop. (Burgess, in Fischer 1978:238)

Ernest Burgess was, of course, talking about the process of modernization in Western societies. In anthropology and aging circles—where the primary concern is with non-Western societies—Cowgill and Holmes (1972) are well-known proponents of the modernization model. In their collection of essays on aging in various cultures, they propose that modernization inevitably weakens the prestige, influence, and power of the old. In a revision of the model, Cowgill (1974) specifies how urbanization, the spread of literacy and mass education, and the introduction of scientific and health technology undermine old people's status. The elderly, the argument goes, were respected for their experience and expertise in premodern societies, where they controlled property and played important roles in the extended family. Their situation, however, is thought to be much worse in the modern world. The aged not only multiply in numbers. They are relegated to less prestigious jobs, or are forced to retire altogether, while the young are better equipped with the knowledge for newer, specialized, and more lucrative jobs. No longer is there a mystique of age or a reverence for the old on the basis of their superior knowledge and wisdom. Indeed, old people's wisdom becomes obsolete.

Introducing another series of articles on old age in non-Western cultures, Robert J. Smith sets forth a similarly pessimistic view. "In societies at present undergoing rapid changes associated with industrialization," he writes, "the alienation of the young from older generations is greatly increased" (1961:84). In many African and Asian societies in this state of change, he goes on, older adults no longer serve as effective role models for the young. Old people's way of life becomes out of date, and the bases of their traditional authority weakens.

Even if they do not directly tackle the question of age and modernization, many ethnographers seem to be guided by the premise that contact with the industrial world is a boon for the young and a bane for the old.

The Historical Critique

It is becoming increasingly clear, however, that the modernization model oversimplifies and distorts changes in age relations in nonindustrial societies.

While gerontological anthropologists have been relatively silent on the subject of the limitations of the modernization model, historians of aging have been much more vocal. Indeed, the central question in most historical writings on old age is the validity of this model (Fischer 1978:268).[1] Lately, historians of aging have marshaled considerable evidence from our own preindustrial past to show how limited the modernization model is.

Of course, historians do not agree on all the particulars. They differ, for example, on the extent to which the aged were respected in early modern England and America and on the timing of, and reasons for, changes in the position of the elderly through the years. Yet certain common themes emerge in historians' general criticisms of the modernization model.

Take the matter of causation. The modernization model assumes that specific social and political changes, including the declining status of the old, followed on the heels of industrialization. Recent historical research indicates, however, that certain changes in the status of the old and in age relations associated with modernization cannot be attributed to industrialization. Laslett shows, for instance, that although England began to industrialize in the eighteenth century, extensive changes in the proportion of the aged in the population did not occur until a century or more later (1977:175). According to Fischer, the dramatic undermining of the authority of age in America came before urbanization, industrialization, and mass education had any effect (1978:102, 231).[2]

Quite apart from matters of causation, historians of aging have criticized the modernization model's before-and-after approach: the notion of a uniformly better "before" for the aged in traditional times, followed by a worse "after" in modern days. The model fits what Laslett calls the "world we have lost syndrome," or the tendency to hold up today's problems against the backdrop of an idealized past (1976:91). According to Laslett, "existent informal dogmatic theory" assumes that "before" the aged were respected, held useful and valued roles, and found a secure place in the family; "after," they have been brutally deprived (1976:89–91). Historical evidence shows, however, that such a view romanticizes the past.

The situation of the elderly in preindustrial Europe and America, it is noted, was no paradise on earth. In Achenbaum and Stearns' words, it "mixed official respect, some real power, considerable economic and physical degradation, and cultural derision, and therefore almost inevitably improved in some respects as it deteriorated in others with the onset of modernization" (1978:309).

Nor can we assume, as the modernization model implies, that the position of old people in preindustrial Western societies was uniform. Their condition varied not only among these societies (Laslett 1976:113–115) but within them—according to class, sex, and racial group, for example (Fischer 1978).

There are also many continuities between past and present. Laslett suggests that, much like today, the aged in preindustrial England may have preferred to live apart from their children (1977:212–213). And we cannot confidently say that the elderly were better provided for in preindustrial England than they are now. We need not suppose, Laslett says, that in the traditional era "deliberate provision was made for the physical, emotional or economic needs of aged persons, aged relations or aged parents in a way which was in any sense superior to the provisions now being made by the children, the relatives and the friends of aged persons in our own day, not to speak of the elaborate machinery of an anxiously protective welfare state" (1977:177). Across the Atlantic, Fischer points out that ambivalent attitudes and conduct to the old have characterized every period of American history (1978:230).

Of course, there have been many changes in the past few centuries, and many of these changes have led to declines in old people's authority and prestige. But to view shifts in old people's situation as a "fall from grace or manifest destiny from a remote point" is, Achenbaum says, risky and naive (1978:166–167). The history of growing old in America, he notes, has been filled with "too many surprises, ironies, and exceptions" to say that changes in old people's situation were ever unidirectional, uniform, or inevitable. Fischer observes that it is impossible to say that the condition of the aged in America became worse—or better—with the passage of time. "It became better in some ways," he says, "and worse in others" (1978:230).

Far from steadily deteriorating, old people's situation has, in the past few decades, improved in many ways—the modernization model running in reverse, as Fischer puts it (1978:267). Several American historians have shown that some time after the eighteenth century old people's prestige and influence did decline. But since the 1930s there have been unmistakable improvements in old people's situation. Although serious difficulties still beset the elderly in this country, increased government health and welfare measures (including the wider availability and size of retirement benefits) have provided crucial services for and improved the condition of the elderly in many ways (see Achenbaum 1978:143–157).

Non-Western Societies

Historians of aging point out the need to look at the modernization model with a critical eye. They have shown that the model does not accurately describe changes in age relations that occurred as Western societies industrialized. What about changes in the non-Western nonindustrial world?

In evaluating the model's relevance for studying old age in non-Western societies, I adopt a narrower focus than that of historians of aging, who range over such diverse topics as the care the aged received in the family, old people's longevity and health, the political and economic influence of the old, and general cultural attitudes toward the aged. The concern here is with the status of the old, that is, with the share of social benefits and rewards that the old obtain through access to various social roles. Is the modernization model right to predict that the status of the old will inevitably decline as nonindustrial societies come under the influence of, and are increasingly incorporated into, the industrial world? And to imply that relations with the young also worsen?

The answer to both questions, I argue, is no—not because such declines never happen, but because they are not *inevitable*.

Taking a cue from historians of aging, the rest of the chapter will show why a simple before-and-after approach will not do. The status of the old does not invariably deteriorate in changing nonindustrial societies. Indeed, in some places old people's status has been strengthened or reinforced in various ways as their societies came under the influence of industrial nations. Where anthropologists have charted changes in the status of the old over the years, a bumpy up-and-down path is often revealed, with the authority or prestige of the old improving at one point in time, for example, but declining at a later stage.

As for the quality of relations with the young, here, too, the scenario is not always bleak. Age-related tensions and conflicts often increase, to be sure, when the status of the old changes. But in some cases such change has actually eased strained relations and reduced the likelihood of open conflict between old and young.

If the rest of the chapter shows why the modernization model, as it presently stands, has serious weaknesses, it may be surprising that I avoid using the term "modernization." In the first place, there is no general agreement as to what exactly modernization is. But if the term is imprecise, a more serious problem is its cultural bias. Modernization too often implies that non-Western societies will replicate social developments that took place in Western industrial countries. This, I believe, is an erroneous assumption. It is true that various structural changes in the economy, polity, and society— such as the spread of mass education and mass communications, the growth of urban centers, and the development of bureaucratic organizations—have followed as nonindustrial societies have come into contact with Western industrial powers. But we cannot assume that non-Western nonindustrial societies will imitate Western patterns of change, or that various changes commonly associated with modernization will sweep through nonindustrial societies with uniform effect. The external influences that triggered changes in these societies have not occurred in uniform sequences, forms, and combinations. And the way external influences have affected the relative status of old and young depends on the particular structural arrangements and cultural beliefs and values in each setting.

Rather than use the term "modernization," I prefer to discuss specific types of changes that have occurred in the nonindustrial world. Unless otherwise noted, the chapter considers changes that have, in the past hundred years or so, affected, and continue to affect, nonindustrial societies. These changes include the imposition of colonial rule; integration into a world economic system with such attendant changes as the introduction of wage employment, manufactured goods, and cash crops; the introduction of new religions, especially Christianity; the emergence of newly independent national governments; and the spread of Western education. While the analysis draws mainly on material from the non-Western world, a few examples are from nonindustrial sectors of Western societies.

Another point concerning the ethnographic data must be noted. In previous chapters, the structural inequalities, tensions, and conflicts analyzed were present at the time of the anthropologist's study or, when mentioned (and in a minority of cases), at some earlier period described by the author. In this chapter, the material on change is drawn from several sources: historical data gathered by the anthropologist; follow-up studies by the same ethnographer or other researchers; and the anthropologist's speculations or inferences about the past.

With the expectation, then, that changes of the past century have had complex and even unforeseen consequences for age inequalities and age relations in nonindustrial societies, let us turn to the ethnographic evidence. What follows is not an exhaustive list of every possibility and permutation. Instead, it offers a broad framework within which some of the wide-ranging consequences of change are considered. We begin with the way changes of the past century have affected the relative status of old and young in nonindustrial societies—first to the detriment and then to the advantage of the elderly.

Social Losses for the Old

Although the modernization model overemphasizes the bleak fate of the old, it is not always wide of the mark. Reports on many nonindustrial societies indicate that the old often suffer social losses as a result of change. Of course, ethnographic accounts are influenced by the anthropologist's theoretical orientations and expectations and so may highlight some consequences of change to the neglect of others. Still, ample evidence shows that in many societies the imposition of colonial rule, the introduction of wage labor and Christianity, and other related changes have undermined old people's position in a variety of ways.[3]

On a general level, several analytically separate but empirically connected processes account for declines in old people's status. The way rewards and valued roles are allocated among age strata may change so that the old hold fewer of them. Roles the old fill that were once highly valued may no longer bring as much esteem, influence, or wealth. These roles can even disappear altogether. And new roles may emerge in which younger folks predominate.

Old people's power may also decrease as sanctions that back up the system of age inequality lose force. And the legitimacy of old people's prestige and power may come under fire. The right of the aged to hold valued roles—and the worth of the qualities they possess—may be seriously questioned.

Valued Roles and Rewards

Let us first take a look at how colonial domination and integration into an industrial economic order have changed the way rewards and valued roles are allocated among age strata.

Material Rewards and New Economic Roles. In the past, old men often had the edge in controlling material resources. The advent of wage labor and a money economy, however, has reduced old people's economic dominance in many societies as younger folks have greater access to a wider variety of relatively lucrative economic roles than before.

In many countries, young men typically spend much of their working life in towns, mines, or plantations, sometimes leaving for months or several years at a time.[4] However long they are gone and whatever their particular jobs, young wage workers sometimes supply a crucial, even major, part of their family's income at home. Older people may depend on young men to provide money for such new needs as consumer goods, house-building materials, agricultural tools, school fees, and clothing (see, for example, Jackson 1977:20; R. LeVine 1965:81; Press and McKool 1972:300; Schapera 1971:242, 245).

Whether or not young men's cash contributions to older men's households represent a reversal of traditional[5] age-related roles is not always clear, however. Before wage labor, young men's productive labor in the fields or pastures, though not a contribution in the form of money wages, was often the backbone of the domestic economy. An important question, then, is to what extent older men now, as in the past, control the fruits of young men's labor. Can young men retain the money they earn and decide how it is used? How does this pattern differ from their economic dependence on senior men before wage labor came on the scene?[6]

More research is clearly needed before we have full answers to these questions. We do know that young men in a number of places kept all, or part, of their savings, even when they were supposed to hand over the money to senior kin. The very form of money, Fortes suggests for the Tallensi, enabled young men to hold back their savings: money, unlike cows or sheep, could easily be hidden (1949:208). In Etal, a Micronesian atoll, young men became bolder over the years. While they used to hand over their wages to clan chiefs, parents, or in-laws, in the 1960s, when Nason lived among them, young men often insisted that their earnings were their own (1981:170).

Reports for numerous societies also indicate that the ability to earn and save wages liberated young men from at least some dependence on older men—and thus lessened older men's dominance in a number of ways. In Arab villages in Israel, for instance, wage work enabled young men to leave their father's extended family and establish independence from him much sooner than was possible in the old days of the purely agrarian economy (Rosenfeld 1968:735; see also Adams 1972:125, on a rural Mexican village). Sometimes, older men's benefits from, or influence over, marriage transactions were affected. Opportunities to earn cash through wage jobs were beginning, in the 1970s, to free young Kpelle men from the need to indebt themselves to older men to obtain wives. Many wage earners did not have to rely on fathers for bridewealth payments. Even brideservice could be avoided by giving money to in-laws (Bledsoe 1980:118–120). Among the Chimbu of New Guinea, to take an example from a different part of the world, young men had more say in choosing their brides now that they earned money while away at work and made important contributions to their marriage payments (Brown 1978:160).

In the case of the Giriama of Kenya, young men's access to new wage-earning opportunities played a role in reducing older men's control over crucial productive resources. Even more important, the whole switch to a cash crop economy was undermining the economic position of Giriama older men. The key players were elders, senior men at least over fifty, and a small group of enterprising farmers under fifty. Influential elders were slowly bankrupting themselves while younger enterprising farmers were becoming increasingly wealthy. This trend presages a major transformation in Giriama society, Parkin argues (1972:100–101). In the 1960s, when Parkin conducted his study, age was already less likely to be correlated with economic success than in the past. In the long run, Parkin predicts that the capitalistic spirit threatens to destroy the Giriama ideal that age is the prerequisite of authority.

Since World War II, a new kind of economy, based on the external marketing of copra (prepared from coconuts), has taken hold in Giriama society. As new ways to accumulate and use capital became institutionalized, at least some younger men had much greater scope than before.

One source of capital these younger men drew on to expand their economic operations was wages earned in the boom period of the 1950s. Another was money from the sale of export crops. A third source was cash from the bridewealth received from the marriages of female dependents. (In the post–World War II period, bridewealth could be paid in cash.) Typically, these successful younger men had been eldest sons, able to strike out on their own—and to buy land and coconut palms (the main productive resources) independently—because their fathers or guardians had died.

Not only were the sources of capital new, so were the uses to which it was put. In the old redistributional economy, wealth—in cattle or palm wine—was more restricted due to technological factors. And it was used to obtain supporters—to acquire wives and thus more children and affines. In recent times, wealthy men have used their money to buy land and palms and have thus gained "absolute and permanent rights in a larger proportion of the most important economic assets" (Parkin 1972:55). Why, to complete the picture, were so many elders willing to sell land and palms to younger men? With involvement in an international economy, funeral and bridewealth expenses skyrocketed. To meet these customary expenses, so crucial to elders' status, they had to sell palms and land.

In his study of the Giriama, Parkin talks about the "scramble for land and palms" (1972:13), a scramble in which elders were on the losing end. In peasant communities in nations that have undergone significant industrialization, however, there is often no longer such a scramble. Old people still hold on to land, but its value has declined. This is the case in rural western Ireland, where opportunities off the farm or out of the rural community are now more profitable and desirable and old people's control of land is no longer a linchpin of their authority.

Irish country life in the 1930s as described by Arensberg and Kimball (1968) is, in many ways, unrecognizable today. Gone are the days of the dominance of old men and elderly parents, the days of the match and the dowry (Kane 1979:142–143). Jobs off the land are more prestigious and better paid. Far from envying the heir to the farm, the one who stays at home to take over the farm and care for his old parents, usually the youngest son, is to be pitied. The lucky ones leave (Scheper-Hughes 1979). Meanwhile, the father, according to Scheper-Hughes, is a broken figure, divested of authority and without wealth or education: "At best . . . humanely tolerated; at worst . . . openly ridiculed by his wife and children" (1979:216).

Many of the examples mentioned so far have shown how the old lose economic authority as new ways of acquiring wealth—that are not under their control—open up. While most young people in nonindustrial societies head for unskilled jobs that demand little, if any, training, a minority move into positions that require new technical skills and knowledge. These educated young people usually surpass the old in income and prestige and become economically independent of seniors.

In the early days of contact with industrial powers, the young were usually the first to receive formal education. Continued technological and scientific advances mean that the young, who are the most recently educated, often still have the most up-to-date knowledge. Thus, some young people in nonindustrial societies have been able to enter prestigious and remunerative jobs in the new economic order such as teaching and clerical work, jobs that are beyond the reach of the old.

Political and Judicial Roles. Educational training has also often given the young the opportunity to fill new political roles. As a result of formal education, the young have frequently had the linguistic, writing, and other new skills that equipped them to be intermediaries in dealings with government and other officials.

A good illustration of how the elderly were superseded in this way is provided by the Asmat hunters and gatherers of New Guinea (Van Arsdale 1981). New skills qualified younger men for new political positions as the highly valued roles old men once filled faded in importance.

As recently as 1950, old Asmat men who were local influentials *(tesmaypits)* arranged raiding, rituals, trade, and the periodic relocation of villages. With the imposition of Indonesian rule, the suppression of headhunting and related rituals, and the establishment of relatively permanent coastal villages, former *tesmaypits* became relatively powerless old men in their communities. Their ritual, political, and headhunting skills, once a source of power and glory, were meaningless in the new situation. It was men under forty, who read, wrote, and spoke Indonesian who were now chosen for local government offices.

In advanced agricultural societies as well, new leaders with new kinds of skills may take over, leaving old men behind. In a rural Irish community in the 1960s and 1970s, for example, cooperatives and unofficial community development groups were replacing parish councils as commercial investment and government-assisted programs for local areas became more important. The "traditional" political skills of the clergy and older generations of men were seen as out of date. Young activists, young professionals, and hired community development specialists with new skills were prominent in community development (Kane 1979:161).

Old men in some societies also find themselves out of the running for new judicial roles. Once able to dominate local decision-making bodies and informal courts on the basis of such factors as seniority, economic control, and ritual expertise, old men frequently have less say in the judicial process under colonial and new national governments. They may still run local councils and informal courts, but positions in new national courts are often beyond their reach. Where education and such characteristics as ethnicity or nationality are now the criteria for becoming judges and lawyers in national courts, old men's sway over the wheels of justice is considerably reduced.

As for important older female leaders, there have been cases where their powers were eroded with colonial domination because colonial administrators recognized only male officials. The powers of Ashanti Queen Mothers, for instance, were reduced—and not even officially recognized by the colonial government—when the British took over (Rattray 1923:81–85).

It may also happen that old men and women leaders are less sought after for informal advice and judgment because their experience and wisdom are viewed as irrelevant and outdated. Nukunya writes, for example, that individuals among the Anlo Ewe of Ghana sometimes bypassed old lineage heads, seeking out the educated young for advice and settling disputes (1969:170).

Ritual Roles and Domestic Authority. Old people's ritual dominance may be seriously threatened as new religions come onto the scene. Among the Asmat, younger men were in the forefront of new religions, leaders in Christian church services as well as in cargo cults. Elsewhere, too, new religions have given young people greater opportunity for leadership roles than they had before. Indeed, the ritual powers of the elderly are often less valued as new faiths take hold.

Although age and seniority may still put the elderly in command of domestic groups, fewer rewards may go with this position. I already mentioned how young men's wage-earning abilities could alter the generational balance of power within domestic groups, and the rural Irish example showed old men's authority over sons in extreme decline. Senior kin may also find their power to choose spouses for their dependents restricted with the spread of new ideals—ideals that are backed up by decisions of national courts and legislatures. For example, as early as the 1930s courts refused to recognize marriage contracts that Nyakyusa fathers made for prepubescent daughters, thus supporting young women's right to reject men to whom they were betrothed when younger. The Tanzania marriage law of 1971 went even further. It allowed girls of eighteen to marry without parental consent and required the free consent of both partners to the marriage (Wilson 1977:112, 193–194). Just how this law will affect marriage arrangements is an open question. Among the Nyakyusa, as elsewhere, parents' approval may still be solicited by young couples before they tie the knot. What is clear, however, is that in many societies younger folks have more say in their own marriages.

Greater freedom of marriage choice can also restrict older men's search for their own spouses. In many societies, men typically married women much younger—sometimes over twenty years—than themselves. These younger wives frequently cared for their very old husbands. As women become freer to pick their mates, they are usually reluctant to marry much older men, and few are prepared to accept offers from old men (see, for example, Colson and Scudder 1981:135; S. LeVine 1978:89). Thus, in the future, very old men's wives, if alive, are more likely to be old.

Sanctions

The power of the elderly in the household as well as in the wider community is also diminished when the sanctions at their command lose force.

Where traditional religious beliefs disappear or decline, mystical sanctions the old once wielded are often less effective—perhaps no longer thought to operate at all. Older people's threats, moreover, may be relatively empty, if young folks can easily pack up and leave home.[7] In many societies, young men have long been able to escape parental control by such means as pioneering new land, joining kin in other communities, or attaching themselves as clients to wealthy men. Yet the imposition of colonial rule usually increased young people's opportunities to flee from their elders' authority. Modern transportation facilities have made long-distance travel easier; the abolition of intertribal warfare and the introduction of national courts have facilitated movement, even to areas where the young have no kin or supporters; and new cities and towns have provided a place where the young can avoid the domination of seniors.[8]

Opportunities for wage employment (or the sale of cash crops) also frequently reduce the effectiveness of senior kin's sanctions. Old men's threats to withhold land, bridewealth, or their consent to marriage are less powerful if the young can use their savings to obtain land or furnish their own bridewealth.[9]

Other sanctions backing up the power of the old also sometimes lose strength. The imposition of new national courts can make it harder for older men to punish the disobedient young. In fact, new courts of appeal have at times provided young men with a sanction at their command, a new way to gain leverage in relations with seniors. In the past, Hamer says, Sidamo elders[10] in Ethiopia settled and mediated disputes (1970:68). In recent years, young men used, or threatened to use, new government courts as a way to win concessions in land settlement cases. Among the Anang Ibibio of Nigeria, "unscrupulous youths," according to Messenger, used British-introduced courts to obtain land rights (1959:298). By going to a district officer known to equate occupancy with possession, young men managed to circumvent traditional pledging customs and to obtain land they had received on pledge and had worked for a time.

Finally, the monopoly of the legitimate use of force by colonial or newly independent governments can put a crimp in old people's style, limiting their ability to punish young offenders.

Legitimacy

The fact that old people have fewer privileges and powers undermines the very legitimacy of their authority. Other changes, too, lead the young to question the right of the old to command respect and to exert influence.

Even where the old still have considerable political and

economic power, new values and ideas often raise doubts about their right to wield it. These new ideas may give legitimacy to, and sometimes actually spur, younger folks' challenges to the dominance of the old. Not, of course, that the young slavishly obeyed their elders or fully accepted the natural justice of age inequalities in the past. Nor that the young necessarily become openly disobedient or disrespectful to the old. Yet Western ideas promulgated under colonial domination, to say nothing of socialist ideologies of independent countries, have frequently initiated or accelerated younger people's questions about age inequalities. And the slipping away of economic, political, and religious control from the hands of the old gives added force to these questions.

"Subversive" new ideas and values are disseminated in a variety of ways—for example, through schools, the work place, political parties, the mass media, courts, and churches. Seldom do the young hear the message through one source only. Indeed, young men who go off to towns and cities are exposed to new ideas not only at work but through much of what they see and hear all around them. Such exposure to new ideas of dominant political groups in African urban centers, according to several accounts, led many young men to dispute elders' authority openly when they first returned home. During their sojourn in South African towns, young Kgatla men in the 1930s, Schapera says, experienced:

relative freedom of a different culture, in which the domestic sanctions no longer affect them directly, where the laws and taboos of tribal life may be broken with comparative impunity, and where the authority of father and chief is replaced by that of the employer and the policeman. They enter into individual contracts, and secure earnings formerly unknown; they acquire new habits. . . . On their return home they soon become intolerant of the traditional forms of family control. (1971:242)

In New Guinea villages, too, Worsley writes, migrants who returned from plantations and towns in the pre–World War II years were no longer content to play a subordinate role to old men who knew nothing of the "world" (1968:40). Real political power, they now knew, lay with European whites, not with local elders.

Schools as well as wage employment broaden young men's horizons and can undercut the legitimacy of old people's privileged position. As Nyakyusa young men became literate, learned a second language, and became more knowledgeable about the outside world than their fathers, they called into question the age hierarchy and a society organized "for elders" (Wilson 1977:19). Educated young men in many places believe they are wiser in some ways than their elders and therefore deserve more authority.

New Christian churches also sometimes undermine the legitimacy of old people's authority. If the elderly are no longer believed to have ritual powers—or special links to spirits or gods—they lose an important sanction at their command. The aura of ritual authority surrounding them and justifying their actions is also significantly reduced.

The premises of age inequality may come under fire in national courts as well. It is not only that courts sometimes assume many of old people's powers. In many cases, their rulings and the legal principles under which they operate directly challenge old men's right to hold certain powers. The pronouncements of new political leaders may also cast doubt on the legitimacy of old people's dominance.

The Positive Side for the Old

This account of old people's declines is only part of the story. Older people's powers do not invariably wither away as their societies come under the sway of the industrial world. In many places, the elderly continue to fill valued roles and command deference from the young.

Younger people may call into question the principles of age inequality, but their challenges are not always successful. Sometimes the elderly not only weather these criticisms but end up with more influence and prestige than before. The old (or the young, for that matter) are not passive players upon whom social forces act. Far from being conservative uphold-ers of the status quo, the old may react to certain changes in new ways that preserve or fortify their position.

Ritual and Political Dominance

The Arapahoes of the Northern Plains dramatically illus-trate these points. In the past 130 years, their age-set system has disappeared; they have been subjugated by the U.S. gov-ernment and have lost their political autonomy; and they have been settled on reservations. Through it all, the elders (men at least over sixty) have maintained, perhaps even increased, their authority. And this despite many serious challenges to their position.

I cannot do justice here to Loretta Fowler's (1978, 1982a, 1982b) detailed historical analysis of change among the Ara-pahoes, from the 1850s to the 1970s, but some of the broad outlines can be sketched.

Consider first some of the threats elders faced. In the 1860s and 1870s, for example, youths (men aged twenty to forty) ac-tive in Indian wars initiated actions the elders did not con-done. Later, federal officials set out to discredit the elders by encouraging young alumni of government and church schools to act as tribal spokesmen and by prohibiting ceremonies the elders directed. Indeed, young Arapahoes thought that their new skills qualified them for more important roles and that they did not need to apprentice themselves to or appeal to aid from the elders. If this was not enough, tribal religious ceremonies were endangered as many of the knowledgeable elders died—the victim of the hardships of reservation life—and as the rituals became less relevant to the concerns of the Arapahoes. New religious movements that appealed to young men—the Ghost Dance and peyote church—threatened to un-dermine old religious leaders.

The elders stayed on top, however.[11] From the nine-teenth century up till the present, elders (especially ceremo-nial elders who supervised all tribal ceremonies) were the rit-ual authorities of the tribe. They had supernatural power and sanctions at their command—the ability, so it was believed, to inflict harm on those who violated or disregarded their opinions. Theirs was the most respected judgment; their opinion is, and has been, required on most important tribal matters. Those who have opposed the elders, who have not sought their judgment, or who have not deferred to the elders' views have not fared well. These rebels have been unable to muster support and have been discredited in the eyes of the group.

One might think the elders held their own by clinging to traditional ways and opposing the new. Nothing could be further from the truth. Fowler skillfully shows how they championed innovations over the years. In present-day political jargon, they "coopted the young" by permitting adjustments in ritual and political spheres, thereby allaying young people's discontent and solidifying their position.

Rather than allow new cults, like peyote ritual, to compete with the traditional religion, elders accepted participation in them as potentially beneficial, while ensuring that the new religions remained subordinate to the traditional one. In fact, two senior priests in the 1970s regularly participated in native religion as well as peyote ritual and Christian services. Not only were new faiths tolerated, but the old one was altered. In the past, rituals were modified to appease federal agents as well as to accommodate the level of training of surviving old men selected to fill leadership roles. Recently, ceremonial elders have introduced religious innovations that not only further centralized their authority but also gave young people in their twenties and thirties greater scope for ritual leadership.

Elders were also flexible in allowing younger Arapahoes fuller participation in the political life of the tribe. Indeed, they recognized that newly educated young men with experience off the reservation were more acceptable to, and more adept at, communicating with whites. From the 1930s on, educated men in their forties and fifties came to dominate the Business Council, the body that manages tribal funds and officially represents the tribe to the federal government. Although elders have not held many council offices, they were ultimately in control. The legitimacy of council authority, Fowler argues, has been based on tribal elders' ritual validation. Council members are no longer directly chosen by elders, as was true earlier in the century, but they usually consult the elders on important innovations. Council members who are unresponsive or do not show respect to elders have lost their popularity—and their seats. The very fact that ceremonial elders are not directly involved in council matters, Fowler suggests, protects their authority (1978:759–760). They are "above it all," insulated from criticism councilmen face if they are unsuccessful in defending tribal interests.

That young "upstarts" do not stand a chance is clear from an incident at a General Council meeting in the 1970s. Young Arapahoes in their twenties, involved in the American Indian Movement (AIM), opposed the tribe's official position on a particular issue and attacked the elders' past strategies in dealings with whites. The ceremonial elders—and the old generally—took umbrage. "Why was I not consulted by my younger relative before he announced to the people that he stood for closing the reservation?" one old man asked as he lambasted the young for not deferring to the tribal elders. "And you [he pointed to a second speaker], can you speak your language? Why don't you answer me?" In fact, this young man did not understand the formal oratorical Arapahoe the older man used. Old women laughed, and the AIM leaders left the meeting, most staying out of sight for several weeks (Fowler 1982a:283).

Two more examples, this time from Africa, show that subjugation by a foreign power was not necessarily old leaders' undoing. Colonial rule, in these cases, actually extended or expanded the power of influential old men.

Consider elderly chiefs among the Nyakyusa of Tanzania. During the middle colonial period, when Monica Wilson (1951, 1977) first lived among them, in the 1930s, chiefs were able to stay in office much longer than had been possible before the British came onto the scene.

In precolonial days, a chief retired and handed over power to his two senior sons at the "coming out" ceremony (usually held when the chief's eldest sons were in their thirties). The new chiefs' rule was fully consolidated when the old chief died, usually soon after the "coming out" ceremony. Indeed, an ailing old chief was smothered by his headmen, for a healthy chief was believed essential to the country's prosperity and the fertility of women, fields, and cattle.

With British conquest, elderly chiefs held on to power long after their sons had "come out." They continued to receive salaries (introduced by the British in the 1920s), and their authority was backed by the colonial police force and army. And it was no longer possible to get rid of an old chief by smothering him. Thus, Mwaipopo, over seventy in 1934, should according to precolonial custom have been retired since his heir had "come out" in the 1920s. Said one informant: "Had Mwaipopo lived in the old days and his heir been alive he would have been buried during his last illness" (Wilson 1959:63). Yet Mwaipopo was still thriving—maintained in office by the British government and drawing his salary as chief, exercising power, and marrying young wives.

Among the Afikpo Igbo of Nigeria it was not a question of a few old men's ability to cling to office after their time had come. Rather the powers of elders (men in this age-set society who were roughly over fifty-five) generally increased under British rule.

Before the British came onto the scene, the elders' political powers were circumscribed by the *amadi*, or Aro patrilineages. This had probably been going on for several hundred years, ever since people from Aro Chuku, a village-group south of Afikpo, had moved into and come to dominate Afikpo society (Ottenberg 1971:23–30). *Amadi* not only controlled shrines but also trade, including the slave trade, and major judicial affairs. The *amadi* held top leadership roles regardless of age and "apparently took part in decisions of village elders and had some veto power over them" (Ottenberg 1971:26).

With British control of Afikpo in the early twentieth century, a new order was ushered in. No longer did the *amadi* dominate trade, and their political influence faded. The British distrusted the *amadi* and refused to give them a dominant place in new councils and courts, and the *amadi* lost their fight to try serious legal cases. The British, Ottenberg (1971:310) says, expanded the contribution of elders as generalized leaders and encouraged the development of a "consensus-oriented gerontocracy" that, despite some recent limitations, was still going strong in the 1950s.

Economic Control

Land. If colonial rule was not necessarily old men's undoing in political affairs, so, too, their economic authority could still be strong. In many societies, old men's control of land has ensured—perhaps, in some places, increased—their economic dominance.[12]

Such is the case in many African farming societies, where the situation, simply put, is this: For most young people, new occupational opportunities have not led to their economic deliverance. Meanwhile, land is a crucial resource, and it is in the hands of older men.

What has happened in these societies is that land has become more and more valued and more and more scarce. This scarcity stems from several changes, including dramatic population increases in past decades (themselves a product of improved medical services). Also, more land has been put into cultivation because cash crops are profitable. Indeed, new techniques permit an individual to work larger areas than before.

Land is valued not only because it is in short supply. It provides basic food staples for household consumption as well as for hospitality. And it yields cash crops, something that is particularly important where nonagricultural income sources are limited and cash needs have increased. In societies where government social welfare benefits are few or nonexistent, land is also a chief source of social security. No wonder that so many young people want their own land. And that old men are in an advantageous position where seniority or age gives them control over it.

Young men's wage-earning power rarely balances the scales. Wage-earning opportunities, to be sure, can, as I discussed earlier, reduce young men's dependence on senior kin. But much depends on wage levels and job availability. Only the lucky, well-trained few get skilled or nonmanual jobs. Too often, available jobs for most young people are unskilled and low paid. Sometimes, it is hard to get wage work at all. Even if young men earn enough to get married and set up a household, older men's control of land often puts a stumbling block in their way to full independence.

Not only are young people's cash savings often small, but their earnings may have limited buying power. Bridewealth inflation can consign young men to bachelorhood for longer than they reckoned. When land is in short supply, it is expensive and difficult to purchase or lease. Indeed, older men may be more reluctant to hand over or sell land to younger men when they can use it for cash crops—and when these crops bring in a good income.[13] Given landholding customs, young people are not always able to buy land independently. In fact, land sales are disapproved altogether in some places (see Gulliver 1961:17, on the Nyakyusa).[14]

Quite apart from the increased value and scarcity of land under older men's control, there is the possibility that older men will have more extensive rights over land than before. This is what happened in Kangra district, northern India, as a result of new legislation introduced after independence. Before independence, sons had the unconditional right to inherit their father's ancestral estate at his death. A 1948 law, however, decreed that fathers were absolute owners of the estate and could dispose of it as they wished. The law thus bolstered a man's authority over his sons—he could now deprive disloyal sons of their share of the ancestral estate—and increased the likelihood that sons would remain in the father's household, in a subordinate position, until he died (Parry 1979:169–171).

Old-Age Pensions. An entirely new benefit has improved the economic position of the old in some societies: old-age pensions. Although pensions are probably a long time coming for most people in the developing world, in some societies, where they are available to the bulk of the population, they have improved or fortified old people's economic position.

Admittedly, the introduction of pensions by national governments can be double-edged. On the negative side, the old are sometimes pressured into ceding property ownership to qualify for government benefits. Old-age pensions, one County Clare woman said, hurried the old into giving up the land, and Irish farmers usually did have to transfer their farms to meet pension requirements (Arensberg and Kimball 1968:120–121). Old Navaho men were persuaded by government agents to transfer livestock to their heirs to qualify for old-age benefits. Although pension payments increased the family income, the old lost managerial authority and prestige in the process. All too often they "were seen as nothing more than an added source of income" (Levy 1967:235).

On the positive side, the introduction of pensions in several North American groups was a blessing to the old (see Goodwin 1942 on the Apache; Hughes 1961 on the St. Lawrence Eskimos; and Williams 1980 on nonreservation Indians in Oklahoma). Old-age assistance, Hughes says for the St. Lawrence Eskimos, gave the old a new value to both themselves and their household mates: "In an economy which is tenuously hanging on the edge of the cash money system of the mainland, such monthly checks make it additionally profitable to be old in this society" (1961:95).

In poor communities where cash is hard to come by, old-age pensioners provide a steady source of income for their households, sometimes even becoming the mainstay of the domestic economy. This can be a a definite improvement, particularly for the disabled old. Thus, before the advent of pensions among the Western Apache, the very old were poor and economically dependent on the young. When Goodwin lived among them in the 1930s, however, the tables had turned

(1942:517). Old people who received monthly army pensions were often the wealthiest members of their families, and younger relatives came to them for money. The very frail old also usually received better care. Younger people, Goodwin says, had an interest in keeping old relatives alive: when they died, the pensions ceased.

Religious and Ethnic Revival Movements

I have already discussed how the lack of jobs for young people—or the low status and poor pay of available jobs—could bolster the economic position of the land-controlling old. Young people's inability to make it in the new economic order may benefit the old in another way. One response of the disaffected young, frustrated by their attempts to gain new economic rewards and frequently stigmatized for their ethnicity, is to become interested in and proud of traditional beliefs and customs as a way to affirm their dignity. Old people may become esteemed for their roles as ritual experts and sources of information about indigenous ways.

An excellent example of this process is provided by Pamela Amoss' (1978, 1981) study of the Coast Salish Indians of Washington State and British Columbia. Renewed interest in Indian culture in the past two decades once again elevated the old to valued positions.

Contact with the white world was initially devastating for the Coast Salish aged. In precontact times, the old, by Amoss' account, were on top: they made real economic contributions to the group, held all leadership roles except in warfare, and were sources of important practical and ritual information. After contact with whites in the nineteenth century, old people lost ground. With the shift from hunting and gathering to wage labor, old people's knowledge became less relevant and their practical skills outdated. New jobs such as logging, which required great physical strength, were beyond their reach. Religious leadership passed to younger men, and old people's supernatural powers were challenged.[15]

So far this sounds like the portrait of the old "in decline" described earlier in the chapter. Yet by the 1970s, old people's status had vastly improved as a result of the revival of interest in indigenous customs. This revival stemmed from the frustrations the Coast Salish experienced in recent decades.

Since World War II, it has been hard for the Coast Salish to get jobs, and most have received some kind of welfare payments. Brought up in a culture that stressed self-reliance and autonomy, they felt that accepting welfare was demeaning. Indeed, it left them with a sense of powerlessness (Amoss 1978:163). In the 1940s and 1950s, many sought solace in various forms of Christianity. Christian churches, however, did not offer the opportunity to feel dignity as Indians, particularly as some ministers attacked Indian belief systems. "Disappointed in revivalistic Christianity," Amoss writes, "these people were ready for something that would offer them a renewed self-esteem as individual Indians" (1978:163).

Traditional religious ceremonies were the answer. Although a number participated in Christian churches as well as revived traditional-type spirit dancing rituals, it was the latter that gave the Coast Salish a sense of self-esteem as Indians. These traditional rituals emphasized their solidarity with earlier generations as well as with present-day Coast Salish Indians. They also offered people a chance to validate their worth as individuals and Indians in a setting from which whites were excluded (Amoss 1978:163).[16]

Old men and women became the focus of Indian identity in this new revivalism. Younger folks wanted to feel proud of their traditional culture, and it was the elderly who claimed and were believed to have preserved traditions from the past.

Old people's role was most central in aboriginal-style spirit dancing rituals.[17] At these ceremonies, held in winter, most of the initiated were young. The old (and some middle-aged persons) ran the show, managing the initiation process, which was the only way to gain full participation in the winter dancing ceremonial system. Many of the elderly actively promoted the revival of Indian religious ceremonies among the young. Some even went so far as to have younger relatives initiated without the young people's prior consent.

The old were well qualified to be prominent initiators.

They were believed to have stronger spiritual power than younger people, and they were sought as advisors and participants in winter dancing ceremonials because they knew the ropes. During the 1940s and 1950s, old-style rituals were on the way out and rarely performed in most communities. The elderly alone remembered when and how they were practiced—how speeches should be made, for example, or the family regalia displayed.[18] In their speeches at these ceremonies as well as other public occasions, the elderly reminded their listeners to respect them and to heed their advice.

How widespread the Coast Salish experience is, or will be, is an open question. We do know that ethnic revival movements need not focus on religion to give the old a prominent place. Linda Cool (1980), for example, describes how young Corsicans in Paris sought to explore and reinterpret their ethnic heritage. They avidly listened to old people's tales, soaking up information about traditional customs on the island. Revering old relatives who actually lived the traditional way of life in Corsica and listening to their teachings was, she argues, a way the young emphasized their ethnic identity. Cool goes further, suggesting that the case of Corsicans in Paris has general applicability. She proposes that ethnic movements that glorify "traditional" culture will inevitably celebrate the old:

Whenever an ethnic group depends for its special identity on a traditional heritage separate from that of the larger sociocultural context, its consciousness of belonging demands respect for the old as individuals who actively lived or were chronologically nearer that different life to which the membership collectively aspires. The old always represent proximity to that mythical time of ethnic purity before the contamination by the larger society and its values. (1980:167–168)

There is reason to doubt the universality of this claim, however, if only because ethnic revival movements sometimes draw heavily on radical political ideologies, which the old may not support. In these cases, it is possible that such movements will further downgrade the old and that young activists will disparage the old-fashioned (or conservative) political views of the elderly.[19]

Complexities of Change

For analytical purposes, I have so far isolated some ways change affects old people's status for better or worse. Yet this black-and-white view usually oversimplifies reality, a point already apparent from many of the previous examples. We now need to refine our view of the consequences of change for age inequalities.

For one thing, the "status" of the elderly is multidimensional so that we cannot simply say changes lead to improvements or declines in old people's status. Rather, we must specify (as I have done in the preceding pages) which aspects of the "status of the old" we are talking about—which rewards and social roles they lose or gain. With change, all components of old people's status rarely vary in exactly the same way. In other words, old people may lose some rewards and valued roles at the same time that they keep or expand the scope of others.

Second, changes in particular aspects of old people's status—say, their political authority—need not be unidirectional over the years. For example, certain changes in the early period of contact with the industrial world may increase old people's political authority; but with later changes, their political authority may decline (or vice versa).

Ups and Downs Through Time

Regarding up and down shifts through the years, let us look again at two of the societies already mentioned.

The Coast Salish example showed how the elderly recuperated some of their losses as their society continued to change. After contact in the nineteenth century, the old lost their central place in the religious life of the people. The rituals they dominated were either suppressed by missionaries and Indian agents or "abandoned as useless by a progressively demoralized people" (Amoss 1981:235). Meanwhile, young men assumed leadership positions in new faiths. In the past few decades, however, the old have played a leading role in the revived Indian religious ceremonies and once more have become valued for their ritual knowledge.[20]

Alternately, an increase in rewards for the elderly may be followed by later declines. Thus, British rule enabled old Nyakyusa chiefs to hang on to power much longer than was possible before conquest. With Tanzania's independence, however, old chiefs were losing their authority while some young men gained leadership positions in the ruling political party (Wilson 1977:98, 187).

Gains and Losses

If old men can first gain, then lose political authority, it is also true that other aspects of their status can, at the same time, vary independently.

Thus, elderly Nyakyusa chiefs no longer had as much political authority in the 1960s as they did in the 1930s. But old men's economic power in the 1960s was as, if not more, solid than it had been thirty years before due to their control of land and reduced wage-earning opportunities for young men.

Take another familiar case. Giriama elders in the 1960s were, as a group, losing economic ground in the community as many sold palms and land to enterprising younger men. Yet elders were still believed to have superior ritual powers, and they were still sought out as the most important witnesses and mediators. In the absence of government registration of land and trees, elders were called in to serve as witnesses in cases involving claims to land and palms. Government courts and local moots regarded these old men as experts on customary law. Notable local elders, in fact, ran the local moots, which were a common place for litigation. As original settlers in their neighborhood, elders could testify on the history of various claims. An added seal of legitimacy to their status as witnesses was their recognition as ritual experts. Younger successful men who were outstripping elders in wealth and who were seeking to expand their holdings thus found they had to depend on elders to prove ownership or rights in land and trees.[21]

I could go on with more examples, but the point, I think, is clear. Old people can lose some and win some, all at the same time. The next question is, How do these gains and losses affect relations with the young?

Tensions and Conflicts

Just as changes of the past century in nonindustrial societies have not inevitably led to the decline and fall of the old, so, too, they have not inevitably exacerbated tensions and conflicts between old and young. Intergenerational relations are often more difficult, but not always. Starting out with the negative side of the picture, let us first explore how changes in nonindustrial societies have increased strains and clashes between old and young before examining how these changes have offered some relief.

Tensions and Conflicts on the Rise

It is possible to identify several often intertwined ways that social change in nonindustrial societies in the past century has increased tensions and conflicts between young and old. Change, for one thing, can lead to or accentuate value differences between them as the young are exposed to, and internalize, values very different from those held by the old. Such value differences can create tensions or spark open conflicts. The young, in addition, may be encouraged to come out from under by new outside forces. And mechanisms for reducing conflict or strain may disappear or become less effective.

New events and circumstances can also lead to changes in the system of age inequality. These changes, in turn, are likely to affect relations between age strata—often for the worse. The shifting distribution of rewards and valued roles among age strata can intensify or create strains. When the ideological underpinnings of the age stratification system come under fire, relations between age strata are frequently more difficult.

New Values, New Questions. In many societies, differences in values and aspirations between old and young have become more pronounced in the last century. Clashes over beliefs and values, including over who is judged to have the right to control resources and make decisions, have thus frequently increased in number and intensity.

Before extensive contact with industrial powers, seniors usually socialized the young in dominant cultural values without much competition from socializing agents with a different message. More recently, older people have faced stiff competition from authority figures—in churches and schools, for example—who espouse and try to inculcate the young with new values and ideas. It is not unusual for young people who accept these new standards to be intolerant of customary practices and beliefs that their elders support. That young people not only accept new ideas and values but have greater political, educational, and occupational opportunities than before can feed into, accentuate, or even spark intergenerational cleavages. The young may openly question the legitimacy of older people's continued dominance and become bolder in protesting their subordinate role.

A number of studies note the difficulty young wage earners have in settling down to a subordinate position at home after tasting freedom from paternal control and exposure to new ideals of equality in urban areas (for example, Schapera 1971:80). Young rebels, of course, often turn into respectable citizens and staunch upholders of customary ways when they become older. While they are still juniors, however, they suffer numerous disabilities at home when senior male kin control important resources, exercise jural authority in the homestead, and demand respect and obedience. Armed with new ideas about the social order, and sometimes considerable savings, some young men assert their independence and even openly challenge their elders' dominance. The often hostile response of older men aggravates strains and escalates conflicts.

Many young Gusii wage earners, for example, openly defied their fathers' authority, a situation that Robert LeVine says represents a new challenge to paternal dominance (1964:81). Rather than wait for their fathers' permission, they simply appropriated some of the marriage cattle brought in for their sisters. Older men did not react to such disobedience passively. Many were furious at this threat to their control and marshaled the support of outside authorities. Some fathers in the 1950s reported their sons to the police as thieves for taking cattle in this way. Several even burned down their sons' houses.

New Support for the Young. That young people increasingly challenge their elders' authority is sometimes compounded by other new developments. Open conflict between dominant old and subordinate younger men tends to be more likely, and more serious, when the young are spurred on and supported by representatives of dominant political and religious groups. Such support may be particularly strong or effective in certain historical periods.

In the 1920s, on the Northern Plains, disgruntled Arapahoe young men were encouraged by the Indian agent (a federal appointee). The agent expanded aid to young men who wanted to farm and raise livestock, thereby hoping to bolster young men's confidence and diminish the elders' authority. Although young men were unable to generate significant support for their (and the agent's) programs, tensions between young and old mounted at this time. More recently, in the 1970s, young members of the American Indian Movement (AIM) have challenged—again unsuccessfully—elders' dominance. Young AIM members were certainly not backed by a representative of the federal government, but ideological and moral support from the AIM in other tribes probably strengthened their confidence and perhaps even played a role in initiating their challenges.

The Tiriki of Kenya offer a good example of how young

men were encouraged to defy tribal elders by new, outside authorities (Sangree 1966). Undoubtedly there were tensions between elders[22] and young men in this age-set society before the British government or Christian missionaries came onto the scene. But in the 1920s, young Christian converts were brazen in their defiance of the elders because they had new and powerful sources of support.

What happened in the late 1920s? With missionary encouragement, a group of a half dozen or more young adult male Christian converts openly challenged traditional customs and the elders' authority by confessing initiation secrets at a meeting of the Friends church in front of the uninitiated. If this was not bad enough for the elders, the young "criminals" were backed by Chief Amiani, the tribal chief who had been appointed by the British in 1924 and who was himself a Christian convert. To the horror of the elders, the chief went along with, indeed furthered, the subversion of traditional initiation customs. He ordered the cutting down of all the circumcision groves. He also joined other Christians in supporting open circumcision ceremonies as well as a reduction in the seclusion period.

The elders were indignant at what was happening. The chief's actions were an insult and threat to their dominance. The traditional initiation ceremonies so important to maintaining their power were being disrupted, and who knew what the chief might do next. The initiation elders held a meeting where they named and cursed those who had revealed the secrets. But the accursed did not repent. Unlike the past, the young men now had powerful allies and were thus more independent of the elders. They had the backing of the tribal chief, whom the British assisted and supported. The missionaries provided them with moral and medical aid. And the young men also received support from converts in other tribes.

The District Commissioner's intervention saved the day for the elders. His compromise solution protected the traditional ceremonies. While he decreed that Christians should be circumcised at the mission hospital or in a shortened African ceremony in the open, he also declared that African or

British Christians had no right to interfere in traditional initiation ceremonies, which could continue according to traditional secret customs.

In the years that followed, the elders shored up their position as leaders of the traditional initiation ceremonies. Whether or not the chief found the elders' obstructions to his duties a problem or feared their sorcery powers, the fact is that in 1930 he paid them a substantial sum to perform a reconciliation ceremony to withdraw the curses uttered against him. He did not tamper with initiation customs again. A new chief, appointed in the 1940s, was sympathetic to the elders and took an outspoken stand against abolition of the traditional initiation rites.

New Distribution of Rewards and Resources. Changes in the way social rewards and valued roles are distributed among old and young can also aggravate strains between them, as I already noted in talking about young people's challenges to the dominant old.

Consider the problems that can arise when the old are on the losing end as a result of change. On the one hand, they resent their losses and often take out this resentment on their young usurpers. On the other hand, old people's continued demands for deference or other privileges can meet with resistance from the young, who are eager to assert their new status.

Relations between the incapacitated aged and their young caretakers can also deteriorate when changes make it more difficult for the elderly to get the kind of support they feel they deserve. The trouble is that many of the old have increased "needs" for cash or consumption items, and the young cannot, or will not, oblige them.

Whatever the needs of the dependent old, the young may find it harder than before to satisfy them. In the new money economy, the young themselves have rising needs for such things as clothing, household goods, school fees, and transportation. Given their limited resources, they have little to spare for dependent elderly relatives. Tensions between the generations may thus increase: supporting the old becomes a more onerous burden; and the old resent not having their own needs met (compare Wilson 1977:98).

Tensions can also mount when young people are the ones to suffer—when, as a result of change, they find old people's dominance more constraining and social rewards harder to obtain. That these problems actually do arise is borne out by several studies of African societies, which found that tensions between fathers and sons increased in the post–World War II period as land became scarcer and more difficult for young men to acquire (see, for example, Gulliver 1961; La Fontaine 1967:257; Shack 1966:117).

The Nyakyusa case is particularly illuminating in this regard. Detailed material for the period between the early 1930s and late 1960s shows how young men's increased land hunger, as well as their desire for marriage cattle, aggravated strains with fathers in this society (Gulliver 1961; Wilson 1977).

In the 1930s, the key conflict between fathers and sons turned on cattle with which to marry. At this time, most young men obtained marriage cattle by combining wage earnings with help from their fathers or older brothers. Although burgeoning opportunities for migrant work and rising wages over the next two decades made it easier for young men to acquire cattle on their own, by the mid-1960s the quest for marriage cattle had become extremely difficult. The rising price of cattle far outpaced wage increases, and job opportunities were scarce now that changing political relationships cut off the possibility of migrant labor in South African mines. To make things worse, fathers were less able to help their sons with marriage cattle as pastures continued to shrink (because of the demand for land for cash crops) and as consumption needs for their own households increased. Thus, Wilson relates how inflation of marriage costs and reduced job opportunities exacerbated conflict between the generations to the extent that one son in the late 1960s threatened patricide because his marriage had been so long delayed (1977:89).

As for land, in the 1930s it was still plentiful and not an issue. Although the best land (in old craters) passed from father to son, young men gained rights to other land by virtue of their membership in an age village. In the 1930s, the "coming out" ceremony still heralded the legal establishment of age villages in most chiefdoms and signaled the redistribution of land. After this ceremony, older men (from forty to seventy) moved aside to make room for their sons and provided adequate land for young men's villages. And within the age village, land was readily available.

Easy access to land did not last long, however. With the near doubling of the Nyakyusa population between 1931 and 1967 and the rapid growth of cash crop farming, land scarcity became a basic feature of life; and it was older men who possessed most of the land. By the 1960s, old men were not moving aside for their sons, and young men were unable legally to establish age villages on their own land. Young men, in addition, were stymied in the quest for land by the fact that land sales were disapproved and purchase was almost impossible. Young men had no alternative but to depend on their fathers for land.[23] Indeed, inheritance became the most common way to acquire land (Gulliver 1961:17). Already in the 1950s, Gulliver (quoted in Wilson 1977:96) reported that most men under thirty in high density regions had little or no arable land and could not hope to attain it until their fathers died.

Fathers and sons thus now competed for land as well as cattle.[24] While older men would have liked to keep all their land under their own control and for their own use, they did make concessions. They gave their adult sons shares in the produce of land. In return, a father expected his sons to work the fields, under his direction (Gulliver 1961:19). Not surprisingly, young men were dissatisfied with this arrangement, especially since the traditional emphasis on their independence was still strong. Sons complained that their fathers expected too much work and subordination and gave them only small shares of food and cash crops. For their part, fathers grumbled that sons did not work hard enough and got more shares than they deserved. Even the growing practice of fathers allocating a strip of land to sons at marriage did not satisfy younger men's demands for land. Land-hungry young men sought unskilled jobs elsewhere, although these, too, were very hard to come by in the mid-1960s. In any case, young men did not want to live away permanently (Gulliver 1961:18). Other than leaving Nyakyusa country, many had little choice but to live in their father's village, unable to come fully into their own until he died.[25]

Conflict-Reducing Factors Lose Effectiveness. The Nyakyusa example suggests another reason why change can heighen strains between old and young and increase the likelihood of open conflicts. Arrangements for physically separating age strata can change. Doubtless one factor responsible for greater strains between Nyakyusa fathers and sons in the 1960s was that, unlike in the past, sons often lived in the same village as, and under the direct authority of, their fathers.

Sometimes other mechanisms that reduce tensions and conflict between old and young cease to operate or become less effective. Sanctions that keep the young in line, for example, can lose force. Recall the Tiriki case, where the curses of elders in the 1920s did not intimidate young rebels who had the British colonial government, missionaries, and converts in other tribes behind them.

In many societies, important outlets for young men's aggression have disappeared. In Africa, intertribal warfare was abolished by colonial governments, and the same was true for Native American groups in this country after pacification by the federal government. The route to prestige as brave and bold warriors was thus cut off for young men. No longer could they release pent-up hostility or resentment they felt toward elders in battles with enemy groups.

Thus, in many societies the kind of tensions observed between old and young men in the colonial or postindependence era may well have been less problematic in precolonial times, when warfare engaged much of young men's energies. So Spencer argues for the Samburu (1965:149). At the time of his study—and in the period I discussed in earlier chapters— warfare was a thing of the past. Before the British took over, he suggests, the thorough involvement of the moran in war-

rior activities "overshadowed any frustrations they experienced at the hands of the elders and even provided an outlet
for their resentment." The moran were occasionally involved
in "spasmodic raids" in the colonial period. But the absence
of warfare meant that their "antagonistic attitudes were no
longer diverted away from the society . . . and they developed into a delinquent faction within it. With no institutionalized outlet for their animosity, they had, in effect, turned
from warriors into angry young men" (Spencer 1965:149).

Reduction of Tensions and Conflicts

Changes in nonindustrial societies over the past hundred
years or so have not always had such adverse consequences
for intergenerational relations. At times, these changes have
eased strains between old and young and made open conflict
less likely.[26]

The reduction of these tensions and conflicts can come
about in a number of ways. For one thing, there are cases where
the elderly lose power over the young. Initially this change
can aggravate strains with the young. But in the long run, relations with the young may be more relaxed precisely because the young do not find old people's domination so oppressive or constraining.

This last outcome is what David Hackett Fischer suggests
occurred in our own society over the past few centuries
(1978:154–156). In colonial New England, old men controlled land almost until they died so that sons were economically dependent on their fathers long after attaining physical
maturity. Sons were expected to show respect to powerful and
privileged fathers. Affection was not encouraged, and emotional distance marked intergenerational relations. By the
nineteenth century, however, older men's formal powers were
much reduced. As fathers became less authoritarian, relations
with sons became more affectionate.

Another example suggests that something similar may
have happened in postrevolutionary Chinese villages with respect to mother-in-law–daughter-in-law relations. Admittedly, this relationship remained a "conflict-prone dyad," ac-

cording to Parish and Whyte (1978). Mothers-in-law still frequently complained that daughters-in-law lacked respect, and daughters-in-law resented the older women's nagging. But young women were in a stronger position than before the revolution because older women had lost some of their power. Whether conflicts between older women and daughters-in-law of long standing were less serious than in prerevolutionary times is unclear. The transition of new brides into their husband's—and mother-in-law's—home, however, became smoother.

Collectivized agriculture had much to do with making older women's domination less oppressive and younger women's incorporation into their new households less difficult. Because older people controlled less property than in the past, they could not use it as a means to dominate the younger couple as easily as before. At the same time, younger women's role in the fields was increased with collectivization. Most women under forty-five now worked regularly in the fields and made major contributions to the family income. Older women with grandchildren or, in any case, women over fifty-five had, by contrast, usually retired from active field labor. Since the household economy depended on younger women being productive and contented workers, they stood to be treated better than previously by their mothers-in-law. Further, with younger women in the fields and older women at home, the two spent less time with each other. Then, too, since more women now married men from the same village, or even the same patrilineage, they had close kin nearby to keep an eye on how they were treated (Parish and Whyte 1978:216–217; 243–244).

Relations with the young can also become less tension-filled when old people improve their status as a result of change. The introduction of old-age pensions can have this effect by making the frail old less of a burden than they used to be. In fact, younger people may depend on old-age pensioners for money and therefore try to avoid alienating and becoming involved in serious conflict with them (see chapter 4 on County Clare, Ireland).

Change can also lead to the emergence of new ways of reducing conflict between old and young. Potential or actual combatants who lived and worked at close quarters in the past now, in some cases, are physically apart most of the time. Chinese mothers-in-law and daughters-in-law, we just saw, were separated for much of the day. In Arab villages in Israel in the 1960s, young married wage-earning men split off from the parental household much earlier than they had ten or fifteen years before, putting distance not only between themselves and their fathers but between their wives and their mothers. Daughters-in-law were thus liberated much sooner from their mother-in-law's day-to-day control, and the likelihood of open conflict between the two women was reduced (Rosenfeld 1968:746).

Opportunities to move even further away, through emigration, have increased in most societies in the past hundred years. Colonial rule and independence usually made travel less difficult and opened up new ways to escape the authority of, and avoid open conflict with, seniors such as in jobs in the army, mines, and urban areas.

New bonds, too, between old and young serve to mitigate sharp conflicts. Where migration to towns or mines has gone on for a long time, young and old frequently share a comraderie based on their common work experiences. Young men among the Gwembe Tonga in the 1950s often followed their seniors to the same work places and sometimes to the same employers (Colson and Scudder 1981:134). (By the 1970s, as jobs became more diversified and the search for work took individuals to more places, this pattern was changing.) It is also possible that old men, having been through the experience themselves, will be more tolerant of young men's desire to go off to work and young men's behavior on return.

Where young people participate in ethnic revival movements, ties with the old can be strengthened. Shared understandings based on a common interest in their ethnic identity have been known to develop between old and young. The young look up to the old for their wisdom and experience; in turn, the elderly become more sympathetic to the grievances and opinions of the young (see Cool 1980:167–168).

Cleavages between old and young, moreover, are sometimes submerged, if only temporarily, in their united opposition to a new, outside enemy or to policies administered by external agencies. Often on opposite sides of political issues, Afikpo Igbo elders and "progressive young men" allied in 1960 to protest the unfair treatment of their village-group in the newly formed District Council and to support a movement for greater autonomy for northern Igbo village-groups (Ottenberg 1971:285). New class loyalties, too, can take precedence over age divisions. When nonindustrial societies become incorporated into nation-states with class systems, class differences begin to interact with and may, at times, become more important than age inequalities at the local level. It is possible that occasions will arise when individuals in the same class, whatever their age, will be in sympathy on particular issues and unite to press their demands.

Opposition to foreign powers, domestic political groups, or national elites can also dissipate hostility that might otherwise be directed against neighbors or kin. In the 1950s, the Arusha vented much of their anger at the acute land shortage onto whites and the colonial government that they said had taken much of their land. "In this social and emotional climate," Gulliver writes, "brother excuses brother, and neighbor is tolerant of neighbor, for both are believed to be similar victims of unscrupulous and powerful outsiders" (1961:24). In many societies after independence, political battle lines at the national level have coincided with ethnic divisions. In these cases, individuals of all ages in local communities frequently blame other ethnic groups for many of their troubles and join in common cause against these ethnic groups on certain political issues.

Finally, in societies where government agencies have assumed significant social welfare responsibilities, younger people still saddled with burdensome duties to aged relatives may direct their resentment against the government bureaucracy for not doing enough for the old rather than against the old people themselves. Thus, in this way, the advent of the welfare state or socialist governments can reduce tensions and conflicts between the frail old and younger caretakers in nonindustrial sectors of industrial, or industrializing, nations.

Conclusion:
Internal and External Forces of Change

The foregoing account has made clear that social changes of the past hundred years or so have not been an irresistible force, relentlessly undercutting the powers and privileges of the old in nonindustrial societies. Nor is there an inevitability about the way these changes have affected the quality of relations between old and young. The status of the old, I have shown, has sometimes improved in certain ways with change. Rather than deteriorate, relations between young and old in some cases have become more relaxed and less conflict-ridden.

Implicit in this analysis has been the notion that the direction and form of change in particular societies are products of *both* external and internal pressures. This point bears some elaboration.

In terms of external forces of change, this chapter has focused on cases where contact with the industrial world, usually in the form of colonial rule, was what initially stimulated change. Obviously, the nature of colonial rule—including administrative programs and policies as well as on-the-spot decisions by colonial officers in reaction to crises—differed from place to place. But if external forces of change were not uniform, neither was the internal makeup of each society. The social structure and cultural beliefs and values in each society clearly affected the way people responded to external events, rulers, and institutions. Indeed, structural and cultural factors peculiar to each society could, in themselves, exert pressure for change.

The central point here is that the age stratification system itself, including inequalities and tensions among age strata, often influenced what happened in the wake of outside pressures for change. Many examples cited in this chapter showed how individuals' location in the age stratification system shaped their reactions to external pressures and trends. Although I am not suggesting that people act purely to further their interests, it is true, nonetheless, that members of advantaged or disadvantaged age strata often "seize the day," responding to new opportunities, values, and allies so as to maintain or improve their powers and privileges. Those on top of the age hierarchy want to safeguard their position, while subordinate age strata often want a larger share of the social goods of their society.

Sometimes, as we saw, the elderly championed customary ways that ensured their dominance and privileges. Tiriki elders, for example, struggled to preserve traditional initiation ceremonies so important to their status. And in many African societies, older men asserted their customary right to paternal authority in the face of defiant wage-earning sons.

In other cases, the old, as well as younger people, supported and actively promoted changes—the introduction of Christianity, for instance, or the revival of traditional rituals—that enabled them to hold on to or expand their influence and prestige. They sometimes even introduced innovations for this purpose. Thus, I discussed how the disadvantaged young in many societies heralded and tried to institutionalize new values and customs that gave them greater scope than before, such as keeping their wage earnings for themselves or selecting their own spouses. In their attempt to institute changes, young people often found themselves directly challenging their elders. As for the old, several examples indicated that they were receptive to changes that propped up or improved their position. Indeed, old people sometimes encouraged and sponsored changes that were to their benefit. Coast Salish elders, to mention one case, promoted the revival of Indian religious ceremonies in which they had a dominant place. And Arapahoe elders brought in religious innovations that strengthened their authority.

Coast Salish and Arapahoe elders were successful innovators. Whether or not efforts to bolster the traditional order or bring about changes are successful elsewhere obviously depends on a wide variety of factors. What is significant is that such attempts are made and that they can affect the status of the old as well as relations with the young.

These comments, like the rest of the analysis in this chapter, have concentrated on changes of the past century. But I do not want to give the impression that nonindustrial societies were static before that time. The question of how the status of old and young—and their relations with each other—shifted before contact with the industrial world is one of the topics I shall consider in the concluding chapter.

8
Conclusion: Inequality Between Old and Young in Nonindustrial Societies

This book has begun to chart and systematize the anthropological study of age inequality. Just as sociologists have documented the existence of systematic age inequalities in modern industrial societies, so this work shows that they are an important feature of nonindustrial societies as well. Beyond this, the book offers an interpretive framework for understanding the wide array of ethnographic material on age inequalities. The principal figures here, as we have seen, are the old. By focusing on the position the elderly occupy in the entire age hierarchy, this study directs our attention to the quality of relations, and thus the potential for strains, cleavages, and conflicts, with younger people.

In exploring the way age inequalities shape the lives of old people and their relations with the young, this book has covered a lot of ground, ranging over societies from all parts of the world. We have looked at the benefits that come with old age as well as the losses, the bonds between old and young as well as the strains. And while noting structural similarities among various nonindustrial societies, we have also been aware of cultural differences.

This final chapter summarizes the central themes and pulls together generalizations about age inequality presented in the book. It also expands on some issues regarding change as well as on the links between age and other forms of stratification that were mentioned in earlier chapters.

In Review

Inequalities between old and young are built into the very fabric of nonindustrial societies. These inequalities are a systematic product of the way rewards and roles are allocated in each society. And they have important consequences for social life.

In many nonindustrial societies, the active and alert old are at the top of the age hierarchy. Because of their age, they have the chance to obtain, or compete for, the social rewards and valued roles their society has to offer. These rewards and roles run the gamut from having many wives and large families, controlling material resources, and exerting power over family and community members to having ritual authority and being recognized and respected for wisdom and experience. Age inequalities exist because younger adults do not have the same opportunities to reap such benefits. They must wait their turn.

But for some old people, their turn has already come—and gone. They are worse off in many ways than younger people. Even in societies where the elderly occupy a privileged place in the age hierarchy, those old people who become physically or mentally incapacitated suffer social losses. Whatever their formal powers over the young, they tend to become increasingly marginal in everyday affairs, and younger adults take on more and more responsibility. By the time advanced debility has set in, the elderly are totally dependent on younger people for care and support, and this, too, is a social loss. Given their position, it is not surprising that the old tend to lose prestige at this stage.

In some places, the old suffer marked social losses even before they are mentally or physically incapacitated. Such is the case in some peasant and age-set societies, for example. Whether or not individuals in these societies begin old age with numerous advantages, at one point in their elderly years, while they are still physically capable and mentally alert, they are obliged officially to give up hard-earned gains—control over the family and economic resources, for example, or political leadership in the community. As the old formally step down from these positions of control, younger adults begin to take over and have greater scope for achievement and independence than before.

Age inequalities found in nonindustrial societies play a role in shaping individuals' hopes and aspirations as well as their perceptions of themselves and others. Like other sorts of inequalities, they are also a breeding ground for conflict. Whether the old are at the peak of the age hierarchy or have experienced serious social losses, strains are likely to develop with the young.

Where the old are powerful and privileged, younger people often have much to complain about. They may not voice their frustrations openly, but inwardly they may be filled with envy and resentment or at least be ambivalent toward old people on top. The young are eager to come into their own, and old people often stand in the way. Indeed, the young are often subject to, and are severely limited by, old people's authority.

Just which relations are particularly subject to strain has a lot to do with structural arrangements that shape patterns of authority, resource allocation, inheritance, and obligation in each society. In some places, there is a general opposition between old and young men in the local community, with young men, as a group, restricted by powerful and privileged elders in what they, the young, can do. This kind of opposition is likely to arise in societies where old men exercise control over and place severe constraints in the way of younger men in the community irrespective of kinship or affinal ties. Age-set membership and age-grade location can provide elders with such power, but community-wide oppositions between old and young men are not confined to age-set societies. How widespread such oppositions are—and whether they also occur between old and young women in some societies—are questions that call for further research.

In many nonindustrial societies, tensions between old and young are most pronounced between particular close kin or affines. Issues of succession often loom large. Additional sources of tension are young people's dependence on senior kin or affines for access to property, wives, or other resources; their obligation to provide these seniors with labor and other services; and their subjection to the old people's jural authority. There is the classic case of strains between fathers and sons in patrilineal societies—and their opposite numbers in matrilineal societies, maternal uncles and sister's sons. Also frequently reported are the difficulties between dominating mothers-in-law and subordinate daughters-in-law in patrilocal extended families. And fathers-in-law and sons-in-law may have tension-filled relations in societies where bridewealth payments or brideservice obligations are heavy and long lasting or where sons-in-law live under their father-in-law's direct authority.

When the tables are turned, and the old are disadvantaged, tensions and friction have different sources. In societies where the elderly officially transfer property or household headship to the younger generation during their lifetimes, they often have trouble accepting their new role and continue to try to run things even though formal control is gone. This can create strains with the young heirs, who want to take over fully. As for the physically incapacitated old, many have a hard time coming to terms with their physical condition and resent the still healthy young—who are also taking over. The frail and feeble aged, in addition, may feel they are not being supported properly, while younger people, on their side, may resent what they believe are exorbitant or unfair demands from the old.

What may aggravate strains between the disadvantaged old and younger people is the inconsistency in the status of the aged. Location in an age stratum, after all, does not necessarily lead to a consistently high or low "age status"—a point, by the way, not explicitly dealt with in writings on the age stratification perspective. Individuals in one age stratum may, on the basis of age, have limited opportunity to acquire some rewards and valued roles while at the same time be in an excellent position to acquire others. For instance, the very old may lose political authority or economic control but rank high on the scale of seniority and have a definite edge in accumulating ritual and practical knowledge. The elderly who still fill some rewarded roles might be particularly unhappy about their losses. While they feel they deserve respect for their experience or seniority, the young, thinking more about old people's social losses, might not agree. Such a situation has the potential for trouble.

Given the grievances of the disadvantaged (young or old), it is hardly surprising that strains sometimes lead to open conflict with those who are making their lives difficult. Disputes and quarrels between old and young are common, and, in fact, in a number of societies witchcraft accusations against particular old people can result. From our perspective, what is harder to understand is why, at least on the surface, relative peace is so often maintained. The stratification approach to age bids us to ask not only about the roots of conflict but also about the sources of accommodation between old and young. In terms of relations with particular relatives and affines, the question is why, despite profound inequality and tensions, open conflict is not more prevalent and, in so many cases, more severe.

There is also the issue of age conflict within the community or society as a whole. Much has been written in the stratification literature on the potential for class consciousness in modern industrial societies—on the likelihood, in other words, that the working class will develop ties to each other, become aware of their common interests, and act together to further these interests (see A. Foner 1979). The question of stratum consciousness among the deprived is also important in the study of age inequality in nonindustrial societies.

The extent to which members of subordinate age strata develop common ideas about their stratum identity and stratum interests is a topic that awaits close and careful ethnographic description. Do the subordinate young or old recognize the existence of age inequalities in their society and their low rank in the age hierarchy? Does a fellow feeling and a conviction that their interests are opposed to those of the privileged age stratum develop among the disadvantaged? Beyond ethnographic description, what structural conditions—residential segregation of young and old, for example—foster the emergence of age stratum consciousness? While these questions have yet to be answered, when it comes to actual behavior, we do know that the underdogs, be they young or old, are unlikely to engage in concerted action to change the age system that puts them at a disadvantage. And we can begin to understand why this is so.

This study suggests that a number of factors reduce the motivation of the less privileged to become involved in serious community-wide *as well as* interpersonal conflict. Considered from the viewpoint of the subordinate young, there is, first of all, the possibility for upward mobility. Since aging is universal and inevitable, the young can anticipate future gains when they grow old. Compensations in the present, such as receiving prestige for some activities, can also blunt young people's dissatisfactions. Moreover, there is the legitimation of inequalities. Young people often believe that the distribution of rewards according to age is justified. Put another way, they may think they deserve what they get because they are so young and inexperienced. To what degree individuals become convinced of the justice or inevitability of the system of age inequality that puts them on the short end of the distribution of rewards is, of course, an empirical question that needs to be explored in each context. The content of legitimizing values as well as the various means by which they are instilled also require more detailed analysis. One function that rituals frequently serve, in fact, is to present symbols of domination in a cogent way and thus to dramatize, reinforce, and validate age inequalities for the participants. In addition to the legitimation of age inequality, close bonds of cooperation draw young people and many of the elderly together in the community. In the family, the young often feel affection for and loyalty toward the very same elders with whom they have strained relations.

Even if the young are seething with anger and are spoiling for a bitter fight, they may think twice before acting in a provocative or aggressive way toward elders. Negative sanctions act as a deterrent in that the young fear that unfortunate and often extremely harsh consequences are apt to follow. Then, too, they may be able to let off steam in "safe" ways, onto other targets. And in many cases they are physically separated from their senior antagonists for much of the time— or required to avoid or behave in a formal manner toward them.

Just which factors come into play varies with the society and the situation. And, we must remember, these factors are not fixed or immutable. Social arrangements that reduce conflict may be altered. Indeed, the very structure of age inequalities and age relations can undergo significant change.

In exploring the dynamic aspects of systems of age inequality in nonindustrial societies, chapter 7 focused on the effects of changes often subsumed under the rubric "modernization." These changes, such as integration into a world economic system, the spread of Western education, and the introduction of industrial technologies, were ushered in by contact with the industrial world in the past hundred years or so. Contrary to the predictions of modernization theory, they were not necessarily detrimental to the old. True, in many nonindustrial societies these changes meant that the old held fewer valued roles and rewards while the young had greater scope than before. But in a number of societies, the old kept, in some instances increased, important powers and privileges. In at least one case, they initially lost, but later regained, certain rewards in response to changes. Indeed, it is likely that finely drawn studies, with considerable time depth, that trace the effect of changes on successive cohorts of the elderly will reveal more such cases.

Similarly, strains and conflicts between old and young did

not inevitably increase as a result of changes of the past century. Of course, intergenerational relations did very often deteriorate. In many places, to mention one pattern, young folks were emboldened by new ideas and allies to challenge the old, and these challenges sometimes sparked bitter conflict. Yet there have been cases where intergenerational relations became less strained and conflict-ridden—in a number of situations, for example, where changes made the elderly less powerful or less of a burden to the young.

What is clear, then, is that contact with industrial nations did not have a uniform or predictable effect on age inequalities and age relations in nonindustrial societies. In trying to understand how contact affected the old as well as other age strata in these societies a variety of factors must be considered. These include the particular external forces of change, such as the nature of colonial rule and subsequent political and economic developments in national centers since independence; the peculiar social, economic, and political conditions as well as cultural beliefs and values in each local setting; and the often unanticipated actions and decisions of individuals in these settings as they responded to, and thereby influenced, the course of change.

It is important to emphasize, too, that age inequalities and conflicts themselves exert pressure for and shape the direction of change (see A. Foner 1982). The way individuals react to various events and changes is, after all, related to their location in a system of age inequality. Those on top of the age hierarchy do not want to give up their privileges, while subordinate age strata often feel they are not getting "theirs" as quickly as they want or need. Thus, old and young people have been instrumental players in the process of change, often jockeying to take advantage of and even actively promoting changes that would improve their influence and prestige while resisting innovations that would hurt their position. Such actions have led, at times, to intergenerational conflicts. In turn, these very conflicts can affect the distribution of social rewards among old and young and thus alter the system of age inequality.

The analysis of age inequalities and age relations closed with an investigation of change, but I only discussed changes of the past hundred years or so. This is because these are the changes we know most about. The study of age inequality and change, however, must have a broader focus. Momentous as the changes were that nonindustrial societies experienced when they came into contact with Western countries, we must remember that nonindustrial societies were not static or changeless before that time—and that more changes are undoubtedly yet to come in the future.

First let us step back into precolonial and precontact times. The major problem, of course, in discerning changes in age inequalities and age relations in this period is that available historical material is sparse. Even though a number of anthropologists and historians have, in recent years, tried to reconstruct the precolonial past in several societies—using such sources as local archives and early published accounts, oral histories, linguistic data, and archeological evidence—they have told us very little about changes in systems of age inequality. It certainly seems likely that such dramatic events as natural disasters, epidemics, or conquest did effect transformations in age systems prior to Western influence (see Riley 1978:45; N. Foner 1984). In fact, there is evidence from some societies that before European domination changes in age systems had already occurred.

Consider the Giriama case. Their age-set system was no longer effective when the British established a protectorate in Kenya in 1895 and began active administration of Giriama in 1912. Earlier, when the Giriama had dispersed from their forest home in the latter half of the nineteenth century, their age-set system—which had generated particular structural tensions between certain old and young men—had broken down. Also, as a result of this general migration some young Giriama had greater economic opportunities than before (Brantley 1979:115; see Brantley 1978 for a discussion of the structure of the Giriama age-set system and the history of its demise). In the New World, among the Blackfeet Indians of the

Northwestern Plains, the disabled old benefited from changes before sustained contact with and subjugation by whites. The introduction of the horse in the early eighteenth century meant that frail old men and women, too feeble to ride alone, were no longer abandoned. Now they could be carried on the A-shaped horse travois (Ewers 1958:106).

Difficult as it is to know just what changes took place in nonindustrial societies before Europeans came to stay, and dominate, the point is that changes did take place at that time, and in some instances they undoubtedly affected the status of the old.

What about the future? After all, in broad historical perspective, colonial rule lasted a relatively short time in most societies, as Monica Wilson points out in the Nyakyusa case, barely seventy years (1977:187). New forms of socialism, to say nothing of other economic and political changes on the horizon, may have just as profound—and unexpected—an effect on old people's situation and on intergenerational relations as the changes of the past century.

Peering into the future is obviously highly speculative. So many factors cannot be predicted. Economic and political events in the national and international arena that we cannot foresee, for example, can affect age inequalities and age relations. So can the unpredictable actions of individuals and groups of individuals in particular localities.

While we cannot foretell exactly how systems of age inequality will change in the years ahead, the predictions of modernization theorists that old people's status will inevitably decline everywhere must be challenged. That is, the erosion of the powers and privileges of the old and the enhancement of younger people's opportunities to fill desired roles and obtain social rewards is only one possible outcome.

For one thing, it is possible that the old will keep many of the rewards they now have. Cultural traditions, we know, often die hard, and age norms are no exception. The idea that age deserves respect may be strongly rooted in some places, especially when seniors are still believed to have moral and mystical power over their descendants (compare Wilson

1977:105). Thus, the old might continue to command deference from younger people.

Even where old people's prestige has already declined markedly, they might recuperate some of their losses with time. One way is familiar. Where ethnic revival movements take hold, the elderly may be revered for their wisdom and experience of customary ways. Another possibility is that the first men to become important leaders when young will try to hold on to power in their old age and so be active, and perhaps successful, agents in trying to maintain or restore some of the rewards of old age. While only too delighted in their younger days to gain political power and supplant their elders, when they advance in years "revolutionaries"might just claim a traditional respect for age (see Wilson 1977:19).

There is also the chance that old men will recover some of their former glory because the privileges of age are so closely linked with the privileges of gender. It may have happened in the past, for example, that changes that reduced old men's status also severely undermined men's position in general. In an attempt to recapture former male prerogatives, men may try to restore a system that gave them a dominant role and that also put senior men on top. This is what Mary Douglas (1963a:269–270) speculates could occur among the Lele. While new cohorts of Lele young men, she says, will enjoy the freedom from gerontocratic restraints made possible by European influence, they may be less happy about their reduced control over women. The new society introduced by missionaries made men more vulnerable to "the vagaries of women." The missionaries protected monogamists, but they could not help a Christian whose wife ran off with another man. The abandoned husband was further humiliated because he could not retaliate or remarry. This experience—or the very real possibility of it happening—might lead men to try to reinstate some of the old institutions that buttressed male dominance and also served the hegemony of the old. "It is conceivable," Douglas writes, "that Lele adherence to deep-rooted ideas about how relations between men and men and between men and women should be conducted may swing them

back into something very like their old society based on seniority and privilege" (1963a:270).

All this talk of old people maintaining or recovering
privileges refers to the still active and capable old. What lies
ahead for the frail elderly who need custodial care? In most
nonindustrial societies, continued dependence on kin for care
and support is a likely prospect.

Chapter 7 indicated that the position of the very old had
improved in several Native American groups where government pensions had been introduced. Indeed, in industrial societies the trend has been for national governments to assume
some of the burden of support through social welfare programs that provide income maintenance and health care to the
aged. Developing nations, however, are unlikely to enact such
extensive government programs. Given the high costs involved, social welfare programs that are instituted in these
countries will probably bypass most of the rural population
for some time to come.

Even in China, where the government has made major efforts to improve rural economic and social conditions, no
general state-funded pension system like that available to urban workers has yet been adopted for rural villagers. Only the
rural elderly without grown sons to care for them are eligible
for old-age support (Parish and Whyte 1978:74–76). If all old
people were supported, said one Chinese authority quoted by
Parish and Whyte, the economy would be in a shambles and
the business of socialist construction hampered. In many other
developing states as well, children will doubtless be the main
support of the frail old well into the future. The kinds of strains
I spoke of in chapter 4 between younger caretakers and the
dependent old will, under these circumstances, probably
continue to arise.

Age Inequality
and Other Forms of Stratification

The focus in this book has been the nature of inequality between old and young—how it is elaborated and sustained and

how it changes in different societies. While I have emphasized age stratification in its own right, age inequalities clearly
do not exist in isolation. They are intricately connected to other
systems of inequality. What are these connections? And just
how important are age inequalities—particularly between old
and young—compared with other types of inequality?

The question of the relative importance of the age hierarchy has come up most recently in the anthropological literature with regard to the comparative weighting of age and
sex distinctions. In trying to make sense of sexual asymmetry
in what they call brideservice societies (where gifts of labor
by the groom to his in-laws are the expected form of marital
legitimization), Collier and Rosaldo conclude that differentiation between senior and junior men is the most publicly sa-
lient form of inequality in these societies (1981:312). Caroline
Bledsoe, in her study of women and marriage in Kpelle society, also writes about the primacy of age inequality (1980:186).
"The distinction between the old and young," she says, "may
ultimately be more important in understanding people's goals
and strategies in many African societies than the distinction
between men and women, even though the latter is the one
to which our attention is most often drawn by anthropologists and natives alike." Speaking specifically about the Kpelle,
she notes that old women may find it in their interests to unite
with old men against "power plays by young upstarts" (Bledsoe 1980:4).

These three anthropologists are unusual in that they focus on sexual inequalities but also recognize the significance
of age inequality. On the whole, the salience of age or sex distinctions in ethnographic accounts depends on the anthropologist's interests, with anthropologists who study women,
for example, highlighting sexual inequality, and anthropologists who study age-set organization concentrating on age inequality. Whether this emphasis reflects the actual importance of age or sex inequality in the society is another matter.

When anthropologists do systematically compare the importance of sex and age inequality in individual societies, they
must specify what is meant by terms like "importance" and
"salience." Is the anthropologist referring to folk beliefs about

whether age or sex inequality is more significant? Or is he or she the one who is making the assessment? And what criteria is the anthropologist using to determine the salience of age or sex inequality? Is it that one type of inequality is more crucial in determining the allocation of highly valued roles and rewards; in shaping individuals' sense of identity; in structuring individual or collective actions; in determining group formation; or in generating strains and conflicts in the society?

Inequality between old and young may turn out to be more significant than sex inequality in numerous societies along many, perhaps all, of the dimensions just mentioned. However that may be, what is clear from ethnographic reports is that age and sex inequalities are linked in many ways.

Age divisions, for one thing, frequently modify or reduce sex inequality. In general, men may be superior to women, but women in many societies, as we saw in chapter 3, look forward to obtaining rewards—often including some of the prerogatives associated with the domain of men—when they grow older. In their old age, women frequently expect support not only from younger women but also from younger kinsmen and sons-in-law. Indeed, they may acquire privileges that are unavailable to younger men, and in certain situations they may outrank the younger men.

Where old and young women have divergent interests, as chapter 3 showed they often do, the likelihood that they will join forces in actions to improve their position as women is reduced. Sharp age cleavages among women may, in fact, prevent them from becoming conscious that they share common concerns as women.

Not only do age inequalities give women the opportunity to improve their lot with age and minimize the chances for all-out struggles between the sexes, but they can also operate to maintain and reinforce sex inequalities. Old women as well as men of various ages often benefit from, and are active agents in perpetuating, the subordination of young women. Old women, for example, have been known to support and even resist changes in such customs as feminine modesty standards and menstrual restrictions that keep young women in an inferior position not only in relation to old women but also in relation to men.

In many polygynous societies, moreover, older men's dominance over younger men depends on sexual asymmetry. That is, older men's control over women is a crucial factor underlying their control over younger men. Earlier chapters showed how older men in many places were the ones who could accumulate many wives and who sometimes even monopolized the right to marry. Rights in wives and subsequently daughters enabled polygynous elders to head large households and command the labor of large numbers of people, to obtain material wealth, and to forge bonds with affines. Meanwhile, younger men were consigned to bachelorhood—because they lacked, and depended on elders for, the wherewithal to marry or because societal rules barred them from marriage until quite late—without wives and households of their own. Maasai moran, like the nearby Samburu moran we spoke so much about, were in this kind of marginal position for many years. Indeed, it is in part because relations with women are so important in the "age hierarchization of men" that Llewelyn-Davies prefers to speak of the Maasai age-set system as the "age/gender organization" (1981:330).

Because the age and sex hierarchies are so closely articulated in many ways, a change in one often has an impact on the other. Where women have greater rights and more power to choose or reject their mates than before, for instance, old men may find their ability to marry young women—or to keep their wives—sorely reduced. Increased freedom for women generally can also undercut the advantaged position of old women. One possibility is that new or expanded wage-earning opportunities for women outside the household will give younger females a greater chance to escape elderly women's domestic authority. Finally, an example from a study done in urban Kano, northern Nigeria, shows how a change in the roles filled by members of one age stratum affected the nature of sexual inequality. Here the age stratum involved was children, not young or old adults. Hausa women in purdah (or seclusion), severely limited in their spatial mobility, were able to pursue independent economic activities because their children performed crucial economic tasks for them outside the household. Western education has brought changing opportunities and roles for children, however. When children attend school, they cannot help their mothers as much as they used to, and this has meant lower incomes for women and a more difficult position within the institution of purdah (Schildkrout 1978:132–133).

In considering the connections between age and sex inequalities, we should not forget that the very structure of the age hierarchy of roles differs for men and women. And while I mentioned that age inequalities among women lessen the probability that women will unite in a "war between the sexes," it is also possible that sex divisions will defuel age antagonisms if women of all ages unite as women against men—or if men band together against women. Also, the sharpness of age antagonisms in a society can be reduced among younger women if they feel sexual inequalities more acutely than those based on age. As for young men, superior position in the sex hierarchy can take some of the sting out of their inferior rank in the age system. Young men, for example, who are subject to the authority of older men may be able to exercise certain rights over young (or younger) women.

These same points are pertinent to the relationship between age and class. The structure of the age hierarchy often varies by class. Economic class differences have long been crucial among peasants in state societies, and they are becoming increasingly important in communities that have recently been drawn into nation-states with class systems. The structure of the age hierarchy often varies by class. Studies of numerous peasant societies show, for example, that it is only well-to-do men who control large amounts of property in their later years. Older men who are poor peasants have little property at their command and are less likely than the better-off to head large extended family units.

As for the question of consciousness of deprivation, individuals in disadvantaged age strata are likely, in some situations, to perceive that their class, rather than their age, interests are the central ones. Strong class interests can thus reduce the salience of age differences to individuals and lessen the possibility of age conflicts. Indeed, people in the same class, whatever their age, may unite to promote their class interests. Landless laborers of all ages, to take one example, may be bound together by similar complaints and actively struggle together against wealthy landlords.

Furthermore, class cleavages may impede solidarity among members of an age stratum, even among age-mates of the same sex. Young men, for instance, may have common grievances over their dependent station in the domestic family but be deeply divided by class cleavages. Well-to-do young men often feel superior to their age peers in the lower class, while poor male youths frequently envy and bitterly resent wealthy young men. Significant as class inequalities are, we should note, too, that other important social inequalities—caste or race, for example—may be linked to age divisions in much the same way and operate like class distinctions in reducing the possibility of age conflicts.

We thus come to the close of our inquiry. Whether inequalities between old and young are viewed on their own or in relation to other forms of stratification, it is clear that these inequalities are crucial in human societies. They affect people's attitudes and their actions; they have an impact on the family and the community; and they can even play a role in furthering or impeding social change.

Because inequalities between old and young impinge on so many areas of cultural and social life, they cannot be ignored. This book has begun to analyze the structure and ramifications of age stratification in different societies. In pointing to the factors that lead to strains and conflicts between old and young, it thus explodes any simple and idyllic myths about the elderly in nonindustrial societies—luxuriating in their power and privilege and living in perfect harmony with juniors, in the secure bosom of the family. Indeed, despite the tremendous variety in cultural and social patterns in different places, this work suggests that tensions may well be inherent in intergenerational relations in all societies. The challenge of the future is to identify the universal features and consequences of age inequality as well as to learn more about how age inequality operates, in all its complexity, in particular and widely diverse cultural and social settings.

Appendix

Some Methodological Issues in the Comparative Study of Witchcraft

A number of questions have been raised about the methodological validity of many witchcraft studies. There have been complaints about the lack of statistics as well as about the absence of extended-case material. Both shortcomings are evident in many studies I relied on in chapter 6. Despite these weaknesses, however, the witchcraft studies I used do illuminate old people's situation and age relations and are thus well worth examining.

Specification and Statistics

First let us begin with the criticisms. The anthropologist most closely connected with the "statistical critique" is Max Marwick. What concerns him is that many anthropologists make general statements about the connection between witchcraft beliefs and social relations on the basis of what he thinks are questionable data. Many witchcraft studies fail to specify the methods of data collection and lack statistical data on large numbers of cases.

Too often, Marwick (1972) complains, anthropologists rely on statements of dogma without also counting up who accuses whom and without investigating the detailed social background to real or believed events in each case. Anthropologists may not even tell us whether they refer to their own or informants' observations of witchcraft accusations. In other words, we may not know if the anthropologists are speaking of folk perceptions of the direction of accusations (stated dogma) or their own observations of actual accusations (aggregated case material). Data drawn from these two sources are not always consistent. Thus Marwick's own field data show that the Cewa said that most witches were women. An analysis of case material, however, reveals that three-fourths of the witches were men (1965:103).

Even when case material is presented, Marwick complains that witchcraft studies may not distinguish between (1) the relationship between the accused and the believed victim (believed attacks of witches) and (2) the relationship between the accuser and the accused (specific instances of witchcraft accusations). Although comparing believed attacks of witches with specific instances of accusations gave a similar picture of social tensions among the Cewa, this, Marwick says, is not always so (1965:283). The relationship between the witch and victim, he claims, points to the estimates people themselves make of the incidence of tensions in their society; the relationship between witch and accuser provides a more objective, external assessment of this incidence (1965:283).

Social Situations

If Marwick is concerned with quantification, Victor Turner also wants to know more about the uncountable. In Turner's (1964) view, witchcraft accusations are the result of a "complex interplay of processes and forces" that are not always elucidated by statistical analysis.

Turner's (1957) Ndembu study dramatically illustrates that recording accusations simply shows who was finally judged responsible for a particular death. It does not indicate all the alternatives canvassed before this point was reached or those occasions when no agreement was obtained (Mair 1969:134). Members of different groups may seek to divert suspicion from themselves onto others, and competing interests lead different groups (and individuals) to choose their suspects. Knowing who was suspected, not just the person eventually accused, may be crucial for understanding tensions in a society.

"The significant point about a given instance of accusation," Turner argues, "is not that it is made by someone against a specific type of relative, but that it is made in a given field-situation." The "total context of social action" must, he says, be studied in considerable time-depth. Among the factors Turner thinks we need to know when analyzing witchcraft accusations are: "the structure of groups and subgroups to which the accuser and accused belong . . . their extant division into transient alliances and factions on the basis of immediate interests, ambitions, moral aspirations . . . the history of these groups, subgroups, alliances and factions . . . demographic data about subgroup and factional fluctuations over the relevant time period" (1964:316).

If a younger person accuses someone older of witchcraft, age status, following Turner's line of argument, may only be "phenotypical." That is to say, the conflict between particular old and young people may have more to do with their allegiance to opposed local factions struggling for authority, for example, or to factions linked to opposed cult groups than with age inequalities.

Assessment

Clearly the data at hand fall short of Marwick's and Turner's prescriptions. This does not mean, however, that they should be ignored.

To reject all witchcraft studies that are not based on the

analysis of a large number of cases would leave us with a small sample indeed. But if the studies I used tend to be weak on numerical data, they do avoid two dangers. Nearly all the studies cited make plain whether a discussion refers to informants' perceptions of the direction of accusations or the anthropologists' observations of accusations. Where numerical data on cases are given, we are told if the cases refer to the relationship between accuser and accused or between accuser and believed victim.

Still, it is true, many accounts described in chapter 6 do not give statistics on cases and rely on witchcraft suspicions or gossip or on cultural images of the witch. Witchcraft suspicions and gossip, which cannot be counted in the same way as accusations, can illuminate the quality of relations between old and young. So can cultural images of the witch. Such images, even when not supplemented by rigorously collected case material, provide insights into structural strains and tensions.

That the Cewa believe women to be witches, even though more men are accused, probably says something about the ambiguities and conflicts that center about women's status in that society. Similarly, where the image of the witch is an old person, this cultural perception, I suggest, reflects ambivalent feelings toward old people generally.

In our society, negative stereotypes about certain categories of people, while not witchcraft stereotypes, do express underlying structural tensions, although they may not be statistically valid representations of reality. If an anthropologist conducting a field study of a middle-class American community were to sum up the native image of the older worker, a picture would probably emerge of generally unproductive workers. Admittedly, there is great variation among older workers. Many old people, often those who are ill and who might be unproductive, are already out of the labor force. Still, most studies show that older workers are as productive as younger workers. In certain respects, they even surpass younger workers—in consistency of performance, for instance (Palmore 1979). Creative productivity is also maintained well into old age. The statistical results of these studies are obviously important. But so is the stereotype. Belief in the stereotype may at least partly reflect strained relations between the generations, stemming from such factors as younger workers' desire to move into the jobs old people hold.

Finally, it should be remembered that statistical methods themselves are not fail-safe. The number of witchcraft accusations collected in a year or two fieldwork period, even given meticulous data gathering, may be not only atypical but small. Marwick managed to accumulate 194 cases of misfortune. (In 101 of these cases, misfortunes were attributed to attacks by witches.) But these 194 cases were only reported by between thirty and forty informants. And generally Marwick had only one person's view of any particular believed attack or accusation (Douglas 1967:74). There are different versions of a believed instance of witchcraft, shaped by the informant's loyalties and social position. Also, as Marwick (1965) is aware, a high frequency of accusations involving those in one type of relationship may be an index of the frequency of interaction as well as the degree of tension in this relationship. There may, for example, be fewer accusations made against dependent old men than dependent old women by younger people simply because there are fewer dependent old men than dependent old women with whom the young interact. And statistics without extended case studies, as Turner points out, may overlook important aspects of accusations.

To limit our analysis to studies that meet Turner's requirements, however, would drastically limit the number of ethnographies available for analysis. In the Lugbara example, Middleton (1960) does use extended case studies to show how struggles for authority are waged in the idiom of witchcraft. But most of the other accounts present few or no extended case histories and rely on synchronic data, and none investigates all the variables Turner feels can be important. Yet as Turner himself shows, individuals' structural position may predispose them to become involved in particular competitive struggles and factions. Old people (or at least some old people) may find themselves in a particular position—and accused or suspected of witchcraft—when the battle lines are drawn.

Admittedly, anthropologists may overlook the role of witchcraft in factional rifts, leaving us to wonder why one old person was accused rather than another. But factional struggles need not be at the root of witchcraft accusations. Moreover, where younger people hold an image of the witch as old or commonly suspect old people of witchcraft, there are bound to be certain strains in relations between old and young. And the structural position of at least certain old people may predispose them to behave in a "witchlike" way. Turner himself observes that the structural position of old Ndembu women makes them likely witchcraft suspects (1957:151–152).

In sum, the data I have had to rely on are far from perfect. Yet the studies I selected provide valuable information on the links between witchcraft and relations between old and young. They thus merit serious attention. Not only do they shed light on the kinds of strains that underly relations between old and young, they also point out one way these strains can be openly expressed.

Notes

1. For a review of the anthropology and aging literature, see Holmes (1976) and Keith (1980).

2. Terray, for one, asserts that classes are found when a dominant minority extorts surplus labor from the direct producers (1975:95). This minority is then able, indirectly or through exchange, to acquire prestige goods, the control of which guarantees its power. Elders, he says, meet these conditions and are therefore a class.

3. Meillassoux briefly touches on the distinction between pubescent and post-menopausal women and calls for research on the different ways they are exploited (1981:76–78). "It is necessary," he writes, "to distinguish different categories of women in terms of the functions they fulfil according to age by which they are not in the same relations of exploitation and subordination" (Meillassoux 1981:78).

4. The age stratification perspective has been developed in a series of books and articles. See Riley, Johnson, and A. Foner (1972); Riley (1971, 1976, 1978); and A. Foner (1974, 1975, 1978, 1979, 1982).

5. There is one exception, a study of tensions surrounding life-course transitions in African age-set societies (A. Foner and Kertzer 1978).

6. Although some anthropologists have objected to the term "stratification," there is agreement that social inequality or ranking based on age is a feature of all societies (for example, Fallers 1973:27).

7. An age stratum is not necessarily a social group. Nor do people in an age stratum usually have "stratum awareness," that is, awareness that they have common interests (see A. Foner 1975, 1979).

8. Unless otherwise specified, in this book the phrases "intergenerational" or "between the generations" refer to cases in which age and generation dovetail—specifically to cases in which those in the senior generation are chronologically old, those in the junior generation chronologically younger. The term "generation" is used here in its genealogical, kinship-related sense to refer to relations between parents and their children, these children and their children, and so on (Kertzer 1982). It is true, however, that seniority by age and generation do not always agree. For one thing, individuals of the same generation may be far apart in age. Where polygynous fathers continue to sire children well into old age, for example, one brother may be in

his teens while another is in his forties. By the same token, individuals of different generations may be close in age. A man and his father's younger brother (his uncle), to mention one possibility, may be the same chronological age. For a discussion of the relationship between age and generation, see Kertzer (1982).

9. Fortes likewise focuses on possibilities of friction that arise out of cleavages inherent in the structure of the family among the Tallensi. At the same time, he is aware that "how long these forces of dissension remain dormant, or how they are handled when they are thrust forward, depends very much on the character of the family head" (1949:79).

1. What Is Old Age?

1. While it is true that a complete understanding of old age as a cultural concept can only be achieved by looking at perceptions and definitions of other life stages as well, this is far too formidable a task to undertake here.

2. The distinction between two categories of old people may not be so new. According to Achenbaum, at least two distinct phases of physiological old age have been recognized throughout American history: "Early Americans once distinguished between a 'green old age' (in which one experienced little, if any, physical restriction in activities) and 'decrepitude' or 'second childhood' (where one's infirmities and debilities precluded working and, in many instances, being able to remain independent)" (1978:3).

3. The "discovery" of a new life stage, according to Hareven, involves several steps (1978:203). Individuals must first become aware of specific characteristics of a given life stage; this discovery is then popularized; the discovery attracts the attention of social control and welfare agencies if it is associated with a major social problem; finally, it is institutionalized when legislation is passed and agencies are created to deal with its special problems.

4. In the nineteenth century, the combination of relatively late marriage, short life expectancy, and high fertility meant that child-rearing tended to be a lifelong job, especially for women (Hareven 1978:205). See also Fischer 1978:56.

5. The same flexibility in defining old age was found in pre-nineteenth-century England. Those who framed and administered the Poor Law, for example, thought of old age in terms of physiological functioning rather than exact chronological age. The authorities considered the aged to be people of advanced years who, due to physical debility, could not support themselves and who also gave the physical appearance of being old (Roebuck 1979:417).

6. There were two major exceptions to this generalization: high-ranking ministers and magistrates who did not even partially retire; and ordinary people who had to retire completely because of incapacitating illness (Demos 1978:275).

7. For example, Peter Stearns, in his study of old age in French history, says that "we have to let aging begin when people think it begins" (1976:16–17). He also notes that definitions varied by individual and by class. Because definitions of old age were so variable, he picked age fifty-five for statistical purposes: "a bit later than some cultural perceptions of aging but anticipating most distinctive behavior . . . associated with biological aging" (1976:16).

8. I will not have much to say about definitions of old men as they differ from or are similar to definitions of old women. The same criteria delineate old age for men and women in many societies. Indeed, Glascock and Feinman (1980) found that, in the societies in their sample, patterns for defining men and women as old were

consistent in that the same criteria (change in social role or chronology, for instance) tended to be used. Many ethnographic accounts, moreover, do not specify whether definitions vary for men and women. Often, only one definition is given, and it is unclear whether it covers old women as well as old men. In this chapter, I indicate those cases where the ethnographer gives different definitions for men and women or specifies whether the definition applies only to members of one sex. Otherwise, I follow the ethnographer's example and speak of old people generally.

9. Glascock and Feinman suggest that, since chronology was found so often as a definition of old age in conjunction with other definitional criteria, the frequent mention of chronology may reflect ethnographer bias, that is, the superimposition of Western modes of definition on native definitions. Whether Glascock and Feinman refer to absolute or approximate chronological age when they use the term "chronology" is unclear.

10. Simmons claims that *all* societies differentiate between the intact old and those in the final stages of physical debility ("the overaged" and "the already dead") (1960:87). Glascock and Feinman's (1980) study, however, does not support this contention. Amoss and Harrell say that it is "nearly universally true" that societies distinguish the physically and mentally able old from the old who are totally dependent and require custodial care and supervision (1981:3).

11. It is not at all clear that changes in physical capabilities are as unimportant in defining old age in their sample societies as Glascock and Feinman (1980) say. They included certain kinds of physical changes under their category "changes in social role." Cases where women were defined as old when they reached menopause were classified as changes in social role. And changes in work patterns—the major type of role change—included cases where people were designated old because they were unable to do work associated with adults of their sex. Glascock and Feinman speculate that one reason changes in physical capabilities (senility, invalid status, and change of physical characteristics such as white hair, alteration in dentition, and deterioration of vision) were rarely benchmarks of old age in their sample societies is that people in these societies tend to be classified as old before they become senile or incapacitated.

12. An anecdote related by Shelton highlights the unimportance of exact chronological age among the Igbo. Shelton tells of a heated argument over a leg of goat with a man five years his junior. The Igbo man insisted that he had the right to first choice because he had more gray hair and was therefore senior to Shelton (1972:33).

13. Middleton uses the phrase "senior in years" (1960:12). I do not know whether the Lugbara calculated age in years when he lived among them.

14. Here, and throughout the section on age-set societies, when I refer to "age" it may be based on social, physical, or chronological criteria.

15. Just what powers men gave up when they "retired" is debated. According to Legesse, a "ruling" generation set had political power. Baxter (1978) insists, however, that only ritual obligations resided in sets. In his view, generation sets did not control anything when they were in office; they did not have power of a directly political kind.

2. Consequences
of Age Inequality: I
Old Men at the Top

1. In many nonindustrial societies, some men in late adulthood, not yet defined as old, may also obtain the rewards and valued roles discussed in this chapter and

also have strained relations with younger men. My concern in this study, however, is with the old.

2. There is some disagreement about how rare old people are in nonindustrial societies. According to Kenneth Weiss, in typical tribal conditions, among hunter-gatherers as well as slash and burn horticulturalists, those over 60 constitute about 3 percent of the population (1981:50, 55–56). (In the United States today, about 11 percent of the population is over 65.) He estimates, too, that in hunter-gatherer societies a person who lived to age 15 had, on average, another 22.5 years of life; in primitive agricultural societies, another 30 years. (By way of contrast, in Sweden in 1965, a 15-year-old girl had another 62.4 years to live.) Indeed, Weiss writes that many bands or villages have few or no individuals over 60, so that those who survive become a rare social asset.

Although the old are rarer in nonindustrial than modern industrial societies, they may not have been so unusual. At least that is what is indicated by demographic data on several societies relatively untouched by modern health developments. Among the Kirghiz pastoralists of Afghanistan, for example, those over 60 represented about 8 percent of the population—in numbers, 148 out of 1,825 (Shahrani 1981:177). Writing about the !Kung hunter-gatherers, Biesele and Howell assert that "old age is and has always been a regular and unremarkable phenomenon" (1981:81–82). Of those who survived to age 14, they estimated that about 60 percent would live to age 45 and about 40 percent to age 60.

Of course, we also need to consider native definitions of old age. The cutoff point of 60 or 65 may bear little relation to the way individuals in particular societies define old age. Indeed, individuals who by our chronological criteria are in their forties and fifties may be considered old so that these people should be included in an analysis of the rarity of old age. Biesele and Howell are aware of this problem (1981:79–80). They make clear that in their demographic analysis "old" refers to those whom they estimated to be over a particular chronological age even though the !Kung did not define old age this way. The suffix meaning "old" was added to the names of people who were no longer bearing or begetting children (in their forties and fifties). And the !Kung had a special term for the extremely old—most of whom, they estimated, were over 70.

3. Whether a man with adult sons will be old depends in part on the age when he began to sire children legitimately and on whether he continued to take younger wives as he aged. In societies where men do not marry until relatively late, they will probably be old by the time their eldest son reaches adulthood and marries. And a man with a young wife (or wives) may continue to father sons well into old age.

4. Where the levirate is the custom, a widow may be taken over by her dead husband's brother or sometimes his son (by one of the dead husband's other wives). The new man, however, is a proxy husband in that the children she bears to him are regarded as the dead man's. In societies with widow inheritance, the widow is also taken over by the dead man's brother or son, but she actually becomes the new man's wife and any children she bears afterward are his.

5. The passage from "young married man" to "old man" was, according to Stirling, vague in Turkish villages and roughly occurred about the age of fifty, when, if economic circumstances allowed, a man no longer did much agricultural labor (1965:223–224).

6. How long a son lived with his father depended on a variety of factors. According to Fortes, a son only desired to go out on his own if he had younger brothers

who would remain at home to work for his father—and there was no motive if he were an only son (1949:206). Sons whose own father had died and who were reared by their father's brother were likely to break away from the parental home much sooner than young men with living natural fathers. Proxy parents assumed the social roles of natural parents, but sons did not feel the same attachment to proxy fathers as they did for real fathers. Sons might resent real or believed injustices toward them by their proxy father, especially as they approached adulthood. Thus, while a man often continued to live and farm with his own father until the latter's death, this rarely happened with a father's brother (Fortes 1949:140).

7. A son's guilt at his father's death might also help explain fears of the powers of dead ancestors. If a younger man felt in some way responsible for his father's death, he might fear retaliation from his dead father. If the son suffered some misfortune, he might well believe it was the doing of his dead father (J. Goody 1962:410).

8. By the same token, in patrilineal societies relations between a man and his mother's brother tend to be easier and more informal than father–son relations.

9. A holder–heir relationship can obtain between mother's brothers and sister's sons in societies with double unilineal descent systems (where descent in the male line is traced for some purposes and in the female line for others). Among the Lo-Dagaba, movable property (money, cattle, and harvested crops)—the property over which divergent interests were most likely to arise—passed from mother's brothers to sister's sons (J. Goody 1969).

10. The term for elders, in the plural, referred to ruling elders of the lineage, men who represented the oldest living generation and who were usually old (Kopytoff 1971a:131; 1965:449). As for the label "classificatory," in systems with classificatory kinship, terms that are applied to lineal relatives—father and son, for example—may also be used for collateral kin. A father's brother, for instance, is called by the same term as father. Here, a man's classificatory mother's brothers were brothers of all women of the lineage in the same generation as his mother.

11. Formal authority in the family rested with in-marrying males, that is, men who were connected only by ties to their wives (a line of women). In fact, a man became a member of his wife's matrilineage for all practical purposes when he married. Inheritance of property followed different rules: the parents' rice fields, orchards, and gardens were divided equally among all their male and female children. See J. Potter 1976 and S. Potter 1977 for a more detailed discussion of family life and kinship patterns in Chiangmai.

12. In cases of formality between grandparents and grandchildren in Apple's study, "the grandchild is submissive, reservedly respectful, not on easy and friendly terms with the grandparents owing to the discipline they exert, and/or must show a high degree of formal esteem to grandparents in comparison with the formal esteem shown to other relatives" (1956:658).

13. Although a specific ceremony marked the transition of an age set to elderhood, not all of the moran married and settled down to elderhood at the same time. Younger men might still prefer to remain as moran for a few more years (Spencer 1965:89–90). See chapter 1 for a discussion of the connection between the wide age span within sets and flexibility in grade transitions.

14. If a moran did not marry until thirty, he would be unlikely to be in a position to join actively in elders' debates until he was forty or to acquire much local influence until he was forty-five or fifty. At this time, he probably would be able to take on a second or even a third wife (Spencer 1970:129–130).

15. Those with a developed sense of respect for elders did not act impulsively, lose their temper, or shirk their duties when faced with unexpected situations. If a young man with a strongly developed sense of respect wanted to water his cattle and found an elder using his waterhole without permission, he simply waited until the elder finished watering his cattle. Or if a young man was hungry and only had a small bit of meat but an elder requested some, he would offer a larger portion to the elder (Spencer 1965:135).

16. Nor did the traditional glamour of warriorhood have significance in an era of relative peace. "With no warfare to divert their energies and endow them with a strategic role," says Spencer, "they have no defined purpose" (1970:131). See chapter 7 on the effect of the abolition of warfare on Samburu age relations.

17. Baxter and Almagor argue that gerontocracy is a recurrent theme in East African age systems because elders control stock, wives, and management decisions: "Sets give open expression, cognitive order and ritual respectability to the velvet-gloved hand of the aged with which they wield their control of productive resources" (1978:19).

18. According to Almagor's classification, the Samburu closely fit the model of an ascriptive gerontocracy (1978b:140). Although some Samburu elders had larger herds and more wives than others, all elders, whatever their individual achievements, had the power to curse and the sole right to marry by virtue of their age set and age grade. The Tiwi were an achieved gerontocracy because individual achievement, through useful alliances and the investment of bestowed daughters, rather than movement in an age group through successive ranks, brought rewards in old age.

19. Successful old men were also ahead in having the longest lists of wives—with perhaps more than twenty wives on their list. A list also included unborn and not yet resident wives who had been promised as well as deceased wives.

3. Consequences of Age Inequality: II Old Women at the Top

1. A notable exception is the recent paper by Judith Brown (1982) on older women in cross-cultural perspective. Brown argues that women past childbearing in nearly all cultures are freed from restrictions and have increased authority over certain kin as well as greater opportunity for achievement and recognition beyond the household. In seeking explanations for these changes, she emphasizes the importance of the bond between mothers and adult children.

2. In many nonindustrial societies, late adulthood, before women are defined as old, may also offer the opportunity to obtain these rewards and also be a time when relations with the young are strained. In this chapter, however, I am concerned with old women.

3. Within the homestead, seniority was based on generational age (within a generation, on birth order) so that a woman was not the senior woman in the homestead as long as her father-in-law had wives, even though these wives could be younger in chronological age than she was.

4. In our own society, we associate widowhood with old age, but this is not the case in societies where women marry men much older than themselves and where polygyny and widow remarriage are the rule. Still, in these as well as other nonindustrial societies old women are often widowed.

5. An old mother's position as "central pillar of her son's domestic establishment" was more honorific than active, according to Fortes (1949:59).

6. Several structural factors explain why Gonja women were likely to spend their last years with their natal kin. The absence of the levirate or any form of widow inheritance meant that if a woman's husband predeceased her she would return to her kin in old age anyway. Women's authority and prestige were greater with her own kin than in their husband's communities. Since women often married several times and since child fostering was common, the home of a woman's natal kin provided a neutral meeting ground where the children of each union visited her and where she could also rear any foster children entrusted to her. Finally, a woman's spiritual well-being was enhanced by living with her own kin since she could approach her ancestors more frequently there and at less personal expense (E. Goody 1973:153–169).

7. I am speaking here of Taiwanese mothers-in-law in their late forties to early sixties. By the time a woman was well into her sixties and seventies (the period Margery Wolf refers to in her chapter on old age), she had usually relinquished control of the household management to her daughter-in-law.

8. In rural Taiwan, a fascinating practice, now rare but popular in the past, resolved this problem. A family would adopt a female infant and raise her to marry their son. The older woman had an ally—not an enemy—in her daughter–daughter-in-law. The young woman was socialized to accept her role in life since she did not know the relative freedom of being a daughter. She also knew the ways of the household and had been trained by her mother–mother-in-law. The girl did not represent a threat to the mother's ties with her son. Indeed, the sexual aversion usually found between the couple precluded the development of a close conjugal bond. The girl's strongest emotional bond was to the older woman. Rather than seek out her husband for support, the girl was apt to go to her mother–mother-in-law. The older woman thus had the best of possible worlds: overwhelming control over her daugher–daughter-in-law and no reason to feel jealous that the girl would turn the son against her. The daughter–daughter-in-law's lot, however, was hardly an enviable one. For a fuller discussion of this practice, see A. Wolf 1968; M. Wolf 1972.

9. See chapter 4 for a discussion of the tensions that arise between the two women in peasant societies after the daughter-in-law officially becomes "woman of the house."

10. Just when young women gained autonomy in their economic activities and moved to their own huts in the homestead varied from place to place. In some societies, for example, this occurred after the birth of a woman's first child; in others, when the husband or husband's brother brought a new bride into the domestic group. In many African societies, it should also be noted, sons often broke away from the parental homestead altogether, putting considerable distance not only between themselves and their fathers but between their mothers and young wives.

4. Consequences
of Age Inequality: III
Social Losses for the Old

1. As I pointed out in the Introduction, the term *young* refers in this work to physically mature individuals who are not considered old. It thus includes middle-aged adults who are often caretakers for the elderly.

2. Jack Goody argues that in those advanced agricultural societies where this kind of early retirement of the senior generation is found, this practice is linked to

structural features of the social system (1976a:120–121). Parents want to attract desirable mates for their children so that sons and daughters will be well cared for and family honor will not be besmirched by marriage to lower-status families. This is done by giving children a portion of the family estate when they marry or reach maturity. Goody argues, too, that a similar kind of retirement of the senior generation also occurs during the older couple's lifetime in some pastoral societies. In these societies, men gradually divest themselves of livestock as sons marry and keep only those animals they alone can look after.

3. This is clear in the rural Irish case, where many "old fellows" had not yet transferred their farms. Among the Sherpa, a couple could still hold a large chunk of the family estate in their later years before all their children had married. In Murelaga, a man and his wife could be well on in years before they transmitted the *baserria* to the selected heir since men did not marry until their late twenties or early thirties (and women not until their early or mid-twenties).

4. In those rare cases when the household was dissolved, the two couples invoked the marriage contract clause that detailed arrangements for breaking up the household. One couple moved out or the household was partitioned into two sub-units. Three disinterested spokesmen decided how the property and possessions were to be divided.

5. We should note, too, that an old couple's ability to affect decision making in the household depended to a large extent on whether they could still actively participate in the household economy. And when one of the older couple died, the other usually became more pliant and subservient to the younger couple. The survivor no longer enjoyed his (or her) spouse's support and was completely dependent on the younger couple. His influence over major decision making diminished (Douglass 1969:118, 110).

6. In Murelaga, the heir was a daughter in a minority of cases. Thus, when Douglass writes that the greatest potential source of conflict in the domestic group was in the relationship between the in-marrying spouse and the heir's parent of the same sex, this occasionally refers to a man and his father-in-law (1969:118). But in most cases it was mother-in-law–daughter-in-law relations that were most problematic.

7. In Murelaga, too, the elderly lost influence in the household when physical or mental declines made it impossible for them to perform economic services.

8. Among the Gusii, to take just one example, infirm men over seventy were feared, particularly if they had not yet divided their property, but, says Robert LeVine, they lost influence and power and "their greater isolation prevented their regulating the affairs of others" (1980:86–87).

9. In many European peasant societies, legal contracts that transferred property to the younger generation also made provision, often in elaborate detail, for the old couple's support. If neglecting the old in these cases meant violating the letter of the law, in preliterate societies, where there are no legal documents, it could lead to such consequences as supernatural punishment or community disapproval.

10. Even in old age, the proportion of people who give assistance to their children in the United States tends to exceed the proportion who receive help from them (Riley and A. Foner 1968:552).

11. Glascock and Feinman found seventeen instances (in forty-two societies) where the elderly were forsaken—that is, not supported by members of the social group, given only scraps of food or no food at all, and given poor or no medical care

(1981:25). Of course, the poorly treated elderly may not openly complain. Indeed, they may even accept the justice of their treatment. See chapter 6 on the legitimation of age inequalities.

12. According to Colson and Scudder, most elders between seventy and seventy-five were active cultivators with satisfying positions in their own homesteads (1981:132). After seventy-five, however, physical and mental declines meant that old men progressively lost control over their livestock and were increasingly disregarded when they tried to guide family affairs.

13. For a fascinating account of how single women in traditional Chinese society ensured old-age support—through, for example, adoption, fictive kin relationships, and support of other spinsters—see Sankar 1981.

14. Having younger wives in old age can be due to several factors. In polygynous societies, a man's economic and political skill may have been involved in securing many wives in the first place. And, polygynous or not, biological accident determines if a man's younger wife or wives survive long enough to care for him.

15. Just how frequent such a sonless condition was is unclear. Jack Goody estimates that, given the high mortality rate in nonindustrial societies, about 40 percent of men will not leave behind a male heir: 20 percent because they have no surviving progeny; another 20 percent because they have only daughters (1976a:119).

16. Among the Tallensi, as in most patrilineal societies with virilocal residence, it is extremely unusual for daughters to take care of incapacitated old parents. Fortes says that the Tallensi thought it unbecoming for old people to join their daughters (1949:217). Perhaps as Winter suggests for the Bwamba of Uganda, it is more difficult for daughters to assume this caretaking obligation because they have to seek their husband's permission (1956:174). Perhaps, too, old men are reluctant to join a daughter if this means leaving the community where they have kin and various economic and political rights.

17. All was not yet lost for a postmenopausal widow among the Gusii with no living sons and whose daughters had married and moved away. She could use the cattle from a daughter's marriage to "marry" a woman who came to live as a wife and had sexual relations with a local man, trying to bear "sons" for the widow's dead husband. These "sons" would inherit the dead husband's land and take care of the widow in her old age (R. LeVine 1980:89–90). Similar forms of woman marriage are found in a number of African societies as a solution to the problem of old-age support for barren or sonless widows.

18. Among Black Caribs, according to Kerns, reproductive and productive incapacity and, to a lesser extent, physical appearance were markers of old age (1980:116). By these criteria, women were defined as old at an earlier chronological age than men.

5. Age Conflict and Accommodation

1. The same frustrations that led some younger men to kill their fathers led others to take their own lives. Of forty male suicide cases La Fontaine analyzed, nearly half for which age data were available were under thirty, and two-thirds were under forty (1960:121). The economic struggle to gain control of land rights and cattle could be more than young men could take. That many young men had returned to Gisuland after a period of working away in their early twenties might have exacerbated

their troubles. Used to being independent when away, they were less willing than before to submit to elders' authority. Having been away may also have attenuated their ties to the community.

2. This is "late Terray." In earlier writings, Terray (1972:167) rejected the analogy between elder–youth relations in nonindustrial societies and class relations in capitalist societies. One reason was that juniors would, according to the normal operation of the social system, one day be elders. Later, Terray (1975) reversed his position, arguing that youths were objectively a class "in themselves."

3. Anne Foner's (1974) analysis of youth rebellions in our own society suggests that, when young people do engage in open protests against the old, aging may limit the effectiveness of their struggles. Thus, she argues that youth movements in modern industrial societies may have trouble maintaining continuity of membership and leadership as adherents move on to the next age stratum. When they become adults, individuals may lose their sense of a common fate as the concerns of youth lose relevance or as they begin to acquire the power and influence of older people. Age mobility, however, sometimes fosters age conflict in modern societies. The short period of youth may remind young people of the urgency of pressing their struggle. And the fact that members of a cohort have a common past and face a common future may enhance solidarity among age peers.

4. Bledsoe (1980) and Murphy (1980) stress that secret society initiations among the Kpelle—experienced by almost all boys and girls—intensified respect for and fear of the elders and the elders' control of knowledge. See also Brain 1977:197–198.

5. Changes brought about by colonial rule enabled men like Mwaipopo to continue as chief and take more wives rather than to retire. See chapter 7 for a discussion of the way changes affected age relations among the Nyakyusa.

6. Spencer suggests that elders discouraged moran from coming into the settlements to keep young men away from their wives. He notes, too, that the association between moran and the bush symbolized their in-between status: they were of an age to marry but could not do so for many years. The Samburu themselves said that the association of moran with the bush had historical roots, dating from the time when it was the duty of the moran to keep watch for signs of trouble from hostile tribes (Spencer 1965:99–100).

7. These older men were just starting to build up their reputations and they were clients of old men. The initiation process usually began at about age fourteen and ended at about twenty-four. After about the age of twenty, however, bachelors remained mostly in their household camps.

8. In our own society, old-age communities can provide similar compensations for the disadvantaged old, a world where they can gain honor and esteem they cannot achieve among younger people. See, for example, Colson 1977, Hochschild 1973, and Myerhoff 1978.

9. While sanctions may prevent or reduce open conflict, they generally do not reduce *tensions* between old and young. There are, of course, exceptions. Various sanctions, for example, may deter powerful elders from authoritarian behavior that would inflame the young. Jural sanctions can also give the subordinate young a means to redress their grievances. Alternately, old people's threats to curse, disinherit, embarrass, or punish the young in other ways can actually add to strains between them.

10. The ability to cause mystical harm legitimately is rarely the sole prerogative of the old. In many societies, parents, whatever their age, are thought to have the power to curse their children, for example, or to harm children through their anger.

Control of ancestor shrines falls to senior kin, who may not be old. In this chapter, however, I am concerned with the way mystical powers buttress old people's position rather than that of parents or senior kin generally.

11. Considerable debate has recently centered on the legitimacy of using the term "ancestor" to describe African beliefs about dead elders. Kopytoff (1971a) claims that the term implies a false dichotomy, not held by Africans themselves, between living and dead elders. Dead elders, he says, merely continue to have the power they exerted as living elders. Other anthropologists insist, however, that Africans in many societies do conceptually distinguish dead ancestors from living elders (Brain 1973; Calhoun 1980; Mendonsa 1976; Sangree 1974).

6. The Old Person as Witch

1. The witchcraft-sorcery distinction, first reported by Evans-Pritchard (1937) in his classic study of the Azande, is in any case not always applicable outside Zande society. In many societies an evil force is recognized that has aspects of both witchcraft and sorcery and does not fit neatly into either category (Lewis 1971:13). Evans-Pritchard (1937) also emphasized the role of witchcraft beliefs in explaining unfortunate events. Important as these beliefs are in accounting for misfortunes, this chapter is not concerned with witchcraft beliefs as an explanatory system but rather with the relationship between witchcraft and social tensions.

2. One of the many problems that would be involved in such an enterprise is that witchcraft beliefs probably have not been reported for all societies where they exist. According to Naroll's analysis of a worldwide sample of thirty-seven societies, ethnographers who stayed in the field for a year or longer were more likely than short-stayers to report the presence of witchcraft. Familiarity with the native language was also associated with reporting witchcraft (Naroll, summarized in Owusu 1978:315). Mary Douglas suggests that witchcraft accounts may be sketchy or absent for societies with centralized political systems because the ethnographers might well have been distracted from the witchcraft theme by their study of the political superstructure (1967:79–80). For a discussion of other problems involved in studies where witchcraft beliefs have been reported, see the appendix.

3. Of thirty-nine cases of invocation by a father against a real or classificatory son, fourteen of the sons (three own sons and eleven classificatory) claimed the invokers were using witchcraft against them (Middleton 1960:227–228).

4. I speak here of old Navaho men, but old women were also mentioned as witches in the tales Kluckhohn analyzed (1967:59). In the cases he collected, 131 of the 184 men and all of the 38 women described as witches were definitely old.

5. The Lele were matrilineal but practiced virilocal marriage. Although there was no regular bride service provided by young men for fathers-in-law, sons-in-law were expected to perform such tasks as clearing or house building for their fathers-in-law from time to time.

6. Witchcraft accusations and beliefs did not come into play in competition for the village headmanship among the Lele because there was no such competition. The village headman did not govern, allocate resources, or arbitrate disputes. And he was chosen purely on the basis of seniority: he was the oldest man of one of the founding clans of the village (Douglas 1963a:68–69).

7. Although rights in cleared forest land, fish ponds, and palm trees were heritable, they were not, Douglas says, sufficiently valuable to affect men's residence

patterns (1963a:29). Land, for example, was not in short supply among the Lele, and disputes about land did not occur (see Douglas 1963a:29–35).

8. David Gutmann briefly mentions the connection between women's increased dominance in later life and the ascription of evil motives to old women. He argues that women past childbearing age are freer to express the anger they have previously had to repress. This "long-closeted anger of old women . . . may revive, in others, archaic fears of the 'bad mother' as expressed in the *persona* of the witch" (1977:312).

9. See also Nadel on the Nupe of northern Nigeria, where, in legends and most case histories collected, witches were older women who attacked younger men. Sex, not age, antagonisms underpinned these beliefs, according to Nadel (1954:163–187). They reflected men's frustration at being economically dependent on successful women traders, a reversal, in men's view, of the rightful order of affairs. Indeed, Nadel's analysis of nine cases shows that women who wished to dominate or oppose men or who rejected the submissiveness expected of women were prime witchcraft suspects.

10. According to law, half of a man's property was subdivided equally among all his children when he died. The other half went to his widow for the rest of her life, after which it was also divided among the children. Often, however, the division did not take place until the widow herself died (Pitt-Rivers 1954:103). A widow, moreover, was considered the legal head of household if no adult son lived in the house (Pitt-Rivers 1977:81).

11. According to judicial records, witches were poor and usually women (Thomas 1971:520). Most indictments unfortunately did not record ages, but the assumption of most contemporaries was that witches were generally elderly. Of the fifteen women accused at the Essex Assizes for whom ages are known, only two were under fifty (Macfarlane 1970:161). Since indictments often described the accused as "spinsters," even when other evidence shows they were widowed, it is also hard to pin down what proportion of the accused were widows (Thomas 1971:562). Available data indicate, however, that a very high proportion of suspected witches were widows (Macfarlane 1970:164; Thomas 1971:562).

12. According to White, the relationship between grandparents and grandchildren protected grandchildren from becoming victims of their grandmothers (1961:66). White does not analyze the accuser–accused relationship because of the difficulty in deciding who was actually the accuser (1961:65). Witchcraft was handled as a joint responsibility of kin, and the group, not the individual, made the charge. Even when diviners were called in, they were, he says, the mouthpieces of corporate hostility toward the suspected witch.

13. Although old women were often considered witches, they were not the only ones in Ndembu society believed to have mystical powers to do evil. Men were accused of sorcery, and sorcery accusations were frequently connected with competition for authority in the village.

14. It is also possible that old widowed and divorced women in all three cases were feared because they lived apart from the direct control of senior men (compare Monter 1976:124; Pitt-Rivers 1977:82–83). Monter suggests, in addition, that old widows or spinsters were liable to accusation in the Jura region of Switzerland and France during the sixteenth and seventeenth centuries because, living apart from male control, they had no recourse to socially approved means of revenge available to others such as physical violence or the law courts. "Thus they had only magical revenge—or at least society assumed they had magical means of revenge, which

amounted to the same thing in terms of both popular fears and legal consequences" (Monter 1976:124).

15. Accusations made at Kamcape operations were not a response to personal misfortunes. They were public and the whole community participated. Day-to-day accusations, by contrast, were initiated by such events as illness or death or loss of livestock. They were basically private and intergenerational accusations were rare (Willis 1970b:192).

16. According to Douglas (1963b), before the poison ordeal was effectively suppressed in the 1930s, old men were less likely to be expelled as witches. Partly this was because the ordeal gave accused witches a chance to clear their name and start anew. If they survived, they were not only proved innocent but they could demand compensation from their accusers. Indeed, since acquittal entitled a man to heavy compensation from his accusers, the poison ordeal limited the freedom with which witchcraft accusations were made. In the absence of the poison ordeal, antiwitchcraft cults such as Kabenga-Benga provided an alternate way for accused witches to start again.

7. Social Change: Age Inequality, Tensions, and Conflict

1. To date, gerontological anthropologists have tended not to evaluate critically the modernization model in light of ethnographic data. One exception is Amoss (1981). In addition, a few anthropologists have noted in passing some of the problems with the modernization model (for example, Keith 1980; Simić 1978a). And, as will become clear, several ethnographers, although not writing with the modernization model in mind, provide data that question many of its premises.

2. Why old people's position changed in certain ways in Western Europe and America is subject to debate. Fischer (1978), for one, places strong emphasis on the role of ideas of liberty and equality in effecting changes in age relations in the United States.

3. Note the phrase "a variety of ways." As I discuss later, the elderly may lose certain privileges and powers at the same time as they hold on to or even increase others so that it is usually too simple to say their position is "worse" or "better."

4. Some take up permanent residence in urban areas. Although the study of changing age relations in urban areas of the Third World is important, in this book I focus on individuals whose main base is in the rural, rather than urban, area.

5. For want of a better word, I use "traditional" to refer to social practices and cultural beliefs from the days before the penetration of colonialism and extensive contact with the industrial world, practices and beliefs that may, in fact, still persist.

6. Other factors, such as the value of the wages, are important in assessing whether young men's earnings give them independence from senior kin.

7. Several anthropologists report that young men who feel oppressed by seniors can escape to towns, mines, and plantations and that the greater possibility of flight lessens parental controls (see Fortes 1949:73, 206; Fox 1978:29; Jackson 1977:166; Schapera 1971:37, 242).

8. For those young men who later returned home, however, elders' sanctions—the ability to disinherit sons, for example—were often important in inducing the returnees to toe the line.

9. In terms of bridewealth, however, much depends on its value and form and whether or not the young are still jurally dependent on seniors for marriage arrangements. See Fortes 1949:213; Lewis 1981:67–68.

10. According to Hamer, most men in this generation-set society became elders in late middle age (1972:18). The oldest, still capable elders, however, had the most influence in settling disputes in elders' councils.

11. Why Arapahoe elders were able to maintain and expand their authority is a question beyond the range of this work. Fowler (1982b) suggests that the nature of the traditional age-set system and ritual authority had much to do with their success.

12. It is difficult to determine whether old men's control of land is an improvement in their economic status. In the past, old men may have controlled other scarce and valued resources such as cattle and wives. Thus, it is possible that they are just as economically dominant today as in the past. The particular scarce and valued resources they control may simply have changed.

13. Although, as in the Giriama case, elders' need for cash for customary obligations may induce them to sell.

14. Robert LeVine puts forward a very different scenario for the Gusii. When the land shortage becomes serious, he predicts, older men's economic control over sons will be reduced. Land scarcity will lead to the fragmentation of holdings, and older men will thus have less land to allot to their sons. Sons will then either have to pioneer new land, if they can find it, or get permanent jobs. Both alternatives, he says, will free sons from paternal control (1964:82).

15. See chapter 1 for a definition of old age in precontact times. In the 1970s, a combination of generational position, appearance, physical vigor, chronological age, and personal choice dictated when a person began to act and be treated as an elder. People now became elders later than in the precontact era (Amoss 1981:237).

16. Another reason Amoss advances for the return to old meanings is that Western culture no longer confronted the Coast Salish as a "self-confident monolith." As doubts about Western culture grew within the white world, "faith in things Indian" flourished again (1978:167).

17. The old also held other dominant ritual roles. Shamans, as well as mediums, were old.

18. In this regard, it is interesting that Gerry Williams observes that among non-reservation Indians of Oklahoma renewed interest in traditional Indian culture and the expectation that the old would know traditional ways were stressful for the elderly who could not remember former ceremonies or life styles (1980:109).

19. Nor, it should be added, do ethnic revival movements always have such widespread appeal among minorities. Rural Mexican villagers, for example, were less than enthusiastic about a middle-class-led Nahuatal revival movement, which sought to encourage villagers to take pride in their indigenous heritage (see Friedlander 1975).

20. The Gwembe Tonga illustrate that elders recouped their losses after a kind of change I have not considered in this chapter: mass relocation of a population. In the 1950s, due to construction of the Kariba Dam, old men's control of land was severely eroded. The next cohort of old men, Colson and Scudder (1981) predict, will, however, be in a much better position. For men in middle age at the time of the move were able to gain control, through their own labor, of the best land in the new locations. And they will continue to control this land as they grow old.

21. For a full analysis of the complexities of Giriama elders' position in the 1960s

as well as for predictions about their influence as witnesses in the future, see Parkin 1972.

22. Judicial elders were roughly fifty-six to seventy, ritual elders seventy-one to ninety (Sangree 1965:71).

23. Since the 1930s, inheritance has shifted from fraternal to filial. Wilson links this change to increased opportunities for accumulating wealth by individual effort and men's feeling that what they earned should go only to their own sons since it was personal, not family, property (1977:175). Gulliver stresses land scarcity and older men's reluctance to see their brothers or brothers' sons inherit their land (1961:18).

24. Court cases reflected the increased competition for land. In the years 1934–1948, most litigation centered around women and cattle; by 1968, there was a noticeable shift to litigation about land and crop damage (Wilson 1977:82).

25. In the late 1960s, youths began to look to secondary education and the prospect of a relatively well-paid nonagricultural job as a way to escape this kind of dependence. How many would actually realize these ambitions is unclear, however.

26. Another outcome is also possible. Rather than become more—or less—serious or numerous, strains or conflicts between old and young may not change much in intensity or frequency. Instead, what may happen is that these strains are waged with different symbols. Or struggles between old and young may simply take new forms—focus on different valued resources, for example. In some societies, to mention one possibility, younger and older men who formerly competed over cattle perhaps now compete, with the same intensity, over land.

References

Achenbaum, W. Andrew. 1978. *Old Age in the New Land: The American Experience Since 1790.* Baltimore: Johns Hopkins University Press.

Achenbaum, W. Andrew and Peter N. Stearns. 1978. "Old Age and Modernization." *The Gerontologist* 18:307–312.

Adams, Frances M. 1972. "The Role of Old People in Santo Tomas Mazaltepec." In Donald O. Cowgill and Lowell D. Holmes, eds., *Aging and Modernization.* New York: Appelton-Century-Crofts.

Ahern, Emily. 1973. *The Cult of the Dead in a Chinese Village.* Stanford: Stanford University Press.

Alland, Alexander Jr. 1975. *When the Spider Danced: Notes from an African Village.* New York: Anchor Press.

Almagor, Uri. 1978a. "The Ethos of Equality Among Dassanetch Age-Peers." In P. T. W. Baxter and Uri Almagor, eds., *Age, Generation, and Time: Some Features of East African Age Organisations.* London: C. Hurst.

—— 1978b. "Gerontocracy, Polygyny and Scarce Resources." In J. S. La Fontaine, ed., *Sex and Age as Principles of Social Differentiation.* London: Academic Press.

Amoss, Pamela. 1978. *Coast Salish Spirit Dancing.* Seattle: University of Washington Press.

—— 1981. "Coast Salish Elders," In Pamela Amoss and Stevan Harrell, eds., *Other Ways of Growing Old.* Stanford: Stanford University Press.

Amoss, Pamela and Stevan Harrell. 1981. "Introduction: An Anthropological Perspective on Aging." In Pamela Amoss and Stevan Harrell, eds., *Other Ways of Growing Old.* Stanford: Stanford University Press.

Apple, Dorrian. 1956. "The Social Structure of Grandparenthood." *American Anthropologist* 58:656–663.

Arensberg, Conrad M. 1968 (1937). *The Irish Countryman.* Garden City, N.Y.: Natural History Press.

Arensberg, Conrad M. and Solon T. Kimball. 1968. *Family and Community in Ireland.* 2d ed. Cambridge: Harvard University Press.

280   References

Aries, Philippe. 1962. *Centuries of Childhood*. New York: Vintage Books.

Balzer, Marjorie Mandelstam. 1981. "Rituals of Gender Identity: Markers of Siberian Khanty Ethnicity, Status, and Belief." *American Anthropologist* 83:850–867.

Basso, Keith H. 1969. *Western Apache Witchcraft*. Tucson: University of Arizona Press.

Baxter, P. T. W. 1978. "Boran Age-Sets and Generation-Sets: Gada, a Puzzle or a Maze?" In P. T. W. Baxter and Uri Almagor, eds., *Age, Generation, and Time: Some Features of East African Age Organisations*. London: C. Hurst.

Baxter, P. T. W. and Uri Almagor. 1978. "Introduction." In P. T. W. Baxter and Uri Almagor, eds., *Age, Generation, and Time: Some Features of East African Age Organisations*. London: C. Hurst.

Beall, Cynthia M. 1984. "Theoretical Dimensions of a Focus on Age in Physical Anthropology." In David Kertzer and Jennie Keith, eds., *Age and Anthropological Theory*. Ithaca: Cornell University Press.

Beattie, John. 1964. *Other Cultures*. New York: Free Press.

Beauvoir, Simone de. 1973. *The Coming of Age*. New York: Warner.

Beidelman, T. O. 1963. "Witchcraft in Ukaguru." In John Middleton and E. H. Winter, eds., *Witchcraft and Sorcery in East Africa*. London: Routledge and Kegan Paul.

—— 1980. "The Moral Imagination of the Kaguru: Some Thoughts on Tricksters, Translation and Comparative Analysis." *American Ethnologist* 7:27–42.

Berreman, Gerald D. 1981. "Social Inequality: A Cross-Cultural Analysis." In Gerald D. Berreman, ed., *Social Inequality: Comparative and Developmental Approaches*. New York: Academic Press.

Biesele, Megan and Nancy Howell. 1981. " 'The Old People Give You Life': Aging Among !Kung Hunter-Gatherers." In Pamela Amoss and Stevan Harrell, eds., *Other Ways of Growing Old*. Stanford: Stanford University Press.

Bledsoe, Caroline H. 1980. *Women and Marriage in Kpelle Society*. Stanford: Stanford University Press.

Bohannan, Laura and Paul Bohannan. 1953. *The Tiv of Central Nigeria*. Ethnographic Survey of Africa. London: International African Institute.

Bohannan, Paul. 1960 (1958). "Extra-Processual Events in Tiv Political Institutions." In Simon and Phoebe Ottenberg, eds., *Cultures and Societies of Africa*. New York: Random House.

—— 1965. "The Tiv of Nigeria." In James L. Gibbs, Jr., ed., *Peoples of Africa*. New York: Holt, Rinehart, and Winston.

Bowen, Elinore Smith (Laura Bohannan). 1955. *Return to Laughter*. New York: Harper & Row.

Brain, James L. 1973. "Ancestors as Elders in Africa—Further Thoughts." *Africa* 43:122–133.

—— 1977. "Sex, Incest and Death: Initiation Rites Reconsidered." *Current Anthropology* 18:191–208.

Brantley, Cynthia. 1978. "Gerontocratic Government: Age-Sets in Pre-Colonial Giriama." *Africa* 48:248–264.

—— 1979. "An Historical Perspective of the Giriama and Witchcraft Control." *Africa* 49:112–133.

Brown, Judith K. 1982. "Cross-Cultural Perspectives on Middle-Aged Women." *Current Anthropology* 23:143–156.

Brown, Paula. 1978. *Highland Peoples of New Guinea*. Cambridge: Cambridge University Press.

Byrne, Susan W. 1974. "Arden, an Adult Community." In G. Foster and R. Kemper, eds., *Anthropologists in Cities*. Boston: Little, Brown.

Calhoun, C. J. 1980. "The Authority of Ancestors: A Sociological Reconsideration of Fortes's Tallensi in Response to Fortes's Critics." *Man* n.s. 15:304–319.

Chapman, Charlotte Gower. 1971. *Milocca: A Sicilian Village*. Cambridge: Schenkman.

Chowning, Ann and Ward Goodenough. 1973. "Lakalai Political Organization." In Ronald M. Berndt and Peter Lawrence, eds., *Politics in New Guinea*. Seattle: University of Washington Press.

Clark, Margaret. 1968 (1957). "The Anthropology of Aging: A New Area for Studies of Culture and Personality." In Bernice Neugarten, ed., *Middle Age and Aging*. Chicago: University of Chicago Press.

—— 1973. "Contributions of Cultural Anthropology to the Study of the Aged." In Laura Nader and Thomas Maretzki, eds., *Cultural Illness and Health*. Washington, D.C.: American Anthropological Association.

Clark, Margaret and Barbara Anderson. 1967. *Culture and Aging*. Springfield, Ill.: Thomas.

Collier, Jane F. 1974. "Women in Politics." In Michelle Zimbalist Rosaldo and Louise Lamphere, eds., *Woman, Culture, and Society*. Stanford: Stanford University Press.

Collier, Jane F. and Michelle Z. Rosaldo. 1981. "Politics and Gender in Simple Societies." In Sherry B. Ortner and Harriet Whitehead, eds., *Sexual Meanings*. Cambridge: Cambridge University Press.

Colson, Elizabeth. 1977. "The Least Common Denominator." In Sally Falk Moore and Barbara Myerhoff, eds., *Secular Ritual*. Amsterdam: Van Gorcum.

Colson, Elizabeth and Thayer Scudder. 1981. "Old Age in Gwembe District, Zambia." In Pamela Amoss and Stevan Harrell, eds., *Other Ways of Growing Old*. Stanford: Stanford University Press.

Cool, Linda. 1980. "Ethnicity and Aging: Continuity Through Change for Elderly Corsicans." In Christine L. Fry, ed., *Aging in Culture and Society*. New York: Bergin.

Coser, Lewis. 1956. *The Functions of Social Conflict*. New York: Free Press of Glencoe.

Cowgill, Donald O. 1972. "A Theory of Aging in Cross-Cultural Perspective." In Donald O. Cowgill and Lowell D. Holmes, eds., *Aging and Modernization*. New York: Appleton-Century-Crofts.

282   References

—— 1974. "Aging and Modernization: A Revision of the Theory." In Jaber
F. Gubrium, ed., *Late Life: Communities and Environmental Policy.*
Springfield, Ill.: Thomas.

Cowgill, Donald O. and Lowell D. Holmes. 1972. "Summary and Conclu-
sions: The Theory in Review." In Donald O. Cowgill and Lowell D.
Holmes, eds., *Aging and Modernization.* New York: Appleton-Century-
Crofts.

Cox, Francis M. and Ndung'u Mberia. 1977. *Aging in a Changing Village
Society: A Kenyan Experience.* Washington, D.C.: International Feder-
ation on Ageing.

Crawford, J. R. 1967. *Witchcraft and Sorcery in Rhodesia.* London: Oxford
University Press.

Cumming, Elaine and William Henry. 1961. *Growing Old: The Process of
Disengagement.* New York: Basic Books.

Demos, John. 1978. "Old Age in Early New England." *American Journal of
Sociology* 84 (supp.):S248–S287.

Douglas, Mary. 1963a. *The Lele of the Kasai.* London: Oxford University
Press.

—— 1963b. "Techniques of Sorcery Control in Central Africa." In John
Middleton and E. H. Winter, eds., *Witchcraft and Sorcery in East Africa.* London: Routledge and Kegan Paul.

—— 1967. "Witch Beliefs in Central Africa." *Africa* 37:72–80.

Douglass, William A. 1969. *Death in Murelaga: Funerary Ritual in a Spanish Basque Village.* Seattle: University of Washington Press.

Edel, May. 1957. *The Chiga of Western Uganda.* London: Oxford University Press.

Erikson, Erik H. 1963. *Childhood and Society.* 2d ed. New York: Norton.

Evans-Pritchard, E. E. 1937. *Witchcraft, Oracles and Magic Among the
Azande.* Oxford: Clarendon Press.

Ewers, John C. 1958. *The Blackfeet: Raiders on the Northwestern Plains.*
Norman: University of Oklahoma Press.

Fallers, Lloyd A. 1973. *Inequality: Social Stratification Reconsidered.* Chicago: University of Chicago Press.

Firth, Raymond. 1963 (1936). *We, the Tikopia: Kinship in Primitive Poly-
nesia.* Boston: Beacon Press.

Fischer, David Hackett. 1978. *Growing Old in America.* Exp. ed. New York:
Oxford University Press.

Foner, Anne. 1974. "Age Stratification and Age Conflict in Political Life."
American Sociological Review 39:187–196.

—— 1975. "Age in Society: Structure and Change." *American Behavioral
Scientist* 19:144–165.

—— 1978. "Age Stratification and the Changing Family." *American Journal of Sociology* 84 (supp.):S340–S365.

—— 1979. "Ascribed and Achieved Bases of Stratification." *Annual Review of Sociology* 5:219–242.

—— 1982. "Perspectives on Changing Age Systems." In M. W. Riley, R. Abeles, and M. Teitelbaum, eds., *Aging from Birth to Death: Sociotemporal Perspectives*. Boulder, Colo.: Westview Press.

Foner, Anne and David Kertzer. 1978. "Transitions Over the Life Course: Lessons from Age-Set Societies." *American Journal of Sociology* 83:1081–1104.

Foner, Nancy. 1973. *Status and Power in Rural Jamaica: A Study of Educational and Political Change*. New York: Teachers College Press.

—— 1978. *Jamaica Farewell: Jamaican Migrants in London*. Berkeley: University of California Press.

—— 1982. "Some Consequences of Age Inequality in Nonindustrial Societies." In M. W. Riley, R. Abeles, and M. Teitelbaum, eds., *Aging from Birth to Death: Sociotemporal Perspectives*. Boulder, Colo.: Westview Press.

—— 1984. "Age and Social Change." In David Kertzer and Jennie Keith, eds., *Age and Anthropological Theory*. Ithaca: Cornell University Press.

Fortes, Meyer. 1949. *The Web of Kinship Among the Tallensi*. London: Oxford University Press.

—— 1950. "Kinship and Marriage Among the Ashanti." In A. R. Radcliffe-Brown and Daryll Forde, eds., *African Systems of Kinship and Marriage*. London: Oxford University Press.

—— 1970. "Pietas in Ancestor Worship." In Meyer Fortes, ed., *Time and Social Structure and Other Essays*. London: Athlone Press.

—— 1984. "Age, Generation and Social Structure." In David Kertzer and Jennie Keith, eds., *Age and Anthropological Theory*. Ithaca: Cornell University Press.

Fowler, Loretta. 1978. "Wind River Reservation Political Process: An Analysis of the Symbols of Consensus." *American Ethnologist* 5:748–769.

—— 1982a. *Arapahoe Politics, 1851–1978: Symbols in Crises of Authority*. Lincoln: University of Nebraska Press.

—— 1982b. " 'Look at My Hair, It Is Gray': Age Grading, Ritual Authority, and Political Change Among the Northern Arapahoe and Gros Ventre." In Douglas Ubelaker and Herman Viola, eds., *Plains Indian Studies*. Washington, D.C.: Smithsonian Press.

Fox, Robin. 1978. *The Tory Islanders: A People of the Celtic Fringe*. Cambridge: Cambridge University Press.

Freedman, Maurice. 1966. *Chinese Lineage and Society: Fukien and Kwangtung*. London: Athlone Press.

Friedl, Ernestine. 1975. *Women and Men*. New York: Holt, Rinehart and Winston.

Friedlander, Judith. 1975. *Being Indian in Hueyapan*. New York: St. Martin's Press.

Fry, Christine L., ed. 1980. *Aging in Culture and Society*. New York: Bergin.

284   References

Gardner, Peter M. 1968. "Gerontocracy and Polygyny." In Richard B. Lee and Irven DeVore, eds., *Man the Hunter*. Chicago: Aldine.

Glascock, Anthony P. and Susan L. Feinman. 1980. "A Holocultural Analysis of Old Age." *Comparative Social Research* 3:311–332.

—— 1981. "Social Asset or Social Burden: An Analysis of the Treatment of the Aged in Non-Industrial Societies." In Christine L. Fry, ed., *Dimensions: Aging, Culture, and Health*. New York: Praeger.

Godelier, Maurice. 1978. "Infrastructures, Societies and History." *Current Anthropology* 19:763–768.

Goodale, Jane C. 1971. *Tiwi Wives*. Seattle: University of Washington Press.

Goodwin, Grenville. 1942. *The Social Organization of the Western Apache*. Chicago: University of Chicago Press.

Goody, Esther N. 1970. "Legitimate and Illegitimate Aggression in a West African State." In Mary Douglas, ed., *Witchcraft Confessions and Accusations*. London: Tavistock.

—— 1973. *Contexts of Kinship*. Cambridge: Cambridge University Press.

Goody, Jack. 1962. *Death, Property, and the Ancestors*. Stanford: Stanford University Press.

—— 1969 (1959). "The Mother's Brother and the Sister's Son in West Africa." In Jack Goody, ed., *Comparative Studies of Kinship*. London: Routledge and Kegan Paul.

—— 1976a. "Aging in Nonindustrial Societies." In Robert Binstock and Ethel Shanas, eds., *Handbook of Aging and the Social Sciences*. New York: Van Nostrand Reinhold.

—— 1976b. *Production and Reproduction*. Cambridge: Cambridge University Press.

Gough, Kathleen. 1961. "Nayar: Central Kerala." In David M. Schneider and Kathleen Gough, eds., *Matrilineal Kinship*. Berkeley: University of California Press.

Gray, Robert F. 1964. "Sonjo Lineage Structure and Property." In Robert F. Gray and Philip H. Gulliver, eds., *The Family Estate in Africa*. London: Routledge and Kegan Paul.

Guemple, Lee. 1980. "Growing Old in Inuit Society." In V. W. Marshall, ed., *Aging in Canada: Social Perspectives*. Toronto: Don Mills, Fitzhenry, and Whiteside.

Gulliver, Philip H. 1961. "Land Shortage, Social Change and Social Conflict in East Africa." *Journal of Conflict Resolution* 5:16–26.

—— 1963. *Social Control in an African Society*. London: Routledge and Kegan Paul.

—— 1964. "The Arusha Family." In Robert F. Gray and Philip H. Gulliver, eds., *The Family Estate in Africa*. London: Routledge and Kegan Paul.

—— 1968. "Age Differentiation." *International Encyclopedia of the Social Sciences* 1:157–162.

Gutmann, David. 1977. "The Cross-Cultural Perspective: Notes Toward a

Comparative Psychology of Aging." In James Birren and K. Warner Schaie, eds., *Handbook of the Psychology of Aging*. New York: Van Nostrand Reinhold.

Hamer, John. 1970. "Sidamo Generational Class Cycles: A Political Gerontocracy." *Africa* 40:50–70.

—— 1972. "Aging in a Gerontocratic Society: The Sidamo of Southwest Ethiopia." In Donald O. Cowgill and Lowell D. Holmes, eds., *Aging and Modernization*. New York: Appleton-Century-Crofts.

Hanks, Lucien M., Jr. and Jane Richardson Hanks. 1950. *Tribes Under Trust: A Study of the Blackfoot Reserve of Alberta*. Toronto: University of Toronto Press.

Hareven, Tamara. 1978 (1976). "The Last Stage: Historical Adulthood and Old Age." In Erik H. Erikson, ed., *Adulthood*. New York: Norton.

Harris, Grace G. 1962. "Taita Bridewealth and Affinal Relationships." In M. Fortes, ed., *Marriage in Tribal Societies*. Cambridge: Cambridge University Press.

—— 1978. *Casting out Anger: Religion Among the Taita of Kenya*. Cambridge: Cambridge University Press.

Hart, C. W. M. and Arnold Pilling. 1979. *The Tiwi of North Australia*. Fieldwork ed. New York: Holt, Rinehart, and Winston.

Hayes, Rose Oldfield. 1975. "Female Genital Mutilation, Fertility Control, Women's Roles, and the Patrilineage in Modern Sudan: A Functional Analysis." *American Ethnologist* 2:617–33.

Hess, Beth B. and Joan M. Waring. 1978. "Parent and Child in Later Life: Rethinking the Relationship." In R. Lerner and G. Spanier, eds., *Child Influences on Marital and Family Interaction*. New York: Academic Press.

Hochschild, Arlie. 1973. *The Unexpected Community*. Englewood Cliffs, N.J.: Prentice-Hall.

Holmberg, Allan R. 1961. "Age in the Andes." In R. W. Kleemeier, ed., *Aging and Leisure*. New York: Oxford University Press.

Holmes, Lowell D. 1972. "The Role and Status of the Aged in a Changing Samoa." In Donald O. Cowgill and Lowell D. Holmes, eds., *Aging and Modernization*. New York: Appleton-Century-Crofts.

—— 1976. "Trends in Anthropological Gerontology." *International Journal of Aging and Human Development* 7:211–220.

Hughes, Charles C. 1961. "The Concept and Use of Time in the Middle Years: The St. Lawrence Island Eskimos." In R. W. Kleemeier, ed., *Aging and Leisure*. New York: Oxford University Press.

Jackson, Michael. 1977. *The Kuranko: Dimensions of Social Reality in a West African Society*. New York: St. Martin's Press.

Jacobs, Jerry. 1974. *Fun City: An Ethnographic Study of a Retirement Community*. New York: Holt, Rinehart, and Winston.

Johnson, Sheila K. 1971. *Idle Haven: Community Building Among the Working Class Retired*. Berkeley: University of California Press.

286   References

Kalish, Richard A. 1975. *Late Adulthood: Perspectives on Human Development.* Monterey, Calif.: Brooks/Cole.

Kane, Eileen. 1979. "The Changing Role of the Family in a Rural Irish Community." *Journal of Comparative Family Studies* 10:141–162.

Karp, Ivan. 1978. *Fields of Change Among the Iteso of Kenya.* London: Routledge and Kegan Paul.

Keith, Jennie. 1977. *Old People, New Lives.* Chicago: University of Chicago Press.

—— 1980. " 'The Best Is Yet to Be': Towards an Anthropology of Age." *Annual Review of Anthropology* 9:339–364.

Keith, Jennie, ed. 1979. *The Ethnography of Old Age.* Special issue of *Anthropological Quarterly* 52.

Keith, Jennie and David Kertzer. 1984. "Introduction." In David Kertzer and Jennie Keith, eds., *Age and Anthropological Theory.* Ithaca: Cornell University Press.

Kerns, Virginia. 1980. "Aging and Mutual Support Relations Among the Black Carib." In Christine L. Fry, ed., *Aging in Culture and Society.* New York: Bergin.

Kertzer, David I. 1978. "Theoretical Developments in the Study of Age-Group Systems." *American Ethnologist* 5:368–374.

—— 1982. "Generation and Age in Cross-Cultural Perspective." In M. W. Riley, R. Abeles, and M. Teitelbaum, eds., *Aging from Birth to Death: Sociotemporal Perspectives.* Boulder, Colo.: Westview Press.

Kertzer, David I. and Oker B. B. Madison. 1981. "Women's Age-Set Systems in Africa: The Latuka of Southern Sudan." In Christine L. Fry, ed., *Dimensions: Aging, Culture, and Health.* New York: Praeger.

Kett, Joseph. 1977. *Rites of Passage: Adolescence in America, 1790 to Present.* New York: Basic Books.

Kleemeier, Robert W., ed. 1961. *Aging and Leisure.* New York: Oxford University Press.

Kluckhohn, Clyde. 1967 (1944). *Navaho Witchcraft.* Boston: Beacon Press.

Kopytoff, Igor. 1964. "Family and Lineage Among the Suku of the Congo." In Robert F. Gray and Philip H. Gulliver, eds., *The Family Estate in Africa.* London: Routledge and Kegan Paul.

—— 1965. "The Suku of Southwestern Congo." In James L. Gibbs, Jr., ed., *Peoples of Africa.* New York: Holt, Rinehart, and Winston.

—— 1971a. "Ancestors as Elders in Africa." *Africa* 41:129–141.

—— 1971b. "The Suku of the Congo: An Ethnographic Test of Hsu's Hypothesis." In Francis L. K. Hsu, ed., *Kinship and Culture.* Chicago: Aldine.

Kracke, Waud. 1978. *Force and Persuasion.* Chicago: University of Chicago Press.

La Fontaine, J. S. 1960. "Homicide and Suicide Among the Gisu." In Paul Bohannan, ed., *African Homicide and Suicide.* Princeton: Princeton University Press.

—— 1962. "Gisu Marriage and Affinal Relations." In Meyer Fortes, ed., *Marriage in Tribal Societies*. Cambridge: Cambridge University Press.

—— 1967. "Parricide in Bugisu: A Study in Intergenerational Conflict." *Man* n.s. 2:249–259.

Laslett, Peter. 1976. "Societal Development and Aging." In Robert H. Binstock and Ethel Shanas, eds., *Handbook of Aging and the Social Sciences*. New York: Van Nostrand Reinhold.

—— 1977. *Family Life and Illicit Love in Earlier Generations*. Cambridge: Cambridge University Press.

Lee, Richard B. 1968. "What Hunters Do for a Living or, How to Make out on Scarce Resources." In Richard B. Lee and Irven DeVore, eds., *Man the Hunter*. Chicago: Aldine.

Leighton, Dorothea and Clyde Kluckhohn. 1947. *Children of the People*. Cambridge: Harvard University Press.

Levine, Nancy E. and Walter H. Sangree. 1980. "Conclusion: Asian and African Systems of Polyandry." *Journal of Comparative Family Studies*. (Special Issue on Women with Many Husbands) 11:385–410.

LeVine, Robert A. 1961. "Anthropology and the Study of Conflict." *Journal of Conflict Resolution* 5:3–15.

—— 1964. "The Gusii Family." In Robert F. Gray and Philip H. Gulliver, eds., *The Family Estate in Africa*. London: Routledge and Kegan Paul.

—— 1965. "Intergenerational Tensions and Extended Family Structures in Africa." In Ethel Shanas and Gordon Streib, eds., *Social Structure and the Family*. Englewood Cliffs, N.J.: Prentice-Hall.

—— 1980. "Adulthood Among the Gusii of Kenya." In Neil J. Smelser and Erik H. Erikson, eds., *Theories of Work and Love in Adulthood*. Cambridge: Harvard University Press.

LeVine, Sarah, in collaboration with Robert A. LeVine. 1978. *Mothers and Wives: Gusii Women of East Africa*. Chicago: University of Chicago Press.

Levy, Jerrold. 1967. "The Older American Indian." In E. G. Youmans, ed., *Older Rural Americans: A Sociological Perspective*. Lexington: University of Kentucky Press.

Lewis, Ian. 1971. *Ecstatic Religion*. Harmondsworth: Penguin.

Lewis, John Van D. 1981. "Domestic Labor Intensity and the Incorporation of Malian Peasant Farmers Into Localized Descent Groups." *American Ethnologist* 8:53–73.

Lisón-Tolosana, Carmelo. 1976. "The Ethics of Inheritance." In J. G. Peristiany, ed., *Mediterranean Family Structures*. Cambridge: Cambridge University Press.

Llewelyn-Davies, Melissa. 1981. "Women, Warriors, and Patriarchs." In Sherry B. Ortner and Harriet Whitehead, eds., *Sexual Meanings*. Cambridge: Cambridge University Press.

Macfarlane, Alan. 1970. *Witchcraft in Tudor and Stuart England*. London: Routledge and Kegan Paul.

Mair, Lucy. 1969. *Witchcraft*. New York: McGraw-Hill.

288   References

—— 1971. *Marriage*. Harmondsworth: Penguin.

Marwick, Max. 1965. *Sorcery in Its Social Setting*. Manchester: Manchester University Press.

—— 1972. "Anthropologists' Declining Productivity in the Sociology of Witchcraft." *American Anthropologist* 74:378–385.

Maxwell, Robert J. and Philip Silverman. 1970. "Information and Esteem: Cultural Considerations in the Treatment of the Aged." *Aging and Human Development* 1:361–393.

—— 1981. "Gerontocide." Paper presented to the American Anthropological Association, Los Angeles, December.

Mayer, Philip. 1970 (1954). "Witches." In Max Marwick, ed., *Witchcraft and Sorcery*. Harmondsworth: Penguin.

Meillassoux, Claude. 1981 (1975). *Maidens, Meal, and Money*. Cambridge: Cambridge University Press.

Mendonsa, Eugene L. 1976. "Elders, Office-Holders, and Ancestors Among the Sisala of Northern Ghana." *Africa* 46:57–64.

Messenger, John C. 1959. "Religious Acculturation Among the Anang Ibibio." In William R. Bascom and Melville J. Herskovits, eds., *Continuity and Change in African Cultures*. Chicago: University of Chicago Press.

Middleton, John. 1960. *Lugbara Religion*. London: Oxford University Press.

—— 1963. "Witchcraft and Sorcery in Lugbara." In John Middleton and E. H. Winter, eds., *Witchcraft and Sorcery in East Africa*. London: Routledge and Kegan Paul.

—— 1965. *The Lugbara of Uganda*. New York: Holt, Rinehart, and Winston.

Monter, E. William. 1976. *Witchcraft in France and Switzerland: The Borderlands During the Reformation*. Ithaca: Cornell University Press.

Moore, Sally Falk. 1975. "Selection for Failure in a Small Social Field: Ritual Concord and Fraternal Strife Among the Chagga, Kilimanjaro, 1968–1969." In Sally Falk Moore and Barbara G. Myerhoff, eds., *Symbol and Politics in Communal Ideology*. Ithaca: Cornell University Press.

—— 1977. "The Chagga of Kilimanjaro." In Sally Falk Moore and Paul Pruitt, eds., *The Chagga and Meru of Tanzania*. Ethnographic Survey of Africa. London: International African Institute.

—— 1978. "Old Age in a Life-Term Social Arena: Some Chagga of Kilimanjaro in 1974." In Barbara G. Myerhoff and Andrei Simić, eds., *Life's Career—Aging*. Beverly Hills, Calif.: Sage.

Murphy, William P. 1980. "Secret Knowledge as Property and Power in Kpelle Society: Elders Versus Youth." *Africa* 50:193–207.

Murphy, Yolanda and Robert F. Murphy. 1974. *Women of the Forest*. New York: Columbia University Press.

Myerhoff, Barbara G. 1978. *Number Our Days*. New York: Dutton.

Myerhoff, Barbara G. and Andrei Simić, eds. 1978. *Life's Career—Aging: Cultural Variations in Growing Old*. Beverly Hills, Calif.: Sage.

Nadel, S. F. 1942. *A Black Byzantium*. London: Oxford University Press.

—— 1954. *Nupe Religion*. London: Routledge and Kegan Paul.

—— 1970 (1952). "Witchcraft in Four African Societies." In Max Marwick, ed., *Witchcraft and Sorcery*. Harmondsworth: Penguin.

Nason, James D. 1981. "Respected Elder or Old Person: Aging in a Micronesian Community." In Pamela Amoss and Stevan Harrell, eds., *Other Ways of Growing Old*. Stanford: Stanford University Press.

Neugarten, Bernice. 1974. "Age Groups in American Society and the Rise of the Young-Old." *Annals of the American Academy of Political and Social Science* 415:187–199.

Nukunya, G. K. 1969. *Kinship and Marriage Among the Anlo Ewe*. London: Athlone Press.

Ohnuki-Tierney, Emiko. 1974. *The Ainu of the Northwest Coast of Southern Sakhalin*. New York: Holt, Rinehart, and Winston.

Oliver, Douglas L. 1955. *A Solomon Island Society*. Cambridge: Harvard University Press.

Opler, Morris E. 1979 (1936). "An Interpretation of Ambivalence of Two American Indian Tribes." William A. Lessa and Evon Z. Vogt, eds., *Reader in Comparative Religion*. 2d ed. New York: Harper and Row.

Orenstein, Henry. 1965. *Gaon: Conflict and Cohesion in an Indian Village*. Princeton: Princeton University Press.

Ortner, Sherry B. 1978. *Sherpas Through Their Rituals*. New York: Cambridge University Press.

Ortner, Sherry B. and Harriet Whitehead, eds. 1981. *Sexual Meanings*. Cambridge: Cambridge University Press.

Ottenberg, Simon. 1971. *Leadership and Authority in an African Society*. Seattle: University of Washington Press.

Owusu, Maxwell. 1978. "Ethnography of Africa: The Usefulness of the Useless." *American Anthropologist* 80:310–334.

Palmore, Erdman. 1979. "Advantages of Aging." *The Gerontologist* 19:220–223.

Parish, William L. and Martin King Whyte. 1978. *Village and Family in Contemporary China*. Chicago: University of Chicago Press.

Parkin, David J. 1972. *Palms, Wine, and Witnesses*. San Francisco: Chandler.

Parry, Jonathan P. 1979. *Caste and Kinship in Kangra*. London: Routledge and Kegan Paul.

Peters, Emrys L. 1978. "The Status of Women in Four Middle East Communities." In Lois Beck and Nikki Keddie, eds., *Women in the Muslim World*. Cambridge: Harvard University Press.

Pitt-Rivers, Julian A. 1954. *People of the Sierra*. Chicago: University of Chicago Press.

—— 1977. *The Fate of Schechem or the Politics of Sex: Essays in the Anthropology of the Mediterranean*. Cambridge: Cambridge University Press.

Plath, David W. 1972. "Japan: The After Years." In Donald O. Cowgill and

Lowell D. Holmes, eds., *Aging and Modernization*. New York: Appleton-Century-Crofts.

Poole, Fitz John Porter. 1981. "Transforming 'Natural' Woman: Female Ritual Leaders and Gender Ideology Among Bimin-Kuskusmin." In Sherry B. Ortner and Harriet Whitehead, eds., *Sexual Meanings*. Cambridge: Cambridge University Press.

Potter, Jack. 1976. *Thai Peasant Structure*. Chicago: University of Chicago Press.

Potter, Sulamith Hans. 1977. *Family Life in a Northern Thai Village*. Berkeley: University of California Press.

Press, Irwin and Mike McKool, Jr. 1972. "Social Structure and Status of the Aged: Towards Some Valid Cross-Cultural Generalizations." *Aging and Human Development* 3:297–306.

Radcliffe-Brown, A. R. 1950. "Introduction." In A. R. Radcliffe-Brown and Daryll Forde, eds., *African Systems of Kinship and Marriage*. London: Oxford University Press.

Rattray, R. S. 1923. *Ashanti*. Oxford: Clarendon Press.

Reiter, Rayna R., ed. 1975. *Toward an Anthropology of Women*. New York: Monthly Review Press.

Rey, Pierre Philippe. 1979. "Class Contradiction in Lineage Societies." *Critique of Anthropology* 4:41–60.

Rigby, Peter. 1969. *Cattle and Kinship Among the Gogo*. Ithaca: Cornell University Press.

Riley, Matilda White. 1971. "Social Gerontology and the Age Stratification of Society." *The Gerontologist* 11:79–87.

—— 1976. "Age Strata in Social Systems." In Robert Binstock and Ethel Shanas, eds., *Handbook of Aging and the Social Sciences*. New York: Van Nostrand Reinhold.

—— 1978. "Aging, Social Change, and the Power of Ideas." *Daedalus* 107:39–52.

Riley, Matilda White and Anne Foner. 1968. *Aging and Society*, vol. 1, *An Inventory of Research Findings*. New York: Russell Sage.

—— 1974. "Social Aspects of Old Age." *Encyclopedia Britannica*. 15th ed., pp. 546–552.

Riley, Matilda White, Marilyn Johnson, and Anne Foner. 1972. *Aging and Society*, vol. 3, *A Sociology of Age Stratification*. New York: Russell Sage.

Roebuck, Janet. 1979. "When Does Old Age Begin?: The Evolution of the English Definition." *Journal of Social History* 12:416–428.

Rosaldo, Michelle Zimbalist. 1980. "The Use and Abuse of Anthropology: Reflections on Feminism and Cross-Cultural Understanding." *Signs* 5:389–417.

Rosaldo, Michelle Zimbalist and Louise Lamphere, eds. 1974. *Woman, Culture, and Society*. Stanford: Stanford University Press.

Rosenfeld, Henry. 1968. "Change, Barriers to Change, and Contradictions in the Arab Village Family." *American Anthropologist* 70:732–752.

Salamone, Frank. 1980. "Levirate, Widows, and Types of Marriage Among the Dukawa of Northern Nigeria." Paper presented to the American Anthropological Association, Washington, D.C., December.

Sanday, Peggy Reeves. 1981. *Female Power and Male Dominance.* Cambridge: Cambridge University Press.

Sangree, Walter H. 1965. "The Bantu Tiriki of Western Kenya." In James L. Gibbs, Jr., ed., *Peoples of Africa.* New York: Holt, Rinehart, and Winston.

—— 1966. *Age, Prayer, and Politics in Tiriki, Kenya.* London: Oxford University Press.

—— 1974. "Youths as Elders and Infants as Ancestors: The Complementarity of Alternative Generations, both Living and Dead, in Tiriki, Kenya, and Irigwe, Nigeria." *Africa* 44:65–70.

Sankar, Andrea. 1981. "The Conquest of Solitude: Singlehood and Old Age in Traditional Chinese Society." In Christine L. Fry, ed., *Dimensions: Aging, Culture, and Health.* New York: Praeger.

Schapera, Isaac. 1971 (1940). *Married Life in an African Tribe.* Harmondsworth: Penguin.

Scheper-Hughes, Nancy. 1979. "Breeding Breaks Out in the Eye of the Cat: Sex Roles, Birth Order, and the Irish Double-Bind." *Journal of Comparative Family Studies* 10:207–226.

Schildkrout, Enid. 1978. "Roles of Children in Urban Kano." In J. S. La Fontaine, ed., *Sex and Age as Principles of Social Differentiation.* London: Academic Press.

Schlegel, Alice. 1977. "Toward a Theory of Sexual Stratification." In Alice Schlegel, ed., *Sexual Stratification.* New York: Columbia University Press.

Schneider, David. 1968. *American Kinship: A Cultural Account.* Englewood Cliffs, N.J.: Prentice-Hall.

Shack, William A. 1966. *The Gurage.* London: Oxford University Press.

Shahrani, M. Nazif. 1981. "Growing in Respect: Aging Among the Kirghiz of Afghanistan." In Pamela Amoss and Stevan Harrell, eds., *Other Ways of Growing Old.* Stanford: Stanford University Press.

Sharp, Henry S. 1981. "Old Age Among the Chipewyan." In Pamela Amoss and Stevan Harrell, eds., *Other Ways of Growing Old.* Stanford: Stanford University Press.

Shelton, Austin J. 1968. "Igbo Child-Raising, Eldership, and Dependence: Further Notes for Gerontologists and Others." *The Gerontologist* 8:236–241.

—— 1972. "The Aged and Eldership Among the Igbo." In Donald O. Cowgill and Lowell D. Holmes, eds., *Aging and Modernization.* New York: Appleton-Century-Crofts.

292   References

Simić, Andrei. 1978a. "Introduction: Aging and the Aged in Cultural Perspective." In Barbara Myerhoff and Andrei Simić, eds., *Life's Career—Aging*. Beverly Hills, Calif.: Sage.

—— 1978b. "Winners and Losers: Aging Yugoslavs in a Changing World." In Barbara Myerhoff and Andrei Simić, eds., *Life's Career—Aging*. Beverly Hills, Calif.: Sage.

Simmel, Georg. 1955. *Conflict and the Web of Group-Affiliations*. New York: Free Press of Glencoe.

Simmons, Leo W. 1945. *The Role of the Aged in Primitive Society*. New Haven: Yale University Press.

—— 1960. "Aging in Preindustrial Societies." In Clark Tibbetts, ed., *Handbook of Social Gerontology*. Chicago: University of Chicago Press.

Skinner, Elliott. 1961. "Intergenerational Conflict Among the Mossi: Father and Son." *Journal of Conflict Resolution* 5:55–60.

Smith, Robert J. 1961. "Cultural Differences in the Life Cycle and the Concept of Time." In R. W. Kleemeier, ed., *Aging and Leisure*. New York: Oxford University Press.

Spencer, Paul. 1965. *The Samburu: A Study of Gerontocracy in a Nomadic Tribe*. Berkeley: University of California Press.

—— 1970. "The Function of Ritual in the Socialization of the Samburu Moran." In Philip Mayer, ed., *Socialization: The Approach from Social Anthropology*. London: Tavistock.

—— 1976. "Opposing Streams and the Gerontocratic Ladder: Two Models of Age Organisation in East Africa." *Man* n.s. 11:153–175.

Spiro, Melford. 1977. *Kinship and Marriage in Burma*. Berkeley: University of California Press.

Stearns, Peter N. 1976. *Old Age in European Society*. New York: Holmes and Meier.

Stephens, William N. 1963. *The Family in Cross-Cultural Perspective*. New York: Holt, Rinehart, and Winston.

Stewart, Frank. 1977. *Fundamentals of Age-Group Systems*. New York: Academic Press.

Stirling, Paul. 1965. *Turkish Village*. New York: Wiley.

Tapper, Nancy. 1978. "The Women's Subsociety Among the Shahsevan Nomads of Iran." In Lois Beck and Nikki Keddie, eds., *Women in the Muslim World*. Cambridge: Harvard University Press.

Terray, Emmanuel. 1972. *Marxism and "Primitive" Societies*. New York: Monthly Review Press.

—— 1975. "Classes and Class Consciousness in the Abron Kingdom of Gyaman." In Maurice Bloch, ed., *Marxist Analyses and Social Anthropology*. New York: Wiley.

Thomas, Keith. 1971. *Religion and the Decline of Magic*. New York: Scribner.

Tonkinson, Robert. 1978. *The Mardudjara Aborigines: Living the Dream in Australia's Desert*. New York: Holt, Rinehart, and Winston.

Turner, V. W. 1957. *Schism and Continuity in an African Society*. Manchester: Manchester University Press.

—— 1964. "Witchcraft and Sorcery: Taxonomy Versus Dynamics." *Africa* 34:319–324.

Turton, David and Clive Ruggles. 1978. "Agreeing to Disagree: The Measurement of Duration in a Southwestern Ethiopian Community." *Current Anthropology* 19:585–600.

Van Arsdale, Peter W. 1981. "The Elderly Asmat of New Guinea." In Pamela Amoss and Stevan Harrell, eds., *Other Ways of Growing Old*. Stanford: Stanford University Press.

Vatuk, Sylvia. 1975. "The Aging Woman in India: Self-Perceptions and Changing Roles." In A. de Souza, *Women in Contemporary India*. Delhi: Manohar.

—— 1980. "Withdrawal and Disengagement as a Cultural Response to Aging in India." In Christine L. Fry, ed., *Aging in Culture and Society*. New York: Bergin.

—— 1982. "Comment on 'Cross-Cultural Perspectives on Middle-Aged Women.' " *Current Anthropology* 23:152–153.

Wallace, Anthony F. C. 1971. "Handsome Lake and the Decline of the Iroquois Matriarchate." In Francis L. K. Hsu, ed., *Kinship and Culture*. Chicago: Aldine.

Weiss, Kenneth M. 1981. "Evolutionary Perspectives on Human Aging." In Pamela Amoss and Stevan Harrell, eds., *Other Ways of Growing Old*. Stanford: Stanford University Press.

White, C. M. N. 1961. *Elements in Luvale Beliefs and Rituals*. Manchester: Manchester University Press.

Whyte, Martin King. 1978. *The Status of Women in Preindustrial Societies*. Princeton: Princeton University Press.

Williams, Gerry C. 1980. "Warriors No More: A Study of the American Indian Elderly." In Christine L. Fry, ed., *Aging in Culture and Society*. New York: Bergin.

R. G. Willis. 1970a. "Instant Millennium: The Sociology of African Witch-Cleansing Cults." In Mary Douglas, ed., *Witchcraft Confessions and Accusations*. London: Tavistock.

—— 1970b (1968). "Kamcape: An Anti-Sorcery Movement in South-West Tanzania." In Max Marwick, ed., *Witchcraft and Sorcery*. Harmondsworth: Penguin.

Wilson, Monica. 1951. *Good Company*. London: Oxford University Press.

—— 1957. *Rituals of Kinship Among the Nyakyusa*. London: Oxford University Press.

—— 1959. *Communal Rituals of the Nyakyusa*. London: Oxford University Press.

—— 1977. *For Men and Elders*. London: International African Institute.

Winter, E. H. 1956. *Bwamba: A Structural-Functional Analysis of a Patrilineal Society*. Cambridge: Heffer.

294   **References**

Wolf, Arthur. 1968. "Adopt a Daughter-in-Law, Marry a Sister: A Chinese Solution to the Problem of the Incest Taboo." *American Anthropologist* 70:864–874.

Wolf, Margery. 1970. "Child Training and the Chinese Family." In Maurice Freedman, ed., *Family and Kinship in Chinese Society*. Stanford: Stanford University Press.

—— 1972. *Women and the Family in Rural Taiwan*. Stanford: Stanford University Press.

Worsley, Peter. 1968. *The Trumpet Shall Sound*. New York: Schocken Books.

Index

Abron (Ivory Coast), 71, 76

Accommodation, xvi, 102, 123-56, 243; and witchcraft beliefs and practices, 185-91

Achenbaum, Andrew, 6, 197, 198, 264n2

Adolescence, 4-5

Adoption, 117

Adultery, 41

Affection, 106, 154, 245; and care of frail aged, 115-16; in family relations, 80, 137-38

Affinal ties, 34-35

Affines, 135; and strains between young and old men, 40-56

Afikpo Igbo (Nigeria), 72, 73, 127-28, 148, 235; and social change, 215-16

Africa, 18, 34, 117, 237, 251, 269n10; ancestor beliefs, 150-51; colonial rule, 214-16; social change in, 216, 229; see also Central Africa

Age: as basis for prestige, 39, 69, 78-79; relative, 10-11, 16

Age boundaries, 3, 6, 8; see also Chronological age; Grandparenthood; Menopause; Physiological change

Age cohorts, xvi-xvii

Age grades, 18-21, 25; defined, 18; of women, 72

Age inequality between old and young, ix, xv-xx; and accommodation, xvi (see also Accommodation); in anthropological studies, xi-xiii; bases of, 31-39, 69-79; and change, 247-50; consequences of old men at top, 29-66; nonindustrial societies, 239-62; and other forms of stratification, 250-56; powerful and privileged old women, 66, 67-91; questioned by young, 211, 225-26, 237; social change and, 193-238; and social losses for old, 93-121; and witchcraft beliefs and practices, xvi, 157; see also Legitimation of inequalities

Age mobility, 130, 155, 244, 272n3

Age segregation, 5, 140-41

Age sets, 10; defined, 18

Age-set societies, 17-26, 36, 57-62, 124, 241-42, 247; formal transitions to old age, 17-19; informal transitions to old age, 19-24; physical segregation in, 140-41; social bonds in, 135-36; transmission of formal leadership in, 95; of women, 72-73

Age stratification, defined, xiii-xv

Age-stratification perspective, xiii-xv, xvi, xx, 243; age mobility in, 130; age strata and boundaries in, 4; definition of old age in, 14; infrequency of organized age conflicts, 155; and social change, 236-37, 247-48

Age stratum consciousness, 243-44; see also Group solidarity

Aging: inevitability of, 129, 130-32, 144; see also Age mobility

Aggression: deflection of, through witchcraft, 185, 186-87; indirect, 125, 146-48; outlets for, 231-32; physical, 125-26

Alland, Alexander, 71, 76

Almagor, Uri, 26, 268nn17, 18

Ambivalence: in father–son relationship, 44; in grandparent–grandchildren relationship, 114; in intergenerational relationships, 241; in mother-in-law/daughter-in-law relationship, 87;